INTERPRETING SHIPWRECK
MARITIME ARCHAEOLOGICAL APPROACHES

Edited by *Jonathan Adams* and *Johan Rönnby*

Södertörn Academic Studies 56

Southampton Archaeology Monographs New Series No. 4

HIGHFIELD PRESS

SOUTHAMPTON MONOGRAPHS IN ARCHAEOLOGY
NEW SERIES Number 4

SÖDERTÖRN ACADEMIC STUDIES 56

© The individual authors 2013

ISBN: 978-0-9926336-3-9

ISSN: 1650-433x

ISBN: 978-91-86069-80-3

A CIP record for this book is available from The British Library

Published by The Highfield Press Southampton, 10 Hiltingbury Road, Chandlers Ford, SO53 5ST, United Kingdom

This book is available from Oxbow Books Ltd, 10 Hythe Bridge Street, Oxford, OX1 2EW or from David Brown Book Company, 28 Main Street, Oakville, CT06779, USA

Printed in Great Britain by imprintdigital.com.

CONTENTS

Contributors

Jonathan Adams is Professor of Archaeology at the University of Southampton and was the first Director of the University's *Centre for Maritime Archaeology* (CMA). His field experience includes the Co-deputy Directorship of the Mary Rose project, and since then, several other ship-related excavations in Bermuda, the Channel Islands, the UK and the Baltic. He started the MA/MSc programme in Maritime Archaeology at Southampton in 1995 and was Head of Archaeology at Southampton between 2008 and 2012. He is an editor of the *Journal of Maritime Archaeology*.

Contact: Professor J. Adams, Department of Archaeology, University of Southampton, Avenue Campus, Southampton SO17 1BF. UK.
Email: jjra@soton.ac.uk

Mirja Arnshav is a maritime archaeologist with a special interest in heritage processes and the archaeology of the recent past. She has worked in the museum sector since 2002. At present she works as a research coordinator at the Swedish National Maritime Museum. In 2011 she received a Fil Lic. degree. Her thesis, Recent wrecks: Contemporary Archaeological Approaches to a New Heritage, examined assessment and valuation of modern cultural heritage. Current themes of research are underwater garbology, sailor's tattoos, contemporary collecting and memories of wrecked submarines.

Contact: M. Arnshav, Research Coordinator, Research Unit, Swedish National Maritime Museums,
P.O. Box 27131, SE-102 52 Stockholm, Sweden.
Email: mirja.arnshav@maritima.se

Riika Alvik is a Researcher at the National Board of Antiquities of Finland. She is also a doctoral researcher at the University of Helsinki in Finland. Her work focuses on the maritime archaeology of ships, in particular the materials and artefacts they carried aboard and their roles in cultural transmission in the Baltic area in the late 18th century.

Contact: R. Alvik, National Board of Antiquities, Cultural Environment Management, Archaeological Field Services PL 913 (Sturenkatu 4) 00101 Helsinki
Email: Riikka.Alvik@nba.fi

Charlotte Gjelstrup Björdal is Professor of Conservation at the Department of Conservation, University of Gothenburg. She has worked for several years with active conservation of waterlogged archaeological wood. During the last 13 years her research has focused on microbial degradation processes in terrestrial and aquatic environments. In situ preservation and protection of shipwreck as well as morphological studies on archaeological wood has been carried out in a large number of National and European funded projects. Recently she coordinated the EU FP 7th project WreckProtect and is involved in the EU FP7 project SASMAP.

Contact: Prof C. Gjelstrup Björda, Department of Conservation, Gothenburg university, Guldhedsgatan 5A, Box 130 SE 405 30 Göteborg, Sweden
E-mail: charlotte.bjordal@conservation.gu.se

Niklas Eriksson was formerly a maritime archaeologist with the Swedish National Maritime Museum, and is currently a doctoral researcher at Södertörn University. He specialises in the technologies of shipping and in the recording and visualisation of historic wrecks. His current research interests focus on the use of space on board ship and maritime processes or urbanism. He is currently working on recently discovered wrecks in deeper water, including the Ghost ship, *Mars* and *Sword*.

Contact: N. Eriksson, Södertörn University, Box 4101, 141 04 Huddinge, Sweden.
Email: niklas.eriksson@sh.se

Yvonne Fors is a postdoctoral researcher at the Department of Conservation, University of Gothenburg and project co-ordinator at the Swedish National Heritage Board. Her PhD (at Stockholm University) investigated the conservation challenges of the warship *Vasa*. Her current research uses different analytical techniques to characterize the mechanisms of chemical contamination and biological activity in the degradation of marine archaeological wood with the aim of developing improved procedures for its preservation. Through this work she also aims to improve communication and collaboration between the scientific community including conservators and archaeologists.

Contact: Y. Fors, Archaeological Research Laboratory, Department of Archaeology and Classical Studies Stockholm University, Wallenberg laboratoriet SE-106 91 Stockholm, Sweden.
Email: yvonne.fors@arklab.su.se

Fred Hocker is Director of Research at the Vasa Museum, Stockholm, Sweden. He is the primary author and editor of the *Vasa* series of archaeological monographs. He was formerly Yamini Associate Professor of Nautical Archaeology at Texas A & M University and is a leading authority on the shipbuilding and seafaring of the medieval and Renaissance periods. He has directed several major shipwreck excavations including the 9th-century Byzantine wreck at Bozburun in Turkey and the 12th-century Kolding cog in Denmark. Before studying archaeology, he was an apprentice shipwright at Mystic Seaport Museum.

Contact: Dr F. Hocker, Vasamuseet, Box 27131, 102 52 Stockholm.
Email: fred.hocker@maritima.se

Minna Lieno is a maritime archaeologist currently working as a researcher at the National Board of Antiquities of Finland in the Archaeological Field Services Unit. She started her diving career in 1995 and was later on certified as an Advanced European Scientific Diver (AESD). She is currently on research leave, writing her doctoral thesis for the University of Helsinki.

Contact: M.Lieno. National Board of Antiquities, Archaeological Field Services, Sturenkatu 4 P.O. Box 913, FI-00101 Helsinki, Finland.
Email: minna.leino@helsinki.fi

Johan Rönnby is Professor of Archaeology at Södertörn University, Stockholm and Director of the *Maritime Archaeology Research Institute* (MARIS). He was Senior curator/diving archaeologist at the National Heritage Board Stockholm 1994-97, STINT fellow at Skidmore College, USA 2005 and has been Docent in maritime archaeology at Helsinki University since 2008. His research has focused on various shipwrecks in the Baltic as well as Viking Age lake dwellings, harbours and underwater prehistoric landscapes. He has also published several studies dealing with coastal landscapes and cultural and social interaction with water.

Contact: Professor J Rönnby, MARIS,
Södertörn University, Box 4101, 141 04 Huddinge, Sweden.
Email: johan.ronnby@sh

Oscar Törnqvist studied archaeology, computer science and human geography, then worked in developer-funded archaeology, focusing on the development of GIS-based analysis. Postgraduate study of maritime archaeology, marine biology and ecology led to work as a geographical analyst, managing projects involving analysing and mapping marine landscapes as well as human environmental impact, mainly on the behalf of the Swedish Environmental Protection Agency. He is now at Södertörn University, writing a thesis on aspects of the human presence in archipelago waters and its impacts on Viking and early medieval society.

Contact: O, Törnqvist, Södertörn University, Box 4101, 141 04 Huddinge, Sweden.
Email: oscar.tornqvist@sh.se

Shaun Wallace Shaun Lee Wallace studied computer science, then worked as an IT professional for 18 years for LIFFE (NYSE Euronext) & Cap Gemini. He studied Heritage Studies before moving to Sweden and maritime archaeology postgraduate study at Södertörn University. He is now a maritime archaeology PhD candidate at Helsinki University, writing a thesis on 'A Floating Baltic Stage - the use of court and theatrical symbolism on the 17th century Swedish naval ship.' He also has an internship at Vasa Museum, Stockholm and is research associate at MARIS on the Ship at War project.

Contact: S. Wallace, University of Helsinki
Email: Shaun.wallace@helsinki.fi

Daniel Zwick read for his Masters in Maritime Archaeology at Southampton and has worked in contract archaeology in the UK and Ireland, as a freelance maritime archaeologist in Bremen and consultant in Lübeck. He is currently completing his PhD at the University of Kiel and has research affiliations with the University of Southern Denmark and the Viking Ship Museum at Roskilde, Denmark. His research focuses on Maritime Logistics in the Age of the Northern Crusades and comprises a re-evaluation of shipwrecks, navigation routes and ports within the broader historical context.

Contact: Daniel Zwick, Christian-Albrechts-Universität zu Kiel, Graduate School "Human Development in Landscapes" Leibnitzstr. 3, 24098 Kiel, Germany
Email: dzwick@gshdl.uni-kiel.de

Acknowledgements

The authors gratefully acknowledge assistance from several research institutions and funding bodies including support from the Östersjöstiftelsen (The Foundation for Baltic and East European Studies) which has been instrumental in much of the research underpinning this volume. Thanks also go to our colleagues in industry at Marin Mätteknik AB, Deep Sea Productions and Ocean Discovery who are partners in several research initiatives carried out through the *Maritime Archaeology Research Institute Södertörn* (MARIS). Collectively the authors would like to thank our anonymous peer reviewers, many of whose suggestions led to beneficial enhancements to various chapters.

The editors are particularly grateful to our respective Universities of Södertörn and Southampton. MARIS and the University of Southampton's *Centre for maritime Archaeology* (CMA) have a longstanding collaboration in field research and training as well as joint-authored publications. However, this is the first collaborative volume appearing simultaneously in the research monograph series of both universities. In this respect we thank all at the Highfield Press, Southampton and to Erland Jansson and Jonathan Robson at Södertörn University for their help and encouragement in expediting publication.

Thanks also to all those who participated in the various research projects discussed in this book but who are too numerous to name individually.

Finally Jon Adams particularly thanks Professor Stephanie Moser at the University of Southampton for drawing his attention to the quote by Thomas Pownall.

Note on the cover illustrations

Front cover: Photograph of the warship *Mars* taken by Tomasz Stacura, surely one of the most dramatic archaeological photographs taken in recent years and we are grateful to him and to Richard and Ingemar Lundgren of Ocean Discovery for its use. The image below it is an engraving by Erik Dalhberg showing the profusion of shipping in Stockholm in the 1690s.

Back cover: Conjuring up a more contemplative side to the study of wrecks, though we hope our research comes across as a little more dynamic than is suggested by the contented ruminant lying next to the wreck! (Photo Johan Rönnby)

1

LANDSCAPES, SEASCAPES AND SHIPSCAPES

Jon Adams and Johan Rönnby

'Should the wreck of an ancient ship ever be discovered, a collection of a multitude of its timbers, knees, ribs, beams, standards, fragments of masts and yards, bolts, planks, and blocks, would be une chose à voire, and would make the learned as well as the unlearned stare and wonder: but the eye of knowledge would find no rest or satisfaction there. Where the truly learned Antiquary (by an analysis of the first principles of naval architecture, and by tracing these principles in all possible combinations which the materials admit of) attempts various experiments of combining these fragments into some form, which, as parts, correspond to some whole – there arises the true spirit of antiquarian learning; there begins genuine and useful knowledge.'

Thomas Pownall, 1782

If we ever allow ourselves to assume that people in the past were not as perceptive and insightful as we are today then a swift perusal of the writings of centuries gone by will quickly disabuse us. The above quote is a salutary example and were it not for the date and perhaps the turn of phrase, one might assume that it was written far more recently. The author, Thomas Pownall was something of polymath: a prominent Governor and administrator in Britain's American colonies, Member of Parliament, political commentator, artist, friend of and collaborator with Benjamin Franklin and member of the Society of Antiquaries to which he was elected in 1768. The latter is the origin of his musings on knowledge of the past gained from things, in this case a shipwreck.

With the development of modern archaeology and in particular in its theoretical development over the last half century, the term 'antiquarian' was often used in a derogatory sense, referring to an interest in the past that was object-orientated, being limited to the value of antiquities as curiosities in themselves rather than in their wider social meanings. Yet here is an antiquarian identifying the necessity of progressing beyond description and essentially expressing what could be defined as a contextual approach exactly two

hundred years before 'contextual archaeology' (Hodder 1982) made its appearance as part of the challenge to the processual archaeology of the 1960s and 70s.

Today, given the various ways that archaeologists approach their studies, one could say that there are many 'archaeologies'. Common to all however, is the study of people and their societies based on a source material consisting primarily (though not exclusively) of material remains. The methods used to investigate and analyse those remains are under constant review but our interpretation of them is of equal importance. This book explores approaches to the interpretation of shipwrecks, an archaeological site type with specific qualities and therefore with associated challenges and potentials. It is not a book about shipwreck archaeology in the sense of methodology, neither is it a study of ship technology in terms of their design and construction processes, nor a synthesis of past work in any general sense. Rather, it is a series of explorations of how we experience and interpret the remains of past human action in the form of one of its most complex manifestations. To that end chapter 2 draws together some of the key issues in understanding ships as material culture and some of the perspectives through which they can be contextualised. So given that a comprehensive coverage of the field of shipwreck studies, let alone the broader subject of maritime archaeology, is beyond the capacity of a single volume, the work collected here is more akin to taking the pulse of the subject at this time, in this place, through ship-related maritime archaeological research.

The place is the Baltic, a region where some of the earliest maritime archaeology was carried out and which in many ways set the pace. But this is a regional perspective only in the sense that most of the case studies are being investigated here. In outlook, the research has international relevance, as do the ships under study, for the Baltic was by no means liminal to global affairs. The ships that are the subject of these investigations were the products of internationally connected (and competing) societies both within the Baltic and beyond. The Baltic Sea has been described as a northern Mediterranean, not in the sense of sun, sea and sand (though it is blissfully habitable from Spring through to Autumn), but rather as a would-be *Mare Nostrum* of the North in which its surrounding states interacted, especially those who had political, mercantile and military agendas. Many of these powers were quite aware of the Roman dominion over the Mediterranean and held it as a model for their own ambition (Rönnby, this volume).

With the rise of nation states in the 16th century, more than three hundred years of mercantile domination of the Baltic by the Hanseatic League was steadily eclipsed, economically by the Dutch but in terms of power and control, by Denmark and Sweden who emerged as the principal political and military rivals. Indeed aspiration to control the Baltic was a key element in the expansionist policies of the Swedish king Gustav II Adolph Vasa (1594–1632), explicitly stated as *Dominium maris Baltici* (Roberts 1979:18; Alexandersson 1982:71). Denmark had identical aims but although it enjoyed the geographic advantage of being able to control maritime traffic passing into and out of the Baltic, it was Sweden that emerged as the dominant power in the 17th and 18th centuries, at least in terms of territory. At its greatest extent Sweden presided over an empire that almost surrounded the Baltic, by that time referred to as *Mare Nostrum Balticum* (our Baltic Sea).

Another intriguing indication of the way the Baltic world was understood at this time is revealed in the extraordinary map 'Carta Marina' created by catholic ecclesiastic Olaus Magnus (Fig. 1.1.). One of the earliest maps of Scandinavia, it shows a maritime world of land, sea and ice that was inhabited, worked, exploited and travelled, by foot, animal, sledge and boat. At first sight it seems fanciful - we are shown strange creatures and giant sea monsters, but in other aspects archaeology and ethnography have shown it to be remarkably accurate, not least in its maritime connectivity. At sea, sailing

alongside the ships of Sweden, Denmark, Germany, Poland, Russia and Livonia, were those of England, France, Holland, Norway, Scotland and many others.

For us, the archaeological legacy of this period (and those preceding) is the inevitable sequence of shipping losses that occurred through the fortunes of war, the pressures of commerce and environmental forces. They occurred in uncountable numbers precisely because of the sheer intensity of maritime activity. That they survive in a state so conducive to archaeological investigation is because of the Baltic's particular environmental conditions. For while the Baltic can be very unforgiving in storm conditions, its almost tideless, cold, dark, low salinity waters are a better preservation medium than almost anywhere else in the world.

Not surprisingly the majority of this seabed database discovered so far dates from the historical period partly because the intensity of traffic increased over time. Not that earlier material doesn't survive, it does but it is far less easily discovered, whereas the more recent wreck sites are easily seen by divers or detected with marine geophysical equipment. Effort is being directed towards maritime prehistory but that is another story. Here then are ways into pasts that may be relatively recent but which are still very alien to our own times.

Data and imagination

From the beginnings of Baltic shipwreck archaeology it was realised that this was a three-dimensional archaeology: an archaeology of structures and that therefore good documentation and a sound knowledge of the source material were of obvious importance. A saying commonly but probably erroneously attributed to Albert Einstein runs: '*Everything that can be counted does not necessarily count; everything that counts cannot necessarily be counted.*' Nevertheless it is a good starting point for this book, for as well as measurements, we require imagination, an ability for theoretical thinking and a capacity to see connections in both past and present contexts for successful interpretation and the increase of knowledge. In the following chapter it is argued that the interpretative context of specific shipwrecks is not predetermined but is part of the process of archaeological work and narrative. As demonstrated in that article and throughout the book, the possibilities are many and varied. There is more than just a single story to tell from a specific wreck. Yet these are not stories in the sense of flights of fancy or make-believe. They could be of course but the veracity and relevance of archaeological interpretation depends on its links to the source material, generated and mediated by our method and theory.

Maritime archaeologists who work under water

Figure 1.1. 'Carta Marina', with its accompanying description is an ethnographic record of a maritime world, continuing an integrated conception of land and sea that extends back to the Mesolithic in this region (Rönnby 2007) (Olaus Magnus 1539).

have expended a great deal of effort in achieving accurate documentation partly because of the obscuring veil of the water itself. As a result, methodological and technical accounts used to be common in most archaeological ship studies. Niklas Eriksson and one of the current authors (JA) however, discuss other means of achieving archaeological interpretations. This concerns intuition and insight, processes related to hermeneutic and phenomenological ways of creating knowledge. But, as shown in their papers, this doesn't mean that measurements and data are unimportant in this process. For us as it is for Eriksson it is in fact rather the opposite. Skilful documentation is a part of a 'softer' understanding. Many of these questions are in fact related to the observation that not everything can be resolved numerically, and thus the distinctions between what is science as opposed to art is open to discussion. A scientific approach could also be an artistic approach.

One thing is certain, whichever approach one takes, the import of a shipwreck cannot be understood unless it is related to a context. Several of the authors in this book demonstrate the different contexts obtainable. Oscar Törnqvist discusses shipwrecks in relation to the topographical landscape, and Minna Leino emphasizes

the new connotations ships receive by being re-used as barriers and wharf infill. Törnqvist is concerned with the seascape of the wreck and the processes of formation but also with the nature of the site in which the wrecking event comprises an arresting process in a cultural continuum that has its own time depth. Leino's paper looks at cultural practices that comprise a different form of wrecking – a transference of a ship from one role to another. In exploring the ways in which they are repositioned in time and place she asks whether their individual biographies might influence the ways in which they are treated and where they are placed?

The concept of artefact biography (Kopytoff 1986; Gosden & Marshall 1999) is particularly applicable to ships, implying accrued meaning that transcends mere utility. Indeed we see this throughout aspects of the design, construction, use and disposal of watercraft. But where does this tendency originate? - perhaps from the nature of watercraft as material culture. Their roles are important enough and their operating environments demanding enough to require the investment of appropriate materials and technologies that are as advanced as a society can command. Time and resources were used to create a vehicle, not just for a single voyage (though some such craft exist) but one that would last a life time. Perhaps it is because the use-life of a ship was often of similar length to a human life that ships are named, gendered and invested with immaterial qualities including personality (Rönnby, this volume, Adams 2013:28).

Such objects, particularly larger ships but even smaller boats, can be highly complex and in many ways this complexity comprises part of their archaeological potential. As archaeological assemblages this of course relates to both the vessel as a thing and its contents. The latter can comprise a bewildering number of different source materials and possible means of interpretation. Riikka Alvik demonstrates how the cargo and artefacts placed on board, as well as carrying meaning related to their associated cultures, can also indicate the way a society changes involuntarily or by design. Her case studies are three wrecks en route to St Petersburg, ultimately in response to that great city's intended role – to provide Tsar Peter's Russia with access to the sea and so to Europe. Each ship provides individual perspectives but collectively they manifest the conscious aspiration to connect and to transform society with knowledge but also with exotic luxuries.

In contrast, Shaun Wallace looks at the ideas and symbolism embedded in the ship itself, in this case the decoration and embellishment in the great cabins on board the warship *Vasa* of 1628. On *Vasa,* the meanings of such adornment are complex and manifested in an almost textual way. Subject matter is represented through various artistic conventions with key images and motifs juxtaposed and arranged in relation to space in ways that would have made meaning evident to its intended audience – the ship's company. It was 'decorative' but in being so it identified graphically (to a largely illiterate crew) space designated for those of the highest status. In tracing the relationships between form and motif, Wallace reveals parallels with and influences from contemporary castles and religious buildings. As such we see norms of social class not simply transferred from the castle great hall to the ship's great cabin but transposed to a specific naval form of shipboard hierachy. The carvings therefore played a role in reifying naval ideology of power and inequality - a very different function than is proposed for the *fluits* of the Dutch merchant marine discussed by Eriksson in this volume.

We must not forget of course that these layered meanings of a ship transcend the thing itself. In rationalising three of the ways in which ships can be understood, Keith Muckelroy identified technological aspects ('the ship as a machine') its society ('the ship as a closed community') and the ship as an 'element in a military or economic system' (Muckelroy 1978:216). As the word 'system' suggests, this was partly inspired by the processual approaches of the time. However, in looking back at how people of historical times have understood ships and their roles, we see rather explicit representations of the 'system' where the technological agency of ships was interwoven with overarching political and economic ideologies and social ideals. An example of maritime enterprise and hard-nosed economic prosperity being represented allegorically is well illustrated in an etching by Ludolf Backhuizen from 1701. It shows the waterfront of the City of Amsterdam with several key features: a warship named *Amsterdam*, (power and security) a merchant ship (prosperity) and in the distance between them the Headquarters and shipyard of the Vereenigde Oost-Indische Compagnie (VOC) the powerful United East India Company (global influence). The scene is transformed from being a simple maritime view by the personification of the city portrayed as a classical goddess drawn through the water accompanied by mythological figures (Fig. 1.2).

These ideas are far from dead today (consider the public furore over the scrapping of iconic vessels or the popularity of preserved historic ships). So together with the historical contexts of ships, of equal importance are the ways we view and engage with their wrecks as archaeological source material and as monuments today. Part of that engagement is the way archaeology critically examines and questions traditional beliefs and interpretations. In her text, Mirja Arnshav demonstrates how the import and significance of wrecks, in this case *modern ones*, are bound up in the values of our contemporary society. While many archaeologists tend to focus their attention on older wrecks, Arnhav's work highlights the often greater significance placed upon younger wrecks by the diving community, primarily because of their greater presence and immediacy. But she then shows how awareness of their significance and importance can play an important role in promoting informed attitudes to cultural heritage in general as well as developing knowledge.

Strongly related to this are the ways of conserving and curating wreck sites and the materials recovered from them. The article by Yvonne Fors and Charlotte Gjelstrup Björdal is a contribution by maritime archaeological conservators - that closely allied science which maritime archaeological fieldwork involving excavation cannot proceed without. Compared with the others, their article has a rather different but nevertheless strongly complementary approach to wreck sites. As natural scientists their text demonstrates that perspective is clearly a matter of choice, and that there are many possibilities involved in the interpretation of shipwrecks. The substance of their paper is of

Figure 1.2. *Personification of the city of Amsterdam riding on a triumphal chariot drawn by horses and nereids. Etching by Ludolf Backhuysen 1701 (Courtesy of the Cleveland Museum of Art, Dudley P. Allen Fund 1924.848.1).*

fundamental importance to anyone connected with the preservation, curation and representation of these sites, particularly as environmental change is posing serious threats to wooden structures in the southern Baltic (Björdal & Gregory 2012).

Something old, something new, something borrowed, something blue

So an old rhyme goes, relating to marriage and luck but it might equally suggest the ways in which archaeology has energetically appropriated theories at will in order to attempt more effective interpretations of its data. In discussing evolutionary theory, Daniel Zwick returns to a topic that has excited considerable debate over the years, namely, do the processes of biological evolution have relevance and utility for archaeology? Robert Dunnell advocated a similar course for archaeology as a whole in the 1980s, seeing the artefact as the cultural phenotype (e.g. Dunnell 1989). Dunnell himself was following hard on the heels of Richard Dawkins who developed the concept of the meme, the cultural equivalent of the gene (Dawkins 1989:192). But the first archaeologist who latched on to the analogous

similarity between biological evolution and the ways cultural things including technology changed, was Augustus Lane-Fox (1827-1900), who as General Pitt Rivers, was an archaeological pioneer of considerable influence (Bowden 1991). He did so having read Charles Darwin's 'On the Origin of Species' (1859) and used the principle of evolving cultural and technological characteristics in the ordering of his collection of thousands of ethnographic objects that now form the basis of the Pitt Rivers Museum in Oxford. Indeed he not only knew Darwin but almost all of the British luminaries of that age. For him the principles of evolution underpinned everything. In Sweden no less a figure than Oscar Montelius was working along similar lines, and in developing the principles of seriation he was building on C. J. Thomsen's Three-Age system, both intuitively compatible with notions of evolution in terms of progressive change. Such analogies are not dissimilar to those that were perceived between 'primitive' societies around the world and peoples of the past believed to be represented by the distribution of archaeological materials, i.e. 'archaeological cultures'. And just as those ideas were vigorously challenged so were essentialist ideas that culture evolved in the same ways as biological species. Of course this was before the mechanisms of biological evolution were known and as more was discovered about genetics, cultural transmission and the nature of human society, new ways in which to explore the apparent relationships have resurfaced at regular intervals. Following Dunnell's evolutionary archaeology, the concept of dual inheritance theory was developed – change resulting from different but interacting genetic and cultural mechanisms (Cavalli-Sforza & Feldman 1981; Boyd & Richerson 1985) while Ben Cullen (1993) came up with 'cultural virus theory'. More recently, extensive analysis of cultural evolution and evolutionary archaeology in general is found in the work of Stephen Shennan (e.g. 2002, 2009, 2011). This is perhaps the first time however, that these issues have been viewed in detail from an explicitly maritime archaeological perspective.

For those who reject or are otherwise suspicious of the notion, the fundamental problem rests in the differences between the 'blind' mechanisms of biological mutation at a genetic level as opposed to the ways in which ideas are transmitted culturally. The latter can occur both consciously and subconsciously, but the 'heritability' of behaviour is the result of highly variable and contingent processes. Dawkins' meme and the subsequent 'discipline' of 'memetics' have not found universal favour by any means and Shennan (2009:39), sees particular problems with them and to an extent sidesteps them altogether.

In regard to explaining technological choices and the production of things, the question centres on whether the analogies between biological evolution and social change get us anywhere? Certainly, as Zwick shows, there is remarkable correlation in many ways but strength of analogy does not in itself provide explanation. However, differences between mechanisms of change do not preclude there being relationships between them. In this case the human being is after all the interface *de facto*. The challenge is therefore to get at what underlies apparent parallels between the ways things change and hence how they are manifested in human behaviour. The meme, dual inheritance or cultural viruses all show, as Zwick acknowledges, that this is a mutli-disciplinary project but one in which maritime archaeology through its analysis of some of humanity's most complex material culture, can make a key contribution.

Shipshape and Bristol fashion

If change in the ways things are created and used are of perennial importance in archaeology, so too are the ways in which people have created and organised space. 'Spatial analysis' is of interest to several disciplines,

geography for example and particularly so in archaeology where the use of geographic information systems (GIS) is now ubiquitous. Within the general field of spatial analysis is the notion of space syntax. Developed in architecture, it offers archaeology a powerful tool for analyzing how humans organize and use space or, as expressed by the title of what became the standard work in the field, 'the logic of social space' (Hillier & Hanson 1984). Perhaps space on board ship offers a particularly rich opportunity for such work. Living in a restricted space, often shared with others (and which is always moving), may raise awareness of the ways space is used and negotiated more sharply than ashore. For example the enforced economy of space and tidiness necessary aboard ship, both for reasons of efficiency and safety, survives in the saying 'shipshape and Bristol fashion'. Eriksson's article applies space syntax among other things to the analysis of *fluit* ships and thereby raises questions that challenge prior interpretations of how shipboard communities must have been. These interpretations were often based in assumptions that some social norms would inevitably be reflected in life on board but as noted with respect to Wallace's work and in chapter 2, societies on board ship can be atypical and not 'miniatures' of parent society at all.

The Devil in the detail

At one time, much of the tension between different theoretical approaches in archaeology (and beyond) centred on the schism between generalists and others. The former tended to focus on broader anthropological questions and regarded particularist concern with the specific event as a lesser calling. Historians and geographers had their own generalist vs particularist debate. The geographer Peter Haggett (1965:3) had stated that "one can do little with the unique except contemplate its uniqueness" whereas others including the idealist geographer Leonard Guelke, in following the historian Collingwood saw no reason to avoid the unique and no contradiction between the analysis of specific events and science (Guelke 1974:193).

Over the last seventy years the broad trajectory of archaeological thought has passed from the normative culture history of the post-war years, to its 'loss of innocence' with the onslaught of the New Archaeology at the end of the 1960s, before that in turn was challenged by post-processual approaches in the 1980s. Perhaps the sharpest and most aggressively expressed contrast was that between the culture-historical school, often disparagingly referred to as 'traditional' archaeology - criticised for being predominantly descriptive, inductive, and lacking in methodical rigour - and the generalist, processual approaches of the New Archaeology. In their turn however, the processualists were criticised for being positivist, determinist and scientist by post-processualists who challenged claims of scientific objectivity and swung the pendulum back towards connections with history and a concern with agency and social context. Admittedly this profile more closely characterises the archaeology of the English speaking world and parts of Europe including Scandinavia but it is justified in terms of the bleed across into the newer domains of nautical - and later, maritime archaeology, which were initially developed in those regions.

In the investigation of maritime sites the pendulum also swung back and forth. The early nautical archaeology of the 1960s and 70s broadly correlated with the 'traditional' normative culture historical archaeology of the time and was criticised for the same reasons (Lenihan 1983; Murphy 1983). Then in 1978 Keith Muckelroy published what was in effect a manifesto for an explicitly scientific 'maritime archaeology', broader in scope, encompassing nautical archaeology (and archaeology under water) within it (Muckelroy 1978:9). In conceiving the ship as part of a system and in his concern with quantitative methods and formation processes, maritime archaeology as rationalised by Muckelroy exhibited influences of the New Archaeology he had studied under David Clarke. However, within it there were seeds of a more inclusive approach and as archaeology explored an ever-increasing range of theory through the 1980s, 1990s and into this century, maritime archaeology also came to encompass more even than Muckelroy had proposed (McGrail 1984; Adams 2002, 2013).

Fred Hocker's paper addresses exactly this dynamic of scale in explanation: His *In details remembered* concerns what at first sight might be mistaken for ephemeral or incidental details of the process of shipbuilding. These are not however, minutiae that have no analytical destiny, rather the opposite. They reveal otherwise unsuspected characteristics of the craft process and human relations. As Hocker relates, *Vasa* was built by a large workforce that was disparate in every way. Using several examples he deciphers the archaeological signature of this complex workforce dynamic and reveals that the grand narrative of shipbuilding (enshrined in the great treatises of the literate and numerate master shipwrights) was manifested, as Hocker puts it, as messy reality. We are used to the notion of working from the specific (our data) outwards to engage with broader questions, but Hocker shows that having identified these questions, moving in the other direction - and tackling the devil in the detail - can be just as revealing.

Diagnosis and prognosis

It is now more than 50 years since George Bass and his team excavated the wreck of a small merchant vessel that had sunk off Cape Gelidonya in Turkey around 1200 BC, achieving the first underwater excavation that would still satisfy modern codes of professional practice. Since then many more wrecks, as well as vessels that were abandoned or ritually deposited, have been investigated all over the world and although acute problems of protection and management remain in some areas, shipwreck archaeology is no longer a liminal interest but a vibrant component of a broader maritime archaeology. Opinions vary of course but even those working within the field either take for granted or fail to realise how much has changed even in the last 15-20 years. It is still a relatively small field but effective development is not all about numbers. A more mature maritime archaeology doesn't necessarily equate to another hundred maritime archaeologists or another hundred sites published, but rather to the ways in which the subject is practiced as well as the degree to which the subject has become institutionalised. By this we mean its embedding in the legislative and policy strategies of heritage management, as well as in the domains of academia, industry (including the planning and development process) and the ways in which it has become more visible through museums, television, films, books and games, etc. In other words where and in what contexts are those hundred maritime archaeologists able to work, how do they work as researchers and what is the impact of that work? Globally of course the answers to these questions are highly variable. In some countries there are considerable resources while in others there is no infrastructure at all and neither expertise nor funding. That is one reason why attempting to represent the entire subject in one volume would result in a caricature rather than a revealing portrait.

As editors, in helping to paint that portrait, we have synthesised the content to a degree but have not tried to homogenise the approaches or the views of the individual authors. Indeed if maritime archaeology was a patient undergoing a health check and the contributing authors were the examining doctors, there would be some difference in their diagnosis, ranging from 'full of vigour and getting stronger' to 'needs to work harder to gain fitness'. There is some correlation here between the age of the contributor and their characterisation of the subject. Those who are older, in viewing where maritime archaeology is now as opposed to where it was twenty years ago, regard it with some optimism, especially given the constraints within which the subject has developed (Adams 2006), while those who have been engaged in the field for less time express more frustration and impatience. It was ever thus! One might therefore divide our views of the subject into those who judge the glass to be half full and those who see it as half empty. Both views are equally justifiable. But to close on a positive note, it needs to be stressed, especially with regard to the subject matter of this book, that recovering maritime data doesn't restrict us

to addressing maritime questions. Quite the reverse, for maritime aspects of culture interconnect with the rest of society, so in a sense maritime questions are never entirely maritime. Therein lies the potential both to marshal detail and address broad questions. In doing so the contributors to this book show that ships are one of our most potent resources, just as Thomas Pownall foresaw.

References

Adams, J. 2002. Maritime Archaeology. In: C: Orser (ed.) *Encyclopedia of Historical Archaeology*: 328-330. London: Routledge.

Adams, J. 2006. From the water margins to the centre ground. Editorial article. *Journal of Maritime Archaeology*. 1.1: 1-8.

Adams, J. 2013. *A Maritime Archaeology of Ships. Innovation and Social Change in Medieval and Early Modern Europe*. Oxford: Oxbow Books.

Alexandersson, G. 1982. *The Baltic Straights*. New York: Kluwer.

Björdal C.G., & Gregory D. 2012. *WreckProtect: Decay and Protection of Archaeological Wooden Shipwrecks*. Oxford: Archaeopress.

Bowden, 1991. *Pitt Rivers: The life and archaeological work of Lieutenant-General Augustus Henry Lane Fox Pitt Rivers*. Cambridge: Cambridge University Press.

Boyd, R, & Richerson, P.J. 1985. *Culture and the Evolutionary Process*. Chicago: University of Chicago Press.

Cavalli-Sforza, L.L. & Feldman, M.W. 1981. *Cultural Transmission and Evolution: A Quantitative Approach*. Princeton: Princeton University Press.

Cullen, B.R.S. 1993. The Darwinian Resurgence and the Cultural Virus Critique. *Cambridge Archaeological Journal* 3: 179-202.

Dawkins, R. 1989 (2nd edition). *The Selfish Gene*. Oxford: Oxford University Press.

Dunnell, R.C. 1989. Aspects of the application of evolutionary theory in archaeology. In: C. Lamberg-Karlovsky (ed.) *Archaeological thought in America*: 35-49. Cambridge: Cambridge University Press.

Gosden, C. & Marshall, Y. 1999. The Cultural Biography of Objects. *World Archaeology* 31: 169-178.

Groot, I. de, & R. Vorstman. 1980. Maritime Prints by Dutch Masters. London: Gordon Fraser. Guelke, L. 1974. An idealist alternative in human geography. *Annals of the Association of American Geographers* 64.2: 193 - 202.

Guelke, L. 1974. An idealist alternative in human geography. *Annals of the Association of American Geographers* 64: 193-202.

Haggett, P. 1965. *Locational Analysis in Human Geography*. London: Edward Arnold.

Hillier, B. & Hanson, J. 1984. *The Social Logic of Space*. Cambridge: Cambridge University Press.

Hodder, I. (ed.) 1982. *Symbols in Action*. Cambridge: Cambridge University Press.

Kopytoff, I. 1986. The Cultural Biography of Things: Commoditization as Process. In: A. Appadurai (ed.) *The Social Life of Things: Commodities in Cultural Perspective*: 64-91. Cambridge: Cambridge University Press.

Lenihan, D. 1983. Rethinking Shipwreck Archaeology: A History of Ideas and Considerations for New Directions. In: R. Gould (ed.) *Shipwreck Anthropology*: 37-64. Albuquerque: University of New Mexico.

Magnus, O. 1539. *Carta Marina*. Facsimile reproduction 1964. Uppsala: Bokgillet.

McGrail, S. (ed.) 1984. *Aspects of Maritime Archaeology and Ethnology*. London: NMM.

Muckelroy, K. 1978. *Maritime Archaeology*. Cambridge: Cambridge University Press.

Murphy, L.E. 1983. Shipwrecks as a database for human behavioural studies. In: R. Gould (ed.) *Shipwreck Anthropology*: 65-90. Albuquerque: University of Mexico press.

Pownall, T. 1782. Account of a singular Stone among the Rocks at West Hoadley, Sussex. *Archaeologia* 6 (January): 54-60.

Roberts, M. 1979. *The Swedish Imperial Experience 1560 – 1718* (Wiles Lecture). Cambridge: CUP.

Rönnby, J. 2007. Maritime Durées. Long-Term Structures in a Coastal Landscape. *Journal of Maritime Archaeology* 2.2: 65-82.

Shennan, S.J. 2002. *Genes, Memes and Human History: Darwinian Archaeology and Cultural Evolution*. London: Thames and Hudson.

Shennan, S.J. 2009. *Pattern and process in Cultural Evolution*. Berkeley: University of California Press.

Shennan, S.J. 2011. Descent with modification and the archaeological record. *Phil. Trans. R. Soc. B* 366: 1070-1079.

2

THE ARCHAEOLOGICAL INTERPRETATION OF SHIPWRECKS

Johan Rönnby

The real challenge

It has been said that the ship is possibly the most technologically complicated human artefact produced prior to the industrial era. Sunken ships are also complex archaeological sites through their structure and the extensive variety of objects that they carried (cf. Muckelroy 1978:3; Adams 2003, 2013). These qualities make shipwrecks an important class of source material with great potential for archaeological interpretation.

An important starting point concerning the archaeological study of shipwrecks is to stress that archaeologists, whether maritime in orientation or not, in the end do not examine objects but people and society. Ships were created and operated within cultural, economic and social contexts and were formed by these circumstances. Like all objects of material culture, shipwrecks then hold significance and value beyond the purely functional. As complex archaeological source material, wrecks therefore have great potential for revealing information about society, culture and human behaviour. However, ship alone is not enough, for archaeological study also involves contextualizing the source material; the object of an investigation must be compared to some other phenomenon beyond itself (cf. the discussion on 'contextual archaeology' in the 1980s, and also for example Moberg 1969). Familiarity with one's source material is of course an important starting point in this process as in all scientific studies. But the skill of the maritime archaeologist in diagnosing the technicalities of frames, joints and lashings, etc., must also be integrated with theoretical creativity, imagination and the power of insight. Comparative material and contexts that provide relevant explanation

for a wreck, are not predetermined nor inherent in the object which is studied, but rather depends on the archaeologist's ability to conceive possibilities for interpretation.

The real challenge for a ship archaeologist is therefore to identify and select relevant contexts for the interpretation of the wrecks and from that construct narratives that are not only scientifically credible but also have relevance for modern society and ourselves (cf. Geertz 1973 in a classic study about construction of narratives). With such a research objective in mind, this paper will broadly discuss different potential and available procedures for the archaeological interpretation of shipwrecks. The examples are mostly from the Baltic Sea but as we have argued above, the scope is hopefully relevant for ships and wrecks in general.

Interpretation as dialogue

Interpretation, whether explicit or not, has always played a major role in archaeology. The post-processual critique of the 1980s highlighted the role of interpretation and individual perspectives in archaeological theory. Much of this discussion had its origin in a general post-modernist, de-constructivist and neo-liberalist theory-building, the purpose and meaning of which can be questioned today (cf. Jameson, already in 1984). This is not to say, of course, that an understanding of the role of interpretation and its importance in archaeology has become overstated or is any less essential. Interpretation plays a significant role in the construct by which any knowledge of people and societies is gleaned from archaeological remains.

It is however, important to emphasise that a focus

on the significance of different perspectives and interpretation in the archaeological process is not the same as an acceptance of a subjective and pluralistic past. If we were to accept that different interpretations of history simply mirror different ways of looking at the past, then we would also have to agree that opinions based on nationalistic, fundamentalist and racist grounds are as 'true' as any other. If this is something we do not wish to accept, then we must stress that even an interpretative, narrative and 'poetic' archaeological text can be open to re-assessment.

A way to do this is to say that archaeological writing differs from fiction in that the former concerns a dialogue between the author and actual physical remains. A methodologically well-documented and published shipwreck provides an opportunity for learning more about people and societies, both in the past and in general. But not all opinions and conclusions connected to the interpretation of the wreck are equally valid. The physical remains provide information that fits various interpretations and narratives differently. Similarities and dissimilarities in the archaeological material are real and recordable and can be tools to expose simplified, manipulated or overly-imaginative interpretations of past societies (cf. Hodder 1992:162).

If knowledge is produced in a dialogue between the researcher and the source material, it is important in archaeological studies to try to record how this "discussion" is performed. A literary and scientific challenge to a writer of an archaeological text, regardless of whether it deals with prehistoric flints or post-medieval shipwrecks, is then to be transparent about one's perspective and experiences during the process of research and interpretation.

Ships and technology

The physical objects of material culture are the products and results of societal conditions and are often studied as such in archaeology. Yet at the same time they constitute a two-way dialectical relationship. Objects and the physical world are also part of an historical frame of reference and reality in which people live and in which *'they make their own history'* as Karl Marx said over a hundred and fifty years ago (Marx 1852). A theoretical discussion on the relationship between people and technology is sometimes (though oddly enough not always) to be found in historical technical research (e.g. Hansson 2002; Sundin 2006). In a general sense, this concerns the classic question of the significance of technology for societal change and historical development. This in particular has been discussed

within historical materialism. In Marxist-oriented historical research, the development of technology is discussed mainly in connection with social opposition and the interests of different groups and classes in society. Changes in the material world should then be understood within a social and economic context of conflict.

The relationship between technological development and society offers ship archaeologists an interesting analytical perspective. A general question concerns of course changes to ships and shipbuilding over time. To what extent are the various changes in society the stimulus for new types of ships, technological innovations in rigging or in hull construction? (cf. Adams 2013). Or alternatively, to what extent might one see such material innovations as prerequisites for economic, political and ideological change? How should one view, for example, the transformation of the naval fleet from the late 15th century onward? Should technology be viewed as an external and separate factor, driven for example by international contacts or even specific skilled individuals? Or, on the other hand, should one emphasise nautical developments as the result of changes in the political and economic conditions that occurred when a new form of state was created in Europe (cf. Glete 1993:60-75).

It has been a common tendency in historical research to accord great importance to dramatic technological innovations and ignore slower developments. However, maritime archaeological studies have shown that, for example, the new, larger, carvel-built vessels and new techniques in shipping that emerged at the beginning of the early modern period were not sudden strokes of genius in ship technology. Large ships and structural sturdiness for example can be proved already during the Middle Ages. During the 15th century many clinker-built ships had a strong internal structure that had developed for various reasons. Thus, the transformation in building technique from clinker to carvel was probably not as dramatic a change as was once believed, but rather the logical sequence of events, as a ship with a strong inner framework had no need for the qualities provided by overlapping strakes.

In this way, archaeological evidence has the ability to show that alterations in building methods are not merely a matter of technology, but must also be viewed in a societal context. It was certainly possible to build big ships during the medieval period, but the explanation for the appearance of great new carvel ships in the beginning of the early modern period has to be seen in connection to powerful new national leaders and various groups in society who now needed that kind of ship (cf. Adams 2013).

Economic systems

Merchant ships can be viewed in an interpretative context as an integral component in economic systems and structures. In the archaeological investigations of the well-known Bronze Age shipwrecks from Cape Gelidonya and Uluburun, the researchers used the cargo and other objects found onboard to reconstruct possible trade routes and complex interconnections going back as far as the second millennium BC. Thus the finds onboard revealed more extensive contacts and exchange of goods within the Mediterranean region, than was previously believed for this early period (Bass 1967; Pulak 1998).

The fluyt is another example connected to merchant shipping. This easily navigated, state-of-the-art, cargo ship was developed by the Dutch at the end of the 16th century. During the following century the fluyt and other specialist merchant ships were the most important elements of the booming international trade conducted by the Dutch republic. Trade with East India and the import of raw materials from the colonies in the New World brought enormous wealth to Amsterdam and other Dutch seaports.

The Baltic Sea trade also increased significantly in connection to this. By the middle of the 17th century thousands of merchant vessels sailed the Baltic each year. The cargo delivered to Scandinavia consisted of manufactured goods, spices, cloth, dried fish and salt. The ships were then loaded in the harbours around this northern inner sea with raw materials such as iron, copper, slaked lime, timber and grain, which were transported to the Continent via the Danish Sound and its customs post. At this time Sweden was advancing as a great European power, and in keeping with the current mercantile politics, such a Continental export trade was not only desirable but vital for financing military campaigns.

The technological innovations of the Dutch went beyond the creation of improved types of merchant ships such as fluyts, pinnaces and east-indiamen. They also included advances in production methods. The organisation of the 16th-17th century Dutch shipping industry, despite its reliance on wind power and windmills, heralded the Industrial Revolution of the 19th century (Unger 1978:2). From an economic-historical perspective, the study of wrecks of merchant ships from this period is integral to an understanding not only of the processes leading to the start of global trade, but also early pre-industrial production.

Several of the Dutch fluyts wrecked in the Baltic Sea have been the subject of maritime archaeological investigation. These include the 'Lion wreck' (c.1650), the Ghost ship (c. 1650), *Anna Maria* (1709), the *Jungfru Katarina* (1747), and the Jutholm wreck (c. 1700). A potential ship-archaeological topic offering great scope for socio-economic studies of the period would be to investigate various economic aspects related to fluyt construction. In what ways do they differ from other ships of the time? Can we determine through analysis to what extent were they easier to build and mass-produce? The fluyt was famous for its full-bodied cargo capacity, but how much more could a fluyt really carry as a result of its hull shape and spatial disposition onboard? Were fluyts really easier to navigate as claimed and did they really require fewer crew members? If so, was the economic advantage conferred by its design great enough to have been a key factor in the economic prosperity of the time, or did mercantile success depend much more on other factors?

An onboard society

Archaeological material on land often survives in a disturbed or fragmentary state as its preservation is affected by a number of adverse factors. By contrast, a shipwreck on the ocean floor can often be considered as a form of 'closed' find - representing a single functional, cultural and social unit. This is related to the fact that the original functioning ship could be understood as an entire system, the remains of which has been deposited 'intact' at the bottom of the sea.

By analogy with Muckelroy's observation about ships as a very special feature in the pre-industrial society, referred to in the opening of this paper, a ship's crew also formed a very special kind of social unit in a pre-industrial society. A crew was a very distinct group of workers with a specific 'maritime culture' that was influenced by the economic and social frameworks of the time, but also characterised by its surrounding marine environment and relationship to the ship *per se* (cf. Flatman 2003:143-157).

The complexity of the 'maritime culture' on 19th-century ocean-going vessels is described in a classic study by Knut Weibust. Most striking is that this special 'shipboard' culture was both non-material in the form of songs, narratives and rituals, etc., and material in the form of special clothing, things and equipment (Weibust 1969).

Research concerning the crews of sunken ships can deal with issues of hierarchy, power and the division of labour. Studying finds and their spatial distribution in a wreck can be a way for a maritime archaeologist to discuss the social order onboard the ship. Were vessels always hierarchically organised as so often claimed? What methods were used to maintain order and discipline onboard? Are there different solutions for this? Pirate ships for example are said to have had a rough but effective egalitarianism onboard with a collectively based authority. How would that effect distribution onboard of artefacts and division of space? Were you allowed to sleep and eat wherever you liked if you sailed under the Jolly Roger? (cf. Rediker 1989; Flatman 2003:149;). What was the situation on smaller trading vessels where the workers were few, and where everyone may have shared the same quarters? How did the captain and others maintain their authority under such conditions (cf. Eriksson, this volume)?

It is also interesting to compare sailors and crews with other groups of workers from contemporary contexts. In what ways are they similar? Are there features that link them? Was there a form of class-consciousness? How was the working class constructed and divided prior to industrialisation?

Another obvious yet often neglected fact of shipboard society is that it often consisted mostly of men, even if we know that women were often onboard to a greater extent than official records and official policy would have us believe. The dominance of males onboard is also historically best known in the West during post-medieval times, while in other periods and places different social situations can have occurred. But the fact remains that many seafaring enclaves in the world were and still remain a male-oriented domain. This creates an opportunity for gender studies and for enquiries related to gender roles. What did a predominantly male shipboard society imply? What happened, for example, to the tasks and equipment that were connected with women on land? What do the power structures and division of categories look like in a world where there is no division based on biological sex?

Experiencing ships

In some well-preserved wrecks in the Baltic Sea it is possible to 'go onboard' either by diving down to them or via remote-control camera. This kind of personal visit into the past can be a source of hermeneutically inspired interpretations (e.g. Adams this volume). The visit to the wreck on the bottom can, following the philosopher Hans-Georg Gadamer, be a journey in which one travels to a new unknown place (Gadamer 1960). It is a kind of "knowledge diving" which gives a personal experience that changes one's perspective. Based on personal insights and reflexion it then may be possible to come closer to aspects of the past and of people's lives that are normally beyond our reach.

The so-called Lion wreck (*Lejonvraket)* and the Ghost ship (*Spökskeppet*) from the mid 17th century

are both exceptionally well preserved small-sized fluyts (Eriksson 2012; Eriksson & Rönnby 2012). The Ghost ship lies at a depth of 130 metres in the middle of the Baltic Sea and is almost completely intact with masts still standing (Fig. 2.1). It has been possible to document the ship with the aid of robotic imaging. To look inside the small cabin in the stern where a crew of six or seven spent much of their time around a simple wooden table offers a unique insight into days long gone. In this very limited space, which often necessitated a crouching position, the crew attended to personal hygiene, drying of clothes and the preparation and consumption of meals. To accommodate everyone, they must have rested and slept in turns. This view is quite different to the impression of hierarchical arrangements offered by, for instance, naval vessels. On a fluyt, not only discipline but also consideration and co-operation must have been prerequisites for an endurable life onboard (cf. Eriksson, this volume).

To 'go onboard' these sunken *fluyts* deepens our understanding of the people behind the internationally successful Dutch sea-borne trade and the rising economy of the mid-17th century. A patriarchal structure, a very strict reformist morality, and constant piety would have characterised personal relations in the single, small, crowded, dark and damp cabin. It has been proposed in a classic study by Max Weber that this mentality and ideology, with its strict work ethic and sense of duty, was a prerequisite for the later development and spread of capitalist thinking (Weber 1904-5 (1978)).

Some warship wrecks on the seabed can be characterised as 'smoking guns'. The Swedish ship *Sword,* which sank in 1676 off Öland in the Baltic, shows evidence of the long and intense final fight it endured before being lost. The partly intact hull still bears the traces of fire and canonball impact, and many of its great bronze and iron guns still protrude from the open gunports, looking as though they were ready to fire (Fig. 2.2). Somewhat similar conditions are also visible on the wreck of the *Mars* from 1564, which also lies in the middle of the Baltic. The newly built ship, known as '*Mars the Miraculous*' because of its great size (60 m long, around 1800 tons) took part in battle against a joint fleet from Denmark and the town of Lübeck. After being boarded by the enemy it exploded while the fighting still was going onboard.

More than 1200 people died on these two ships. Blinded by smoke and deafened by the noise from the guns, the seaman and the soldiers onboard were shot, burned to death or drowned. The cold, dark water of the Baltic Sea has preserved these naval battlefields so we are able to visit and experience them. An archaeological challenge is to turn the investigation of these unique places from mere documentation of early modern

Figure 2.1. The Ghost wreck, an almost complete Dutch Fluyt lying in 130m of water in the Baltic. The ROV hovers by the stern port to film the stern cabin. To the viewer, the HD cameras give the sensation of going aboard (Photo: MMT).

Figure 2.2. A 36-pound iron gun, still in place on the lower gundeck of the 'Sword' (1676). Even at 90m depth and hundreds of years later, one can still sense the heat of this sunken battlefield (Photo: Deep Sea Production/Jonas Dahm).

battleships, into an anthropological study of war and its conditions (cf. e.g. Thorpe 2003; Waterstone 2009).

Ships with agency

The dialectical relationship between material culture on the one hand and people and society on the other implies that objects also participate actively in societal changes. We are, of course, influenced by our physical world in general, and some things are used and even created for the specific purpose of exerting an influence, to preserve or to instigate change. A discussion about the social agency of non-human actors (e.g. artefacts), as mentioned earlier in this article, goes back to Karl Marx and the 19th century at least. Also in archaeology, dealing with things as symbols highlights the role of material culture in change and influence (see for example Hodder 1982). Discussions about the agency of things is also to be found in the so-called Actor Network Theory (Latour 2005; for a specific discussion in relation to the field of archaeology, cf. Dolwick 2009; Olsen 2010).

According to a perspective where material culture "acts", merchant ships transported not only goods and objects, but also ideas and new customs embedded in the things onboard. When Russia underwent cultural, social and political change at the beginning of the 18th century, the new culture was transported by ship across the Baltic Sea to the newly established town of St. Petersburg. Finds of luxury goods in the form of paintings, wine, ice skates and gilt carriages onboard the wrecks of the *Vrouw Maria* (1671) and *St. Michael* (1647) in the southern Finnish archipelago provide material evidence of the Europeanization of Old Russia (cf. Alvik, this volume). Objects found in the wrecks of these ships represent a frozen picture of the purpose and ideology of the transformation process.

Also ships as types and constructions can be "actants"(cf. Latour 2005: 64-86) changing people's perceptions and outlook and in turn the society. When people along the Baltic coasts spotted the silhouettes of the new "German" cog (see Crumlin-Pedersen 2000) in the beginning of the 13th century they probably realized that a new time was coming. The effect that the first sight of the European ocean going ships had on indigenous people in America and Australia is also well known.

Another interesting example of this can be seen on 17th century drawings showing the harbours and city centres. On Erik Dahlberg's engraving of Stockholm from around 1690 one can see the old town in the background, but the foreground is dominated by ships (Fig. 2.3). Some of them are warships but most of them are ships for trade and commerce: galleasses, galliots, crayers and fluyts. It is a manifestation of floating Dutch architecture and ideology which has almost

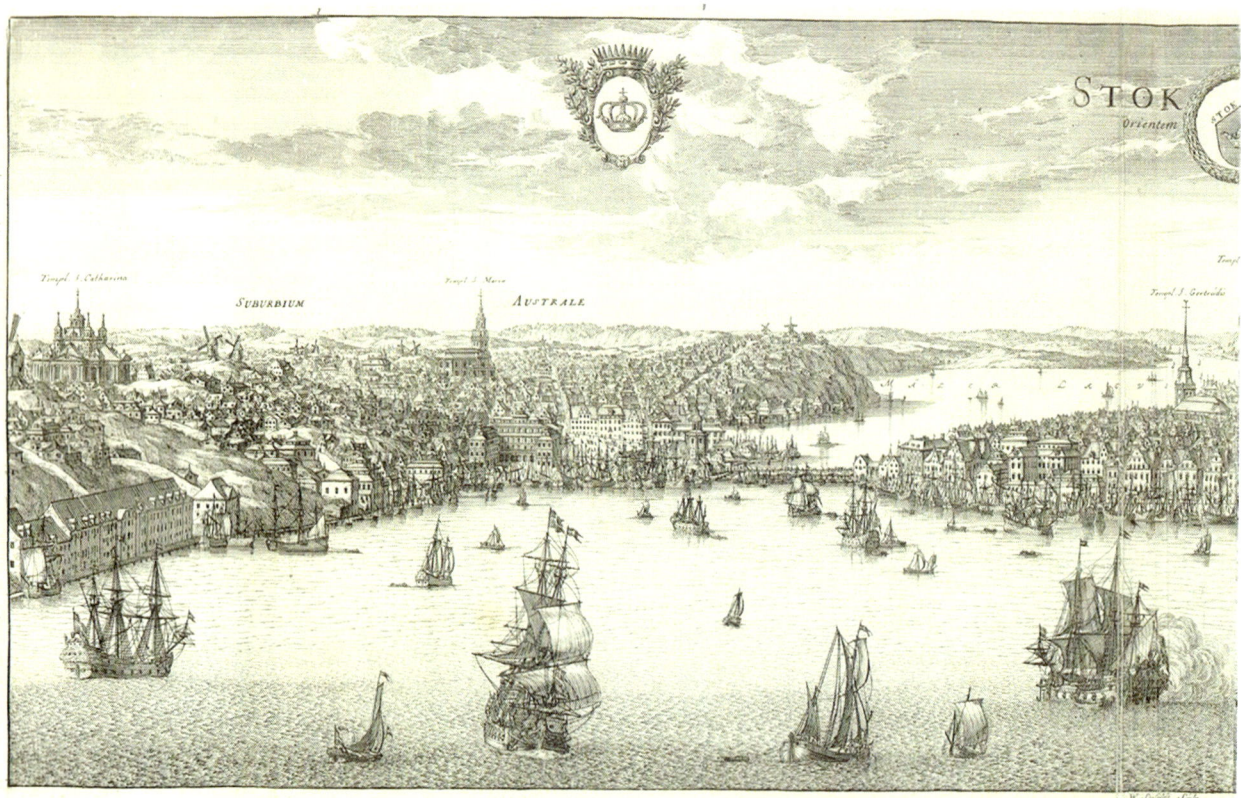

Figure 2.3. (above and opposite) View of Stockholm from the East, by Erik Dahlberg. c. 1690.

taken over old Stockholm (Eriksson forthcoming). The characteristic fluyts with their high sterns and rectangular shape in the water in front of the medieval town and the Royal castle, can in a way be seen as "floating 17th-century usb-memory sticks", foreign objects loaded with new culture and ideas about what was important in the world (pers. comm. Jerzy Gawronski).

Regarding large ships of war, their role as social actors and senders of specific messages is even more obvious. The care invested in sculptured embellishments and elaborate transoms on the largest ships of the Baroque period is ideology carved in wood. These ships were of course war machines, but also symbols of the wealth of their monarch and the country. They were built to impress foreign visitors and enemies, but perhaps above all to demonstrate the sovereign's power over his own subjects. Often anchored in the centre of towns for long periods, such ships became a part of the architectural landscape and shared the iconic message communicated by elaborate buildings. In this sense the larger ships can be compared with castles and palaces (cf. Johnson 2002).

The *Vasa* (1628) and *Kronan* (1676) are two world-renowned shipwrecks from the Baroque period, or more specifically, from Sweden's time of great sovereignty. The construction of impressive naval ships during this period formed an integral part of Sweden's exercise of power and politics.

They also housed miniature multifaceted societies. Both the nobility and the poor farmhands are represented on a large ship such as the *Kronan*. Should the ship, then, be interpreted as a mirror of the contemporary society? Or should we instead view this small, controllable, shipboard hierarchy as an ideal held by the powerful leaders for the way to organise the world? Were the big warships a kind of floating ideological display?

A recurring analogy of the time as used by, for instance, Axel Oxenstierna, the powerful Swedish Lord High Chancellor, was that Sweden and its society resembled a great and elegant naval ship - a 'societal ship' - which under the leadership of its captain sailed diligently forth on a sea teeming with enemies and dangerous reefs. In this way we can see that this miniature society was not in fact a simple facsimile of society at large. The shipboard context instead sheds light on the desired values of the contemporary society.

Wrecks and the landscape

In terrestrial archaeology it is common to reach an interpretation by relating finds and ancient monuments to the landscape. Such a connection is less apparent for shipwrecks at sea. The extent to which the find spot of a wreck should be seen as random or not, must be

judged in each individual case. By analysing landscapes, harbours and sailing routes it is sometimes possible to see a causal connection that is not apparent at first glance (cf. Törnqvist, this volume) (Fig. 2.4).

In some cases ships can also be given a new context and new associations during their 'lifetime'. They can be reused and thereby acquire new meaning. The clearest examples are when ships are submerged to function as defence works or as the foundations of harbour constructions and quays. These wrecks become structures with a new specific purpose. The potential of these kinds of wreck to produce archaeological knowledge is unusually complex and is directly related to the find site (cf. Leino, this volume).

Wrecks can also be seen as part of the history of different provinces and regions (Edberg 2002). On the 'peninsula' of Södertörn, south of Stockholm, people have lived and laboured in a coastal region of the Baltic Sea since the Ice Age (Rönnby 2003, 2007). Traces of activities of these former coastal dwellers are everywhere in the landscape. The prehistoric islands and islets, which now lie 70–80 metres above the sea due to isostatic uplift, contain traces of the region's first Mesolithic fishers and seal hunters. Rock surfaces along silted-up straits exhibit rock carvings of ships from the Bronze Age. Monumental burial cairns crown the tops of the moraine hills overlooking the water. Hillforts, cemeteries and harbours from the Iron Age lie in relation to former bays and inlets. The present-day coast contains remains of coastal inns, fishing huts and stone cairn markers. Sailing routes that have been used for centuries criss-cross between islands and islets, and in the entrances to narrow bays there are the remains of ancient barricades and defence works. In addition, the place-names in the region have a strong maritime association, and the area has a living oral tradition relating to seafaring, shipwrecks and plunder.

The island of Landsort (Öja) lies off the tip of Södertörn. It represents the southernmost outpost of the Stockholm archipelago. Here, the archipelago finally meets the open sea, which makes the region a rather dangerous place. This is evident not least from all the shipwrecks lying on the seabed between the islands. Considering all the wrecks, it is not surprising that in the 1530s King Gustav Vasa established Sweden's first official pilot station here. Landsort was also the site of Sweden's first lighthouse, built in 1669.

The small island of Krogen, just north of Landsort, housed a seaside inn in earlier times. The earliest written evidence for an inn here dates from the 1690s, but the inn itself is probably considerably older. Its buildings were burned down in attacks carried out by Russian galleys in the Stockholm archipelago in 1719. The activity of the inn soon began anew, however, and

continued in existence until 1829. The significance of this place as an important natural harbour and sea haven on the border between the open sea and the archipelago is underlined in literary evidence from the beginning of the 19th century. At times more than thirty large sailing ships lay at anchor outside the small island. Surveys of the waters around Krogen have documented building remains and more than ten shipwrecks. A large amount of find material has been located scattered on the seabed immediately surrounding the entire small island, and in particular at the better landing places. Judging by the large amounts of broken glass, broken clay pipes, and cracked ceramic plates, nightlife on the island could become quite rowdy!

The hundreds of shipwrecks from different periods found in the region of Landsort and Krogen form a part of the long maritime history of the Södertörn landscape. It therefore feels natural to view and discuss these shipwrecks in connection with the landscape and the multitude of other archaeological and historical remains here, rather than as an isolated nautical object.

Combining history and archaeology

When it comes to ships from historical times, written sources can often be studied in parallel to the material remains of the ship. Empirical information about building techniques, measurements, etc., can be found in publications about shipbuilding or shipbuilders' manuals. Early examples of such manuals are Witsen (1690) and Rålamb (1691). On a more general level, the combining of different sources is obviously not only a matter of obtaining new technical information but also a way of studying people and society from all possible perspectives. A wreck can then function as a kind of 'prism' that casts assorted light on a range of questions and problems. The museum exhibitions concerning the *Vasa* in Stockholm and *Kronan* in Kalmar exemplify the scope of such a perspective when applied to wrecks. Here a wreck becomes a portal to discussions for example of diet, hygiene and discipline in the relevant period. Maritime archaeology, which often attracts much public attention, can then be a very effective pedagogical tool for generating interest and stimulating discussion in many different fields.

Most shipwrecks lying on the seabed are anonymous and will continue to be so. But for wrecks that are only a few hundred years old there are sometimes salvage records in archives, and court documents available concerning the ships and their crews. One procedure when it comes to combining literary evidence and archaeological material is therefore to try to identify the wreck and integrate the two types of sources. Since the 1980s this has been one of the main ways of working

Figure 2.4. A maritime landscape: the lagoonal inlet of Kuggmaren in the Stockholm Archipelago, Sweden. The name suggests a connection with medieval cogs and the trade carried in them. This association became all the more plausible when a wreck lying in shallow water, assumed to be 19th-century (foreground) was shown to be a cog dated by dendrochronology to 1215 (Adams & Rönnby 2002).

when it comes to research on historical shipwrecks in the Baltic Sea (cf. Cederlund 1981, 1982, 1983; Kaijser 1981, 1983; Ahlström 1997). However, it is of course not desirable that all nautical archaeological research is directed toward identifying shipwrecks and relating them to written history. The identity of a wreck is not a scientific goal in itself and neither is it necessary for conducting meaningful archaeology. Identifying a ship by means of written material should instead be seen as one approach among other possible research perspectives. To combine archaeological and historical source material can give rise to new questions and inspire in-depth studies. Detailed knowledge about a specific identified ship and its loss can also generate powerful 'moments from the past' that offer the researcher historical insights not easily obtained from the ship's structure or from the written evidence alone. One example of this is the wreck of the *Jungfru Katarina.*

Katarina

In the middle of the 1980s a group of sport divers together with several marine archaeologists decided to investigate some shipwrecks near the island of Högskär situated on the coast of southern Sweden. Surveys at the site, as well as trial excavations and analyses, gave concrete information about the sunken ship. The vessel had been about 40 metres long, with a round stern and good carrying capacity. Among other things, it had transported lime and iron. A canon and ammunition revealed that it had also been lightly armed. Based on artefacts found onboard, the ship was thought to have gone down sometime in the period 1730–50. The construction of the ship proved to be of Dutch origin.

On the basis of these results, an investigation was conducted in several archives to see whether there was any information about such a ship. In the Military Archives, old pilot reports were found telling of a Dutch ship by the name of *Jungfru Katarina* that was lost at Högskär in 1747. In addition, the county archives of Södermanland contained documents telling how a salvage company in the years 1747–50 worked at the site and retrieved 'rigging and other nautical equipment'. Thus, thanks to a combination of underwater archaeology and archival research, the unknown wreck at Högskär had got its name back. With the help of written information from archives in Sweden, Denmark and Holland, a remarkable story could also be told about the wreck (Francke 1998; Rönnby 2002, 2004a).

The Dutch fluyt *Katarina* had made dozens of voyages between her home port of Amsterdam and different cities on the Baltic Sea. On 16th July 1747 she had passed through the Sound, heading for St. Petersburg. The precious cargo onboard included ginger, dried cod, steel wire, and several kinds of wine. The commander of the ship was Captain Dirk Pietersen Reuwekam, an experienced seaman who had several times previously sailed the *Katarina* to Archangel in the White Sea, and elsewhere. The crew was fairly small and consisted of around ten members. Most of them had sailed with Captain Reuwekam before and they must have known each other well. After being loaded with iron, hemp and wax on the Russian side of the Baltic Sea, the *Katarina* left St. Petersburg in mid October and set its course for the south again. It was late in the season and a perilous time of the year for sailing in the Baltic. Perhaps the weather suddenly worsened when the ship left the Gulf of Finland. In any event the captain made an error of judgement and the fluyt sailed straight into the dangerous reefs and sandbars that lay north of Fårö. On Salvorev, where many ships before and after the *Katarina* have met their fate, the Dutch

ship ran aground on 28th October 1747 and thereafter drifted in to Fårö island.

The crew hurried to rescue everything they could before the ship broke apart. Under the captain's direction, parts of the cargo were salvaged. Most likely the crew was assisted in the salvage work by enterprising fisher-farmers from the island of Fårö who were accustomed to wrecks and to the extra income such accidents could bring. Captain Reuwekam, however, had problems co-operating with the Fårö residents, and in a letter written later he complained about 'a week of sorrow and hostility'.

The salvage work was never completed, however. Suddenly the ship was gone. Perhaps the wind changed in the night and the ship glided away from shore, off on a last, lonesome voyage across the Baltic. After several days the unmanned ship may have been sighted briefly off the beacon of Hävringe båk, which was under construction at this time. Drifting on its own, with its sails in tatters, the ship must have then moved further north along the coast of Södermanland toward Högskär. There, the vessel was thrown against the cliffs at the southern tip of the peninsula, where the port side was crushed and the remains of the ship sank to the bottom. On 16th November the diving commissioner Petter Cederberg in Nyköping wrote about a three-masted vessel that had gone down at Högskär. The assiduous commissioner suspected that the ship may have been carrying contraband.

Captain Reuwekam must have been convinced that his ship and the cargo that could not be saved were lost forever when the ship disappeared in the night. He and his crew then travelled home to Amsterdam. Therefore, it must have been quite a surprise for the captain when he received a letter six months later requesting that he travel to Nyköping on the Swedish east coast to represent his employer's interests in the sale of wrecked goods from the *Jungfru Katarina*.

Another history?

A warning is sometimes sounded that historical archaeology should not be reduced to being a mere complement to the written source material. The question is, however, whether one needs to be so worried. As mentioned earlier, shipwrecks often stimulate people's curiosity and interest. Maybe it can sometimes be enough if the wreck constitutes a catalyst for further discussions and deeper studies. Nonetheless, if one wants to avoid letting the archaeological material be a mere illustration in a concrete historical context, it is necessary to make comparisons. How does the find material from a wreck compare to material from, for example, towns and rural areas? What symbolism can be seen in the shipwrecks as opposed to that which is expressed in the architecture or art of the same period? Is the environment onboard a trading ship radically different from that of a naval ship? Uniquely for archaeology performed in historical time, is that these comparisons do not have to be limited to other archaeological materials, but can also be incorporated with texts and images. This provides an opportunity for a kind of 'triangulation' (see Moberg et al. 2009; cf. Hjulhammar 2010).

An interesting circumstance occurs when the archaeological evidence shows something different from that written or depicted. An archaeological study of a historical shipwreck can, then, provide an opportunity to critically examine the period of the wreck as well as established historical myths and truths. Perhaps this critical opportunity represents historical archaeology's greatest scientific potential?

King Gustav Vasa, for instance, has a special position in Swedish written history. He is thought of as the 'father of the nation' and in his war against the Danes he is said to have laid the foundations of the modern Swedish state. Through the medium of chosen chroniclers, Gustav Vasa himself initiated the myths and colourful anecdotes about the war of independence that this first king of the Vasa dynasty conducted. This notional royal history was then reinforced by reiteration over the centuries. A shipwreck in the Stockholm archipelago, however, tells a somewhat different story about this 16th-century Swedish ruler.

The revolt led by Swedish nobleman Gustav Vasa against Christian of Denmark in the early 1520s was swift and effective, conquering fortress after fortress. However, since Gustav Vasa lacked a fleet it was impossible for him to take Stockholm. The Danish admiral Sören Norrby, being faced with no resistance at all, was able to bring in necessities and fresh manpower to Stockholm. It was not until Gustav Vasa himself purchased more than a dozen ships from Lübeck that Stockholm could be conquered. The German ships that arrived at Slätbaken in May 1522 are usually depicted in national romantic military history as the origin of the Swedish naval fleet. It was, however, a mixed collection of ships that the Swedes had bought. Most were probably small clinker-built vessels that had previously functioned as trading ships. Some of the ships, however, such as the flagship, *The Swan of Lübeck*, were specially built as naval ships and constructed in the carvel technique that was new at the time.

A wreck that is very likely one of the first carvel-built vessels in Gustav Vasa's first fleet have been found off the island of Franska Stenarna in the centre of Stockholm's archipelago (Adams & Rönnby 1996, 2013). This small island forms the crest of an underwater hill that rises steeply from the flat bottom of Nämdöfjärden. Today there is a small lighthouse on the island that warns seafarers with its soft blinking light. Five hundred years ago, however, this was a dangerous reef that was difficult to detect. The collision when the ship struck the rock must have been violent, and the ship would have gone down quickly. Thirty-five metres under the surface of the water, the ship came to rest on a cliff ledge with its main mast still standing high.

Visiting this old ship is a fascinating venture into history. However, as the site became more recognizable during the course of archaeological investigations, the feeling grew that the ship was not an elaborate and majestic carvel-built vessel. Rather, it was a large cargo boat, full of lethal but also rather primitive and crude weapons.

There is something grim and harsh but also rather small and plain about this old carvel-built ship of Gustav Vasa. The underwater archaeological evidence reveals a different history from the traditional one. Down in the dark at the bottom of the sea, the ship and its master come across as less distinguished than we expect. We are given an archaeological insight into the exercise of power and the mentality of the period. It gives the impression of the type of world and personalities described by Machiavelli in his treatise on political power *The Prince*.

Shipwrecks and long-term history

Archaeological material and sites, and perhaps shipwrecks above all, have great potential for providing a detailed glimpse into specific historical cases and situations. However archaeologists are also given the opportunity to turn their gaze from the specific object and instead adopt a wider long-term perspective. How do the changes in the material objects mirror the cultural and social development and modifications in a region?

For maritime archaeologists the Baltic Sea is a highly rewarding place for such a perspective thanks to its particular ability to preserve shipwrecks. A primary reason for this is that several of the organisms that normally destroy wood in the sea, including the shipworm *teredo navalis*, are missing in the cold, brackish waters of the Baltic. There are of course other places in the world with the same kind of physical conditions for preserving wood and other organic material, such as the Great Lakes in North America and the Polar seas. But the Baltic has witnessed intensive maritime traffic for millennia for subsistence, industry, trade and warfare. Intensive communications and relatively peaceful maritime contacts can be traced back to prehistoric times and the resulting number of shipwrecks is considerable. Seafaring and the practical material prerequisites in the form of boats and ships, is central to the history of the region, which includes all the countries along the Baltic Sea. In this respect the Baltic is a northern Mediterranean (Kirby 1990; Kirby & Hinkkanen 2000; Gerner & Karlsson 2002; Djerw & Rönnby 2003).

There are tens of thousands of written accounts of wreckings in the Baltic and the ones we have discovered comprise only a fraction of all the vessels lost through the centuries. Certain categories are not even represented among the known finds. This applies especially to older vessels, for example the out-rigged canoes from the Stone Age and the boats depicted in Bronze Age rock carvings. However, through finds of pottery and other artefacts we know that seafaring around the Baltic was already extensive during these periods.

In most parts of the Baltic region, the harbour sites from the Stone and Bronze Ages lie far inland due to shoreline displacement. But inevitably some prehistoric boats must have been wrecked among the islands of the archipelago and on the open sea. A find of such a boat would give us knowledge of early boat construction as well as a glimpse into prehistoric seafaring, transport, and exchange.

Certain types of ships have come to acquire a very special meaning in the traditional history writing of the Baltic region. These include the 'light, supple and beautiful Viking ships'. Viking ships have been found on the seabed off Denmark and outside Foteviken in Scania. In these cases the vessels had been submerged and reused as underwater barricades. Scattered parts of boats have also been found outside the Viking town of Birka in Lake Mälaren.

The similarities in Iron Age artefacts around the Baltic Sea, and the contacts they reflect, are linked to seafaring and ships. The same is true for the founding of early urban centres such as Birka, Hedeby and Wollin. The estimates of necessities needed per day at such places, in relation to marine archaeological data about the hold capacity and size of ships during the relevant period, can provide interesting information about the extent of seafaring and the need for harbour constructions. The different functional aspects of the Viking Age ships, their origin and various types, but also their ideological meaning as symbols of power and status, are interesting research issues with regard to the Baltic Sea during the Viking Age (Varenius 1992).

Another 'classic' ship for northern Europe and mentioned earlier in the article is the cog. The sturdily built and heavy cog has been given a very special place in history writing, namely as the ship of the Middle Ages and of the German merchants. Due to the north German expansion and the establishment of a number of new port cities, there developed a German Baltic sea culture during these centuries whose traces can still be seen today.

In the Middle Ages, marine operations took place in an unstable society. This volatile aspect is reflected in shipbuilding, regardless of whether the ships are cogs or other medieval clinker-built ships. The need to transport new 'bulk goods' but also to stay abreast of competitors, called for new types of ships. Ships that we define today as cogs have been found and investigated outside Oskarshamn and at Kuggmaren in the Stockholm archipelago. These ships are flat bottomed amidships, have heavy frames, and are dated to the first half of the 13th century (Adams 1995, 2013; Adams & Rönnby 2002).

During a hundred year period from the middle of the 15th century, the small, single-masted, medieval ships were replaced by larger vessels with several masts. This innovation in ship design, as discussed above, can be seen as connected with the building of new nations and the royal need for effectively exercising power. Rulers invested extensive resources more than ever in shipbuilding. The development of ships was also very much a matter of necessity for naval and transport vessels in the competition for resources in newly discovered regions on the other side of the oceans (cf. Glete 2000, 2002).

Many Danish, Swedish, German and Dutch naval ships that set out during the struggle for control of the Baltic Sea in the early post-modern period, lie at the bottom of the sea today. The same is true for thousands of the merchant ships that were loaded with bulk goods and sailed across the inland sea in the 17th and 18th centuries. Seafaring on the Baltic had then become part of a world economy involving the global transport of raw materials, but also depending on slavery and colonialism.

During the course of the 19th century the traditional wooden sailing ships began to encounter strong competition from the new mechanised ships with metal hulls. The latter reflected the technological innovations of the time and the bourgeois belief in the future. The design and decoration of the first passenger steamboats at the beginning of the century can also reveal the mentality, spirit of the time, and class awareness that characterised early industrialisation (cf. Cederlund 1987).

Change took place, however, at a fairly slow pace, and intensive vernacular seafaring and the ever increasing need to transport cargo and goods in the 19th century are reflected in the thousands of brigs, schooners and full-rigged ships lying on the seabed. Their histories, as well as those of the 20th century vessels, not least those that sank during the two World Wars, are also exciting future challenges for ship archaeology in this area. They constitute part of its long-term maritime history.

Other ways of understanding?

Archaeology has traditionally been a field that has placed considerable emphasis on examining and documenting physical objects, structures and places as methodologically as possible. An empirical ideal has also largely dominated the field of maritime archaeology and nautical research. Modern ship archaeology has, however, started to draw inspiration from qualitative research in other disciplines and from contemporary theoretical discourse. There are numerous opportunities for maritime archaeologists to allow their experience, impressions and feelings become part of the process of understanding people from sunken ships from the past.

Neither historians nor archaeologists should of course give up the attempt to reconstruct and understand the past as truthfully as possible. There are many good reasons for researching and discussing how things worked and were organised in times gone by. However, there may also finally be other ways of motivating studies of shipwrecks which could complement these strict historical and archaeological perspectives.

Physical remains could for example also be a good starting point simply for general humanist reflection (cf. Burström 2004; Rönnby 2004b). Ruins, graves and old boats as well as simple everyday things, can, when extracted from their original context, become stimulating starting points for existential questions as to who we are and why we exist. The history and fate of a shipwreck can then become a compelling allegory of our own lives (Figs 2.5 & 2.6).

Figure 2.5. Another perspective: Birth, life, death - and rebirth - of the ship. The first of a series of sixteen prints by Sieuwet van der Meulen in the early 1700s, entitled 'Navigiorum aedificatio', illustrating the life story of a ship (de Groot, & Vorstman 1980).

Figure 2.6. Numbers 2 to 16 of 'Navigiorum aedificatio'. The ship takes form in the shipyard and is born into the water, there to grow and achieve full stature with masts and spars and adornment. Careened, armed and fully provisioned the ship puts to sea to face the vicissitudes of life:- plain sailing, warfare, storm-tossed seas, perhaps to be cast ashore and wrecked or with luck, reaching old age where, in the hospice of the breaker's yard some of its timbers and perhaps even its name are passed on to a new generation of ships. (See discussion in Adams 2003:30).

References

Adams, J. 1995. The Oskarshamn Cog - Hull recording. In C. O. Cederlund (ed.) *Medieval Ship Archaeology*. Stockholm: Stockholm University/ Nautical Archaeology Society.

Adams, J. 2003. *Ships, Innovation and Social Change*. Stockholm Studies in Archaeology 24. Stockholm: Stockholm University.

Adams, J. 2013. *A Maritime Archaeology of Ships. Innovation and Social Change in Late Medieval and Early Modern Europe*. Oxford: Oxbow Books.

Adams, J. & Rönnby, J. 1996. *Furstens fartyg. Marinarkeologiska undersökningar av en renässanskravell*. Stockholm: Sjöhistoriska museet / Länsstyrelsen i Stockholms län.

Adams, J. & Rönnby, J. 2002. Kuggmaren 1: the first cog find in the Stockholm archipelago, Sweden. *International Journal of Nautical Archaeology* 31.2: 172-181.

Adams, J. & Rönnby, J. 2013. One of his Majesty's 'beste kraffwells'. The wreck of an early carvel-built ship at Franska Stenarna, Sweden. *International Journal of Nautical Archaeology* 42.1: 103-117.

Ahlström, C. 1997. *Looking for Leads. Shipwrecks of the past revealed by contemporary documents and the archaeological record*. Helsinki: Finish Academy of Science and letters.

Bass, G. F. 1967. Cape Gelidonya: a Bronze Age Shipwreck. *Transactions of the American Philosophical Society* 57.8: 1-177.

Burström, M. 2004. Archaeology and Existential Reflexion. In: H. Bolin (ed.) *The Interplay of Past and Present*. Södertörn Achaeological Studies 1. Södertörn: Södertörn University.

Cederlund, C. O. 1981. *Vraket vid Älvsnabben. Fartygets byggnad*. Statens Sjöhistoriska museum rapport 13. Stockholm: Statens Sjöhistoriska Museet.

Cederlund, C. O. 1982. *Vraket vi Jutholmen. Fartygets byggnad*. Statens Sjöhistoriska museum rapport 16, Stockholm: Statens Sjöhistoriska Museet.

Cederlund, C. O. 1983. *The Old Wrecks of the Baltic Sea*. BAR International Series 186. Oxford: BAR.

Cederlund, C. O. 1987. The Eric Nordevall . An early Swedish paddle steamer. In: G. Burenhult et al. (eds) Theoretical Approaches to Artefacts, Settlements and Society. Studies in honour of Mats P. Malmer. BAR international series 366 (ii). Oxford: British Archaeological Reports.

Crumlin-Pedersen, O. 2000. To be or not to be a cog: the Bremen Cog in perspective. *International Journal of Nautical Archaeology* 29.2: 230–246

Djerw, U. & Rönnby, J. 2003. *Treasures of the Baltic Sea. A hidden wealth of culture*. Stockholm: Swedish National Maritime Museum.

Dolwick, J. S. 2009. 'The Social' and Beyond: Introducing Actor-Network Theory. *Journal of Maritime Archaeology* 4.1: 21-49.

Edberg, R. 2002. *Färder I österled. Experiment, källor, myter och analogier*. Stockholm Marine Archaeological Reports 2. Stockholm: Stockholm University.

Eriksson, N. 2012. The Lion Wreck: a survey of a 17th-century merchant ship - an interim report. *International Journal of Nautical Archaeology* 41.1: 17-25.

Eriksson, N. *Urbanism under sail*. DPhil thesis, Södertörn University (forthcoming).

Eriksson, N. & Rönnby, J. 2012. The Ghost Wreck. An Intact Fluyt from c.1650 in the Middle of the Baltic Sea. *International Journal of Nautical Archaeology* 41.2: 350–361.

Flatman J. 2003. Cultural biographies, cognitive landscapes and dirty old bits of boat: 'theory' in maritime archaeology. *International Journal of Nautical Archaeology* 32.2: 143-157.

Francke, J. 1998. The Voyage of the Dutch Merchant Ship "Juffrouw Catharina" 1741-1747. Unpublished report: Södertörn University.

Gadamer, H-G. 2004 (1960). *Truth and Method*. London: Bloomsbury.

Geertz, C. 1973. Notes on the Balinese Cockfight. In: *The Interpretation of Culture*. New York: Basic Books.

Glete, J. 1993. *Navies and Nations: Warships, Navies and State Building in Europe and America, 1500-1860*. Stockholm Studies in History, No 48. Stockholm: Stockholm University.

Glete, J. 2000. *Warfare at Sea. Maritime Conflicts and the Transformation of Europe*. London: Routledge.

Glete, J. 2002. *War and the State in Early Modern Europe. Spain, the Dutch Republic and Sweden as fiscal-miltary states, 1500-1660*. London: Routledge.

Gerner, K. & Karlsson, K-G. 2002. *Nordens Medelhav. Östersjöområdet som historia, myt och projekt*. Stockholm: Natur och Kultur.

Groot, I. de, & R. Vorstman. 1980. *Maritime Prints by Dutch Masters*. London: Gordon Fraser.

Hansson, S. 2002. *Den skapande människa: om människan och tekniken under 5000 år*. Student dissertation on file. University of Lund.

Hjulhammar, M. 2010. *Stockholm från sjösidan. Marinarkeologiska fynd och miljöer*. Stockholm: Stockholmia Förlag.

Hodder, I. 1992. *Theory and Practice in Archaeology*. London: Routledge.

Jamesson, F. 1984. Postmodernism, or the cultural logic of late capitalism. *New Left Review* 146. 1: 53 – 92.

Johnson, M. 2002. *Behind the Castle Gate. From the*

Middle Ages to the Renaissance. London: Routledge.

Kaijser, I. 1981. *Vraket vid Älvsnabben*. Statens Sjöhistoriska museum rapport 13. Stockholm: Statens Sjöhistoriska Museet.

Kaijser, I. 1983. *Vraket vid Jutholmen. Last och utrustning*. Statens Sjöhistoriska museum rapport 17. Stockholm: Statens Sjöhistoriska Museet.

Kirby, D. 1990. *Northern Europe in the Early Modern period: The Baltic World 1492-1772*. London: Longman.

Kirby, D. & Hinkkanen, M-L. 2000. *The Baltic and the North Seas*. London: Routledge.

Latour, B. 2005. *Reassembling the Social: An Introduction to Actor-Network-Theory*. Oxford: Oxford University Press.

Marx, K. 1852. *Eighteenth Brumaire of Louis Bonaparte*. Gloucester: Dodo Press.

Moberg, C-A. 1969. *Introduktion till arkeologin*. Stockholm: Natur och kuktur.

Mogren, M., Roslund,M., Sundnér, B., & Wienberg, J. 2009. *Triangulering. Historisk arkeologi vidgar fälten*. Lund Studies in Historical Archaeology 11. Lund.

Muckelroy, K. 1978. *Maritime Archaeology*. Cambridge: Cambridge University Press.

Olsen, B. 2010. *In Defense of things. Archaeology and the ontology of objects*. Lanham: Altamira Press.

Pulak, C. 1998. The Uluburun shipwreck: an overview. *International Journal of Nautical Archaeology* 27.3: 188-224.

Rediker, M. 1989. *Between the Devil and the Deep Blue Sea: Merchant Seamen, Pirates and the Anglo-American Maritime World, 1700-1750*. Cambridge: Cambridge University Press.

Rönnby, J. 2003. Land`s End. In: J. Rönnby (ed.) *By the Water. Archaeological Perspectives on Human Strategies around the Baltic Sea*. Södertörn Academic Studies 17. Huddinge: Södertörn University.

Rönnby, J. 2004a. En flygande holländare i Oxelösund. In: A. Åkerlund (ed.) *Kulturell mångfald i Södermanland*, del 2: 123-133. Nyköping: Länsstyrelen i Södermanland.

Rönnby, J. 2004b. Archaeology and the Contemporary.

The Limestone Industry at Lörje, Gotland, Sweden. In: H. Bolin (ed.) *The Interplay of Past and Present*. Södertörn Achaeological Studies 1. Huddinge: Södertörn University.

Rönnby, J. 2007. Maritime Durées. Long-Term Structures in the Coastal Landscape. *Journal of Maritime Archaeology* 2.2: 65-82.

Rönnby, S-E. 2002. Jungfru Catharina – en flygande holländare vid sörmlandskusten. *Sörmlandbygden. Södermanland hembygdsförbunds årsbok*. Nyköping.

Rönnby, J. & Adams, J. 1994. *Östersjöns Sjunkna skepp. En marinarkeologisk tidsresa*. Stockholm: Tiden.

Rålamb, Å. 1691. *Skeps byggerij Eller Adelig Öfnings Tionde Tom Medh behörige Kopparstycken*. Published by Niclas Wankijf Stockholm 1691.

Sundin, B. 2006. *Den kupade handen. Människan och tekniken*. Carlssons. Stockholm.

Thorpe, I. J. N. 2003. Anthropology, archaeology, and the origin of warfare. *World Archaeology* 35.1: 145-165.

Unger, R. 1978. *Dutch shipbuilding before 1800. Ships and guilds*. Amsterdam: Van Gorcum.

Varenius, B. 1992. *Det Nordiska Skeppet. Teknologi och Samhällsstrategi i Vikingtid och Medeltid*. Stockholm Studies in Archaeology 10. Stockholm: Stockholm University.

Waterstone, A. 2009. *An Anthropology of War. Views from the Frontline*. New York/Oxford: Berghahn Books.

Weber, M. 1904-5 (1978). *The Protestant Ethic and the Spirit of Capitalism* (trans Stephen Kalberg). Oxford: Blackwell.

Weibust, K. 1969. *Deep sea sailors. A Study in Maritime Ethnology*. Stockholm: Nordiska Museum.

Witsen, N. 1690. *Architectura Navalis et Regimen Nauticum. Ofte Aaloude en Hedendaagsche Scheepsbouw en bestier*. Amsterdam.

Personal communication

Jerzy Garwonski: Professor of Archaeology, Amsterdam.

3

THE SKELETON IN THE DUNE. UNLOCKING THE EXPLANATORY POTENTIAL OF SHIPWRECKS THROUGH PHYSICAL LANDSCAPE STUDIES

Oscar Törnqvist

In this chapter, the inherent potential of viewing wrecks and other maritime archaeological features within the context of the physical landscape is explained and its necessity for their study is emphasized. The measurable natural forces and processes that act on the land- and seascape are examined. Some archaeological sites are presented in a discussion on methodological implications and solutions for seascape analysis. It is concluded that not only is it important to understand the physical landscape in order to interpret each shipwreck in a meaningful manner (site-formation studies), but studies at landscape level provide substance to the black dots on distribution maps, permit maritime cultural landscape studies, and also capture important knowledge imperative to the interpretation and re-interpretation of terrestrial near-shore archaeological sites. It is essential to integrate environmental relationships and quantitative models borrowed from oceanography, sedimentology and other related disciplines to best understand 'the skeleton in the dune'.

Introduction

It is well known that maritime archaeology, as well as any other research disciplines, historically has been struggling with the definition and status of its own discipline, both as an independent field of research and as a sub-discipline of archaeology as a whole (the latest comment coming from Myrberg Burström 2012, an earlier voice in Carpenter 1991). Whereas some consensus has been reached concerning methods and

aims (first attempted by Muckelroy 1978, later by Babits and Van Tilburg 1998), there is still within many research communities a lack of self-reflection as to the position of research *vis-à-vis* terrestrial archaeology in respect to the level of inquiry which underpins research, for instance illustrated by Hawkes' ladder of inference (Hawkes 1954). More specifically, the question of how documenting ship timbers contributes to social sciences or inquiries within the field of the humanities, is often not raised, sometimes making at least ship archaeology in practice a sub-discipline of the history of technology, not of any socially or ideologically relevant archaeology.

Thus, maritime archaeology is still often criticized, mainly by actors within other archaeological disciplines, for being isolationist, object-fixated and over-descriptive by placing too much focus on documentation and ship-building techniques. Today this critique is only partially relevant. Much has been happening to the standard of research during the last two decades, partly by elevating research from a technical, processualist anthropology and creating a more post-modern social archaeology (cf. Adams 2003:17ff). The intellectual maturity has improved and the subject has become more integrated with many adjacent research communities (Adams 2006).

However, the basic challenge principally remains. How do you make basic recordings of rotting timbers relevant to the humanities or social sciences? Many scholars have investigated this from the standpoint of methodology (e.g. Gould 2000, most recently Markoulaki 2009) and implications of ideology for the writing of history (Cederlund 1997), concluding that this limited focus can be readdressed by creating a framework for research where the subject of study becomes the societal systems that rely on maritime activity (such as trade, fishing, warfare, etc.) rather than the physical remains of these activities (first by Muckelroy 1978, later Flatman 2003; Oka & Kusimba 2008; Dolwick 2009), the classical "archaeology is about people, not things". Accordingly maritime archaeology should be able to complement other fields of archaeological enquiry in creating more complete societal narratives and interpretations (Adams 2001).

Looking at the *de-facto* results produced from research, it soon becomes evident that the discipline seldom comes close to realizing its inherent potentials as outlined by its most ardent proponents. While the subjects raised and the questions posed often address complex issues (Flatman 2003), the actual results of ship archaeology are still dominated by what in terrestrial archaeology would be labelled descriptive and particularistic documentation, lacking major relevance or ramifications for other historical or archaeological fields of study. Ships are often interpreted in a societal context, but society is rarely re-interpreted by using shipwrecks (Ahlström 1997 for an example, Svenwall 1994 and later Adams 2003 as contrasts). In many instances the inheritance from the 1980s where identification and interpretation of the ship was central (evident in e.g. Cederlund & Kaijser 1981, 1982; Cederlund 1983), still colour much ongoing research, today best illustrated by the vast number of salvage and documentation projects undertaken and presented mainly by north American archaeologists. This is an ironic turn-around from the early 1980s when the 'shipwreck anthropologists' cast disparaging glances towards their particularist European counterparts (see Lenihan 1983; Murphy 1983).

A plank adrift

The many hull-intact shipwrecks in the Baltic sea have not only made the area earn renown, but also to some extent directed research. The traditional work on artefacts and technology of e.g. the *Vasa* ship has paved the way for a more socially directed archaeology of architecture (Eriksson in this volume). Often forgotten and neglected, however, are the numerous more derelict wreck assemblages. But the attraction to the more ostentatious wrecks is not only a matter of aesthetics. It is also an effect of inherent research friction. Posing socially relevant research questions to a pile of planks is not done without some effort. In this respect, wrecks as such share some common characteristics. One can point out some general properties of wrecks and ship-wrecking and how this complicates the elevation of

archaeological analysis to the level of social science:

- Mobility: Being 'lost at sea', wrecked ships represent a mobile aspect of culture which *de facto* creates an archaeological record often void of any external context. Conversely, a settlement or grave is always part of a larger cultural landscape that serves to explain the features located within it. Ship timbers without context can be equated with stray finds in a terrestrial setting and the challenge then arises to create some kind of context by analyses of the intrinsic properties of the assemblage.

- Intentionality: A shipwreck is often the result of an accident. Hence the wreck site lacks context according to expressed human intent. As the event of wrecking lacks intentionality, the analysis must strive to uncover the meanings behind the phenomenon, a challenge not normally faced in a terrestrial setting. However, the 'biography' of the wreck site also creates new opportunities, as we can start to trace the intentionality of the primary action behind the voyage and also of the events and contexts leading up to the wrecking, by carefully studying the wreck and wreck site. Terrestrial archaeology often has to face much more complicated intentionalities behind sites, such as settlements and ritual landscapes.

- Representativity: Terrestrial landscapes are surveyed and investigated systematically. Shipwrecks are discovered by chance and maritime regional surveys are still sporadic, though getting more frequent. The processes of underwater site formation not only influence the existence (through wrecking) and state of submerged sites (through formation processes), but are also not adequately understood. Cultural heritage management as well as scientific surveys and assessments of the cultural significance behind site distribution patterns and the methodology used for location and documentation all rely on the relationships between object, landscape and natural (and anthropogenic) forces. Both prerequisites for heritage management and the interpretation of the "large picture" rely on the formation processes – and our ability to understand them.

- Complexity: Primarily affecting the study of prehistoric and early historic wrecks, comparatively fewer wrecks have been studied than terrestrial sites and monuments. The sites that are encountered represent one or several of many complex societal subsystems (trade, fishing, warfare, etc., – it is often unclear which) that may originate from any period in history. A ship's construction, architecture and decoration are often the result of multifaceted social and economic systems. The same applies to the find assemblages on-board. A technique common to terrestrial archaeology is to either explicitly (through statistics or GIS) or implicitly (though judgement, comparison) treat assemblages and associations in a quantitative manner, but this requires a comparative base collection. As for wreck studies, there are often too few well-studied ship sites to support comparative, quantitative studies or conclusions based on statistics and spatial analysis. There are too many variables in the equation and too little empirical data to feed into it; the data at hand does not match the complexity of the study, so to speak. In the terrestrial field, it would, by analogy, be impossible to study social ranking through grave finds without several hundred sites and graves to compare with (but that is in itself a problematic task). However, due to preservation issues, there is almost always a *qualitative* advantage to submerged studies, where many objects survive that would soon be destroyed at a terrestrial site. The key, again, is to understand formative processes for site location, creation and preservation.

Mountains or molehills?

Three concepts regarding the explanatory potential inherent in shipwrecks have gained widespread acceptance, perhaps as a counterweight to the above mentioned complications [1], namely:

- 'Closed find': Everything on a wreck originates from one particular discreet point in time.[2] There is no interference from other periods and all objects are contextually related and meaningful, in contrast to the constantly exploited and altered terrestrial areas (e.g. Kalmar läns museum 2012).

- 'Time capsule': The notion that this rich and undisturbed 'closed find' offers a unique hermeneutic possibility for experiencing an authentic whole from a specific period of time, a frozen moment, is envisaged as having great explanatory potential (Bass 1983; O'Shea 2002:211; Vuijsters 2004:12).

- 'Society in miniature': The interpretation of life onboard a ship as contemporary society in miniature stems from the concept of wrecks as 'time capsules' and 'closed finds'. (Flatman 2003; Einarsson 1996a, 1996b). Indeed, Einarsson (1996b) goes so far as to say that society on-board the man-of-war *Kronan* actually represented a full-scale society; its crew representative of a Swedish 17th century small town, and that this society can be studied using ship archaeology.

It is easy to criticize the idea of a wreck as an archaeological 'society in miniature'. As Muckelroy (1978:221ff) pointed out long ago, societies on-board ships were closed and relatively fixed, but were in no way representative of anything else than themselves. A mirror or reflection of society isn't the same as a miniature society. The approach must be that each ship had its own, unique society resulting from a mix of economic, military, social, cultural and societal needs, jurisdictions, preferences and pragmatic solutions. As these are unknown to us, rather than using simplistic analogies looking for correlations between historic facts and archaeological remains, the opposite approach is relevant; to expose differences between the archaeological record and the wider society (Adams 2003:31ff). Thus the wreck and the ship in its original state prior to wrecking are two very different things. Whereas a complete and untouched wreck could in theory be considered a 'closed find' offering the experience of a 'time capsule', only a negligible portion of known wrecks display such potential[3] and to understand the 'biography' of a decomposed shoe or scattered timbers becomes an imperative task, again to reduce the effects of site formative 'scrambling' and 'extraction' filters (Muckleroy 1978:165ff) to create a more solid base for societal interpretations.

As it happens, a vast majority of all known wrecks exhibit such scrambling and extraction filters, whether natural (erosion from waves, ice scour, etc.) or anthropogenic (e.g. salvage operations, deliberate destruction or damage from fishing or anchorage). These filters alter the content and spatial relationships on a site in such a way that it becomes impossible to treat the wreck as a 'closed' historical context. Surely the study of site formation processes, together with excavation technique including stratigraphic analysis, all allow us to better identify disturbance features. Even in disturbed sites there are often parts of the site that are undisturbed where contextual relationships survive. Again, understanding formative processes will increase the source value of the ship wreck. Furthermore, the few opportunities for studying 'time capsules' run the risk of rewriting the history not of a maritime culture but of a specific kind of vessel that was perhaps not so common, e.g. the most durable transport vessels and men-of-war from the 17th to the 19th centuries. This creates an interpretative and discursive bias. In the Nordic countries, for instance, we have no archaeology of the small vernacular coastal vessel, simply from the effects of site formation processes and survey methodologies; we have not found the wrecks.

Flatman (2003:149) overstretches the potential of maritime (ship) archaeology to include the possibility of studying such aspects of society as leisure activities (dancing and performances, conversation and swimming, etc.) and festivals (Christmas, births and deaths, baptism, etc.). This is surely rather optimistic, considering the limitations and biases inherent in the material record already mentioned. The distance between 'planks adrift' and societal narratives is vast, no doubt the reason for the failure of wreck archaeology to deliver the kind of knowledge it really should be capable of, if the wreck is re-contexualised in respect to 'biography', formation processed and other spatial contexts.

Methodologically inclined archaeologists partially addressing this dilemma have acknowledged the need to understand the processes that shape wrecks (e.g. Manders et al. 2009, first expressed in Muckelroy 1978:157ff). Site-formation studies must act as precursors to any interpretation, by explaining relevant preconditions. While this type of research is necessary it does not by itself give the full leverage to the idea that wrecks are transmitters of social, cultural, ideological and economic history. Severely eroded wrecks or sites of minor complexity offer little more than the obvious to site formation studies; all we really have at hand is a pile of broken planks. The key which is suggested here is to combine the study of formative processes with studies of other spatial relationships in a landscape context, trying to recreate the 'biography' and wider context of the ship and site. Besides basic information on e.g. dating and technological solutions, a re-contextualisation of the pile of planks can start conveying the usage, disposal and life-trajectory of the wooden skeleton, which makes it relevant to richer social narratives.

Site chaos and landscape logic

Maritime site formation can be understood as the result of spatial processes; human or natural, site-specific (e.g. salvage) or general (e.g. waves, climate). At the same time, many of these factors or processes are what create wreck sites in the first place. For instance, wave climate is a factor that not only shapes the site of a wreck but is often one of the causes of the wrecking itself.

Returning to the initial problems inherent in wreck studies as outlined here, we must understand that the apparent problems of mobility, intentionality and representativity both depend on and can be explained by forces acting in the landscape. Shipping lanes in the archipelago are governed by wind movements, but so too are drifting wrecks. Besides being part of a larger complex cultural landscape, the location of harbours

relate to wave climate, especially in an archipelago or semi-sheltered environment. The same forces shape the coastline, hiding not only shipwrecks but whole cultural complexes. Representational issues can only be tackled when a better understanding of the nature of the seabed is obtained; a natural component in the apparent absence of wrecks might be explained in terms of destructive wave energy, ice scour or recent sedimentation.

Clusters of maritime features have a much better chance of meaningful interpretation if coastal processes and the dynamics of the underwater landscape are understood. A shift of focus from site formation on a local level to the forces of formation at landscape level suddenly turns the 'black dots' on distribution maps of wreck sites from arbitrary debris to significant pawns on the maritime chessboard (see O'Shea 2002 for an attempt). Such an approach is connected with the possibilism observed by environmentalists, in that it acknowledges that while cultural adaptation always takes the environment into account, it is not always dictated by it. To understand cultural development in a harsh climate, we must also understand the natural forces at play.

Landscape and seascape archaeology

A few words may be said concerning the methods and aims of landscape archaeology when advocating a landscape (or rather, 'seascape') archaeological approach. This is especially suited to interpreting underwater sites and wrecks which hold very weak inherent explanatory power. Few well-preserved wrecks have been investigated, as most wrecks are largely stripped of their content and context (hence 'the skeleton in the dune'). The large number of finds and salvage operations may have accumulated a large database of ship timbers (Flatman 2007) but with very little ramification outside ship archaeology.

Such a situation is not new to archaeology. In terrestrial landscape archaeology, it is common to use scatter plots of sites, monuments or finds identified only by type rather than by precise content, to create meaningful patterns of spatial dependency. The large number of recorded wrecks and other maritime sites and monuments makes them ideal for a similar type of seascape analysis, if the inherent problems of interpretation are understood. Luckily, these problems relate to the landscape/seascape context itself so we here have one analytical level facilitating both the understanding of single sites and assemblages as well as the relationship between sites: the natural preconditions and factors that are partially responsible for the shape of the maritime cultural landscape.

Landscape of the elements

The natural landscape of the coast and open sea is particularly harsh. The forces acting in the landscape are partially responsible not only for shaping, but also for creating sites. An understanding of these basic forces is required in order to decipher the meaning behind the contents and state of the maritime cultural landscape, including mobile cultural residues:- the wrecks.

There is plenty of data and many applicable models to use for this purpose, originating from various environmentally focussed disciplines (marine geology, sedimentology, oceanography, etc.). Basic factors suitable for study include:

- Wave energy and the wave base: Wave energy increases with wind force and fetch (the distance over which wind travels without hindrance), but decreases with depth down to the wave base where wave impact upon submerged structures is negligible (Bekkby et al. 2008; Håkansson & Bryhn 2008:30ff). Wave models explain where and how waves will affect the material record, the locations of exposed and protected areas and what this implies for the preservation and breakdown of wrecks etc. This delineates favourable and unfavourable areas for preservation and aids the interpretation of spatial patterns.

- Sedimentation processes: Fine-grained material and nutrients are transported from seabed abrasion, river runoff and rain nutrition, by wave force and sea currents to deeper, calmer areas creating accumulation of sediments in some areas and mobile basal substrates or basal erosion in others (see Jonsson 2008 with refs; Karlsson et al. 2009). A recognition of the sedimentation rate affecting wreck burial and an identification of areas of object movement/breakdown due to erosion is essential for understanding spatial patterns in the maritime archaeological record.

- Wind energy and wind-wave interaction: This concerns how wind forces act together with waves in the coastal zone and archipelago to form prerequisites for harbour installations, shipping lanes, etc. Study of the relationship between wind-wave exposure and coastal installations unveils important patterns of where and how coastal cultures have employed the coastal zone. To take a modern example, our exposed coastlines encourage few but large harbours, while protected archipelago shores encourage small and simple jetties (Törnqvist 2009). This factor has a relative effect on the organization of private vs. communal

economic activities in these environments.

- Coastal dynamics: In the temporal context of ship archaeology, the location of the shoreline and the character and stratigraphy of the beach zone are products of the above forces, as well as tidal regimes, the latter being neglible in our examples from the Baltic Sea. The zone not only depends on land upheaval through isostasy (Lilje et al. 2007), and the related processes of eustasy (Ekman 2001) but often locally depends more on the movement of mobile substrates in the upper few metres of the water column closest to the shore. Coastal dynamics are a key to understanding the location and preservation of shoreline structures (e.g. boat houses, jetties) and similar studies are needed when recreating ancient landscapes, studying historical maps, etc. (cf. Hoffman & Barnasch 2005 for an example).

Seascape archaeology - some examples

The strength of natural landscape studies is that once a quantitative relationship between a factor and its effects on the archaeological record, in terms of site location or site formation, is established, that knowledge can be applied to the whole landscape. If, for instance, it can be established that a wreck has broken down after a certain number of years in one type of landscape regime (wind, wave, currents, etc.), other parts of the landscape exhibiting similar conditions will yield similar preservation prerequisites. (cf. Muckelroy's early attempt to classify the impact of natural factors in 1978:160ff) Given enough data, mathematical models can be formed, allowing prediction of processes such as site formation.

It is also possible to use qualitative reasoning based on natural landscape studies. Important issues can be addressed by this method on a level where explanation and interpretation are directed by probabilistic reasoning. We can for instance conclude on the basis of qualitative experience that a person does not try to erect a wooden jetty where the waves will engulf it and tear it down during the first autumn storm. Quantitative analysis can enable us to calculate where such prerequisites exist.

Three examples follow below where the relationship between the natural environment and maritime archaeological sites is studied using existing environmental methods and numerical models. It will be shown that understanding the natural environment when investigating or interpreting archaeological sites, will not only give important input into the interpretation of the specific case, but also help understand the landscape context in which the specific case must be interpreted to leverage its full explanatory potential. For the sake of readability, mathematical formulae and calculations are omitted from the examples. Conclusions drawn within the examples are numbered within parenthesis.

Example 1: Relevance for ship archaeology

The early 16th century man-of-war designated *Kraveln* (the carvel) rests collapsed on the slope of a rocky reef in the Stockholm archipelago, at a depth of *c.* 35m (Fig. 3.1). The wreck has been partially investigated and mapped with non-invasive methods by Adams & Rönnby (2009, 2013). The wreck, with a large proportion of equipment and armament present, can be described as collapsed, with timbers still in quite good condition. Looking at the wreck site from a natural landscape perspective, one can conclude from existing models that the wreck lies below the wave base; the reef is situated in the middle of the protecting archipelago. Hence, (1) wave action is negligible on the shipwreck. No ice scour reaches this far down inside the relatively sheltered bays in the area. These observations prove that the collapse of the wreck is due to a violent destructive impact, followed by natural decomposition, not to any ongoing physical forces. The distribution of ship timbers and artefacts corroborate this, showing no geographical misplacement of items due to currents, ice action or waves. The conclusion is that (2) the

wreck has collapsed in a natural way. Interpreting the breakdown process, one must also be aware of the fact that the impact of the ship upon the reef might have been powerful. A theory advocated by Adams & Rönnby (2009, 2013) holds that a portion of the hull got dislodged at the moment of impact. This would no doubt contribute to the derelict state of the hull today.

With these observations in mind, one can look at another wreck from the same period, situated in a different part of the sheltered archipelago of east-central Sweden; the wreck known as *Ringaren* (Svenwall 1994). Being of the same date and situated in a similar landscape context, this vessel of comparable size (c. 27x8 m) is likewise situated below any ice or wave impact (at a depth of 21 m) but is nevertheless severely eroded and decomposed; while almost all hull planks have dislodged from the stem and stern and fallen away, a lot of the cargo and rigging are still *in situ*.

What do these two examples imply? A tentative conclusion is (3) that the clinker construction of early 16th century ships carries inherent structural weaknesses, lacking support from strong beams, resulting in a natural decomposition when rivets and nails start to snap from corrosion and erosion, which means that vessels of this age will never be found hull-intact today; the construction will collapse by itself due to a weaker design compared to the 17th century carvels (e.g. the wrecked Dutch *fluyts* known as the Ghost and Lion ships, see Eriksson 2010a, 2010b & 2011). A corollary will then be that shipwrecks in general will

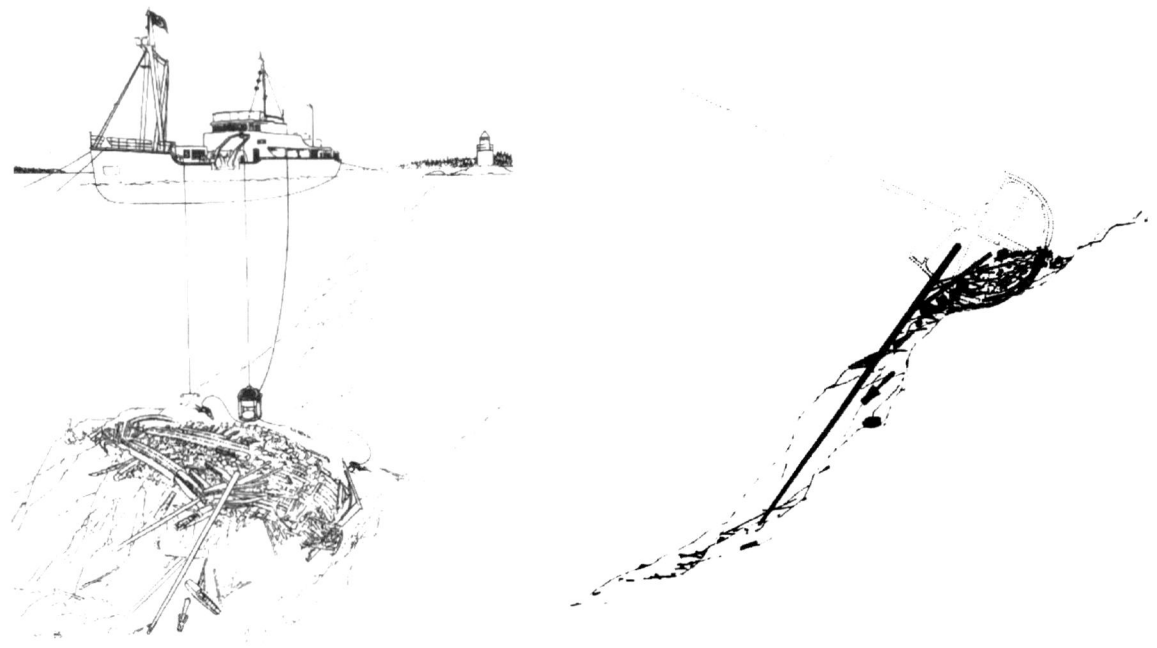

Figure 3.1. The early 16th century carvel shipwreck at Franska Stenarna, seen obliquely from above and from the side, illustrating its natural decomposition resulting primarily from a combination of its violent impact, method of construction and age rather than any physical forces. (Adams & Rönnby 2009, 2013).

only last hull-intact for *c*. 450 years in the Baltic, at the very best unless they come to lie in more estuarine locations and become partially buried, just like the sturdily built *Elefanten*, also from the 16th century, well-preserved in shallow waters in the Kalmar sound because of surrounding and partially covering rocks, put there for the support of the jetties constructed during the (failed) salvage operation during the 1560s. We can also from the above discussion (4) expect any 16th century wrecks resting on the flat seabed to protrude no more than one metre or so above the sea bed, which gives us an idea of what methods to use (and avoid) when surveying, especially in areas with ongoing sediment accumulation. Landscape studies and site formation studies together give important methodological feedback to the employment of survey techniques.

Example 2: Relevance for maritime archaeology

The *de facto* standard when surveying an area in conjunction with for example the construction of an underwater pipeline is to use side-scan sonar equipment to look for submerged cultural remains. A survey conducted near the Viking proto-town of Birka in Lake Mälaren, east-central Sweden, revealed over one hundred wreck finds, to the astonishment of the surveying archaeologists and recreational divers (Fig. 3.2). Over a couple of years, a dozen wrecks were inspected and to the dismay of the divers, all were revealed to be from the 19th or even the 20th century (Törnqvist 2003).

Using the landscape approach to study the scatter-plot of side-scan sonar indications in the context of the marine geological situation, it only takes a minute to conclude that over 90% of the wreck indications are located in areas with ongoing sedimentation (Fig. 3.2). Studying sampled cores from the seabed in the area (Olli 2007; Olli & Destouni 2007), one can further conclude that the sediments have grown between *c*. 1 and 2 metres since the Viking period. From numerous previous investigations of early medieval ships in the Mälaren area (e.g. Varenius 1989), the conclusion can be drawn that most likely all wrecks from that period are collapsed and very flat. Hence, they will be totally buried in sediments and invisible on a side-scan sonar image. Not only was (1) the survey in this example unfit for the purpose; (2) all maritime archaeologists doing surveys in areas where similar sedimentation occurs must resort to other methods than using side-scan sonar if older wrecks are to be located. Thus, (3) one can directly discern a representation issue, as the apparent wrecks will not be representative of the

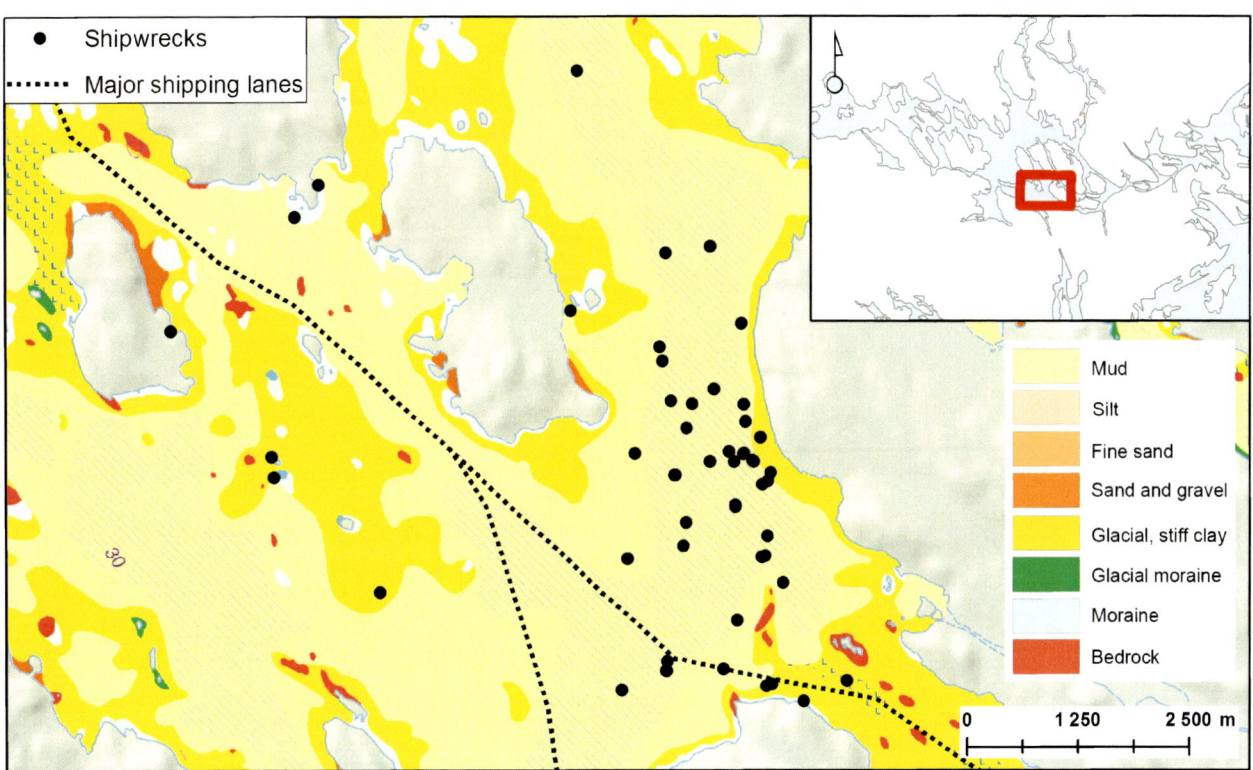

Figure 3.2. Wrecks discovered by using Side-scan sonar near Birka, lake Mälaren. Mainland and islands shown in grey. Almost all indications are found in areas with ongoing sedimentation (hatched in the map), implying that almost none of the indications can point to wrecks of medieval or Iron Age origin. (Base map: National Geological Survey of Sweden).

seafaring in the area.

Lake Mälaren is not severely exposed to wind and wave action. However, if the average wave force acting upon each unit of lake surface is analysed and the most distinct indications in the side-scan sonar diagram in figure 3.2 (mostly comprising 19th or 20th century barges) are plotted onto this wave exposure analysis, an interesting pattern appears (Fig. 3.3). All of the wrecks are located to areas near historical shipping lanes and where wave exposure is relatively high (but absolutely low on a Baltic scale). The fact that several wrecks are located more or less on top of each other implies that they are scuttled and sunk here (cf. Richards 2008), but the relatively high wave exposure suggests that (4) at least some of them have been wrecked there by natural causes. A tentative conclusion is that the area was designated as a ships' graveyard after a couple of wrecking accidents, and was used accordingly in a deliberate manner, in effect creating an *aqua nullius*, an area where fishing and anchorage became impossible. The dense cluster in Figure 3.3 with modern barges (5) must thus be explained in a landscape shaped by natural forces reinforced by cultural values and actions. This, in turn, (6) is relevant for cultural studies in that it gives clues to a shift in mentality and a dramatic break

in behavioural patterns during the industrialization process, resulting in completely different attitudes to material objects, waste and ships as disposables, as well as attitudes to space and the employment of locations.

Example 3: Relevance for terrestrial archaeology

The Kronholmen cog was found buried in sand when digging at a near-shore golf course at Västergarn, Gotland (Fig. 3.4). A fossil landscape from the Viking and early medieval periods had previously been discovered in the vicinity. The maritime cultural landscape includes a wall-enclosed settlement, a harbour, jetties, a pole barrier etc. (Rönnby 1996). Examination of the wreck and the context of the wreck highlight two aspects directly relevant for the interpretation of the cultural landscape in a broad as well as site-specific sense. The first aspect is the cultural context: the existence of a cog implies Hanseatic trade and contacts. But this cog seems to be special, as it is constructed in a way suggesting perhaps a local origin. (1) The centralization of power to Visby during this period and the abandonment of the harbour community at Västergarn must be studied in the context of this hybrid cog, this 'strange bird';

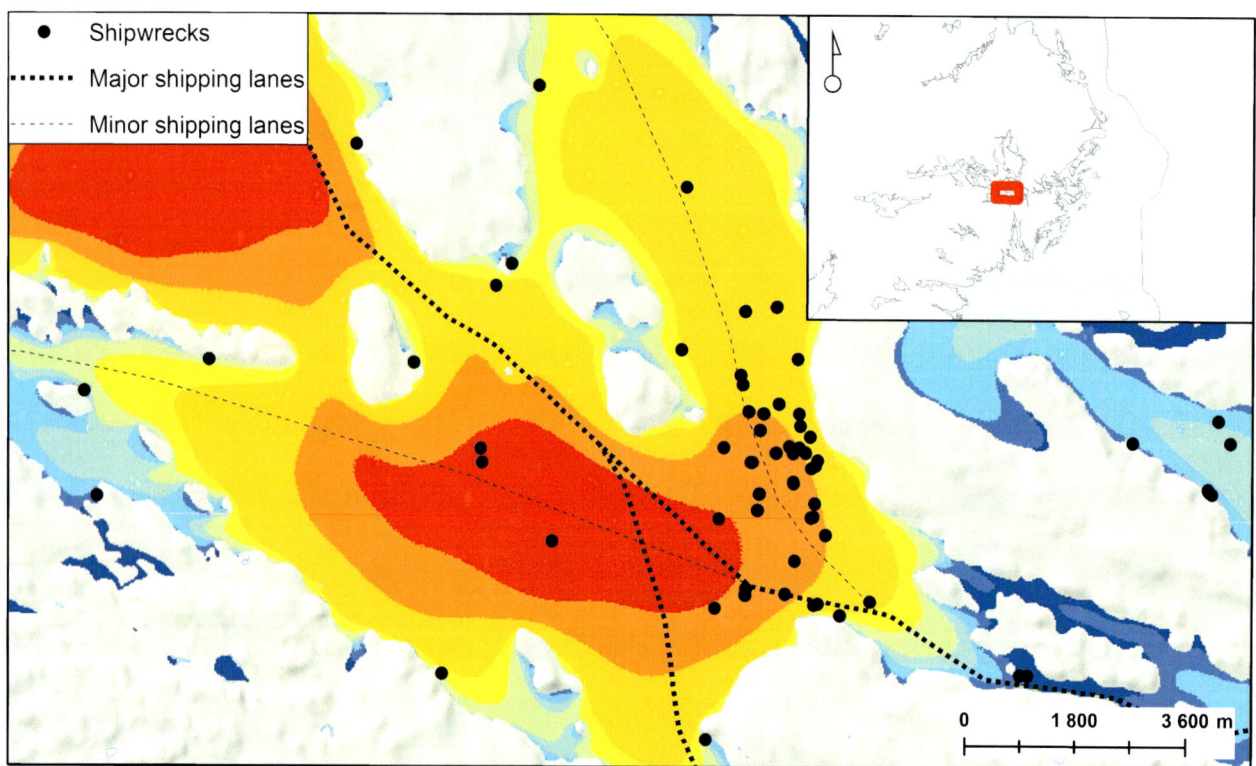

Figure 3.3. A wave exposure model showing the relative exposure of the lake surface due to wind-wave interaction for the medieval sea level. Red indicates high exposure, blue indicates very low exposure. Major shipping lanes in black, secondary lanes in grey. Wave model based on Isæus (2004). Note the relative high exposure and proximity to a secondary (but not major) shipping lane of the central cluster.

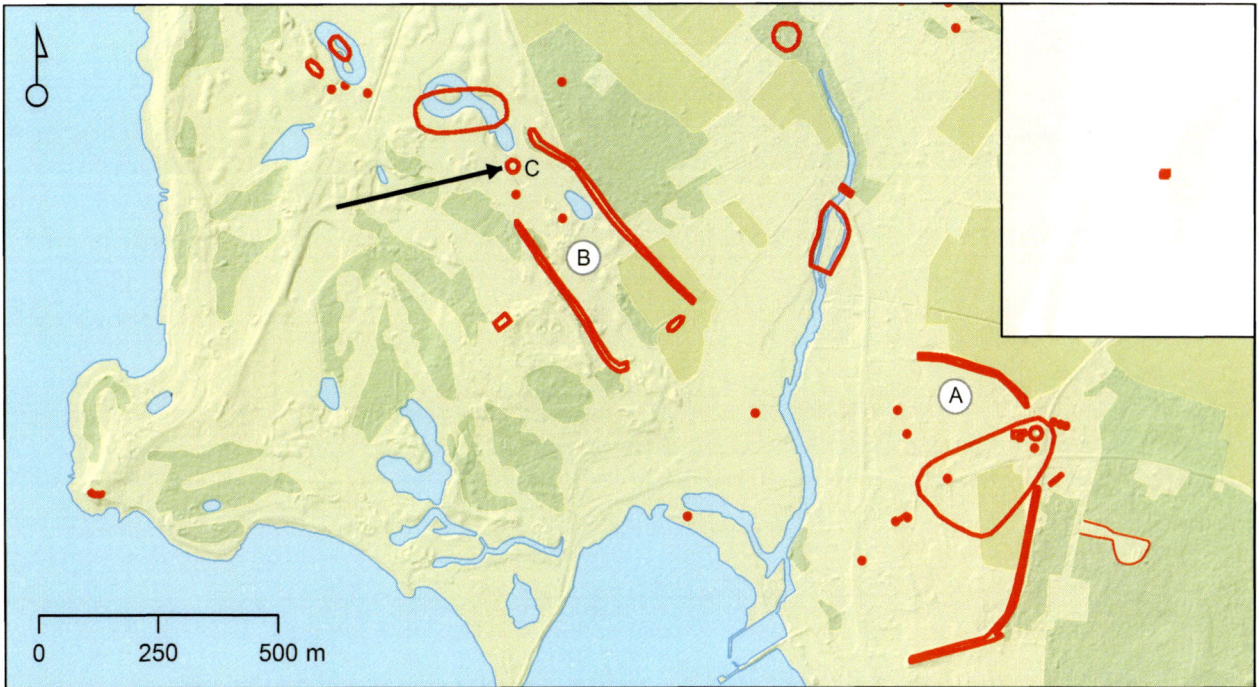

Figure 3.4. The complex fossilized cultural landscape at Kronholmen, Gotland. A = early medieval manufacturing and settlement site, including an earthen wall or rampart. B = medieval harbour, C = the cog, found in the middle of a golf course. Prehistoric and early mediaeval remains shown in red. (Map sources: National land survey of Sweden and the National board of Antiquities)

a key artefact for understanding the whole site. The physical context is thus imperative to interpretation.

The second aspect is the natural environment in which the cog appears. By studying historical maps and land upheaval models, there is no way of predicting the existence of a medieval harbour at the site of the cog find, which owes its existence to the wind/wave-driven aggregation of sand and resulting coastal plasticity. The nearby archaeological features (2) can thus be determined effectively to be a harbour through the presence of the wreck. Furthermore, by understanding sand transport and beach morphology in the littoral zone through the existence, use and dating of the cog, (3) it is possible to gain a better understanding of the character and rate of shoreline change, and the implication this has for surveying, mapping and understanding near-shore communities and ancient shorelines in a similar or comparable environment. The cog is in this context a key to a stratigraphical, chronological and geological comprehension of the sandy coasts of western Gotland.

Conclusion

Observation of the landscape and the totality of material remains, yield important knowledge for ship archaeology, maritime archaeology and also terrestrial archaeology, despite the fact that the objects studied often are little

more than a pile of planking. Quantitative models and known environmental relationships can be applied to a maritime archaeological context for this purpose with some success. A handful of relationships and methods, studies involving sedimentation and wave/wind impact upon site creation and site formation, can be used in every aspect of maritime research, from ship archaeology, via heritage management to the interpretation of maritime and near-shore archaeological sites. Understanding the relationship between nature and culture in the harsh maritime environment is essential for leveraging the explanatory potential of 'the skeleton in the dune'.

Notes

1 See the dictionary at http://www.abc.se/~pa/mark/ordlista.htm, pertaining to a very popular and influential site on marine archaeology.

2 Concerning the man-of-war *Kronan*, see http://www.regalskeppetkronan.se/fynden/fynden.php?lang=sv c.

3 Cf. Lars Einarsson, "Regalskeppet Kronan - en marinarkeologisk och historisk kunskapskälla" at http://www.infoartefact.se/fastaknappar/artiklar/artiklar6.html.

References

Adams, J. 2001. Ships and boats as archaeological source material. *World Archaeology*, 32. 3: 292-310.

Adams, J. 2003. *Ships, innovation & social change: aspects of carvel shipbuilding in northern Europe 1450-1850.* Stockholm Monographs 24. Stockholm: Stockholm University.

Adams, J. 2006. From the water margin to the centre ground? *Journal of Maritime Archaeology* 2006.1: 1-8.

Adams, J. & Rönnby, J. 2009. Kraveln. Marinarkeologiska undersökningar av ett skeppsvrak från tidigt 1500-tal I Nämdöfjärden, Stockholms skärgård. In: Schoerner, K. (ed.) 2009. *Skärgård och örlog. Nedslag i Stockholm skärgårds tidiga historia.* Konferenser 7:73-102. KVHAA, Stockholm.

Adams, J. & Rönnby, J. 2013. One of his Majesty's 'beste kraffwells'. The wreck of an early carvel-built ship at Franska Stenarna, Sweden. *International Journal of Nautical Archaeology* 42.1: 103-117.

Ahlström, C. 1997. *Looking for leads: shipwrecks of the past revealed by contemporary documents and the archaeological record.* Helsinki: Suomalainen tiedeakatemia.

Babits, L. E. & Van Tilburg, H. (eds) 1998. *Maritime archaeology: a reader of substantive and theoretical contributions.* New York: Plenum.

Bass, G., 1983. A plea for historical particularism in nautical archaeology. In: Gould, R. (ed.) *Shipwreck Anthropology*, 91-104. Albuquerque: University of New Mexico Press.

Bekkby, T., Isachsen, P. E, Isæus, M & Bakkestuen, V. 2008. GIS modeling of wave exposure at the seabed: A depth-attenuated wave exposure model. *Marine Geodesy* 31.2: 117-127.

Carpenter, S. P. 1991. Fra undervattensarkeologi til maritim arkeologi. Seminar paper, Universitetet i Tromsø.

Cederlund, C. O. & Kaijser, I. 1981. *Vraket vid Älvsnabben.* Stockholm: Statens sjöhistoriska museum.

Cederlund, C. O. & Kaijser, I. 1982. *Vraket vid Jutholmen. Fartygets byggnad.* Stockholm: Statens sjöhistoriska mus.

Cederlund, C. O. 1983. *The old wrecks of the Baltic Sea: archaeological recording of the wrecks of carvel-built ships.* PhD thesis. Stockholm: Stockholm University.

Cederlund, C. O. 1997. *Nationalism eller Vetenskap? Svensk marinarkeologi i ideologisk belysning.* Stockholm: Carlssons Förlag.

Dolwick, J. S. 2009. 'The Social' and Beyond: Introducing Actor-Network Theory. *Journal of Maritime Archaeology* 4.1: 21-49.

Einarsson L. 1996a. *Faktablad om Kronan.* Kalmar: Kalmar läns museum.

- 1996b. Vraket av regalskeppet Kronan - ett samhälle i miniatyr? *Populär Arkeologi* 2: 41.

Ekman, M. 2001. Computation of Historical Shore Levels in Fennoscandia due to Postglacial Rebound. *Small Publications in Historical Geophysics* No. 8, Summer Institute for Historical Geophysics, Åland.

Eriksson, N. 2010a. *Jutholmsvraket - ett handelsfartyg från sent 1600-tal.* Rapport 2010:1. Stockholm: Sjöhistoriska Museet.

- 2010b. Recording a big three-dimensional ship-structure - thoughts rendered from the Dalarö wreck project. *Proceedings of the third International Congress in Underwater Archaeology*, London.

- 2011. The Lion wreck - a survey of a 17th century merchant ship - an interim report, *International Journal of Nautical Archaeology* 41.1: 17-25.

Flatman, J. 2003. Cultural biographies, cognitive landscapes and dirty old bits of boat: 'theory' in maritime archaeology. *International Journal of Nautical Archaeology* 32.3: 143-157.

Flatman, J. 2007. *The Illuminated Ark. Interrogating Evidence from Manuscript Illuminations and Archaeological Remains for Medieval Vessels.* BAR International Series 1616. Oxford: BAR.

Gould, R. A. 2000. *Archaeology and the social history of ships.* Cambridge: Cambridge University Press.

Hoffman, G. & Barnasch, J. 2005. Late Glacial to Holocene coastal changes of SE Rügen Island (Baltic Sea, NE Germany). *Aquatic Science* 67:132-141.

Hawkes, C. 1954. Archaeological Theory and Method: Some Suggestions from the Old World. *American Anthropologist* 56.2: 155-168.

Håkansson, L. & Bryhn, A .C. 2008. *Eutrophication in the Baltic Sea.* Berlin/Heidelberg: Springer-Verlag.

Isæus, M. 2004. *Factors structuring Fucus communities at open and complex coastlines in the Baltic Sea.* PhD thesis, Stockholm: Dept of Botany, Stockholm University.

Jonsson, P. 2008. *Sedimentationsförändringar I Ådfjärden, Mälbyfjärden och syd Skramösund.* Report, Djurhamn: JP Sedimentkonsult.

Karlsson, M., Jonsson, P., Malmaeus, M. & Rydin, E. 2009. *Sediment studies in the Stockholm archipelago 2008.* IVL Report U2519, Stockholm: Swedish Environmental Research Institute.

Lenihan, D. 1983. Rethinking Shipwreck Archaeology: A History of Ideas and Considerations for New Directions. In R. Gould (ed.) *Shipwreck Anthropology*: 37-64. Albuquerque: University of New Mexico.

Lilje, M., Eriksson, P-O., Olsson, P-A., Svensson, R. & Ågren, J. 2007. *RH 2000 och riksavvägningen.* LMV Rapport 2007:14, Gävle: Swedish National Land Survey.

Manders, M., Oosting, R. & Brouwers, W. (eds). 2009. *MACHU Final Report*. Rotterdam: Educom Publishers.

Markoulaki, P. 2009. Archaeological Thinking and Practice in Maritime Archaeology. *Journal of Maritime Archaeology* 4.1: 87.

Muckelroy, K. 1978. *Maritime Archaeology*. Cambridge: Cambridge University Press.

Myrberg Burström, N. 2012. Händelser vid vatten. *Marinarkeologisk tidskrift* 3/2012: 11-15.

Murphy, L. E. 1983. Shipwrecks as a database for human behavioural studies. In R. Gould (ed.) *Shipwreck Anthropology*: 65-90. Albuquerque: University of Mexico press.

Nilsson, A. 1996. *Metodstudier och tolkningsmöjligheter*. Riksantikvarieämbetet Avdelningen för arkeologiska undersökningar Skrifter nr 20, Stockholm: National Board of Antiquities.

Oka, R & Kusimba, M. 2008. The Archaeology of Trading Systems, Part 1: Towards a New Trade Synthesis. *Journal of Archaeological Research* 16: 339-395.

Olli, G. 2007. Determination of the historical variation of the trophic state in lakes using sediment stratigraphies. In: *Hydrology and Earth System Sciences* 11: 1747-1756.

Olli, G & Destouni, G. 2007. Long-term Heavy Metal Loading to Near-Shore Lake Sediments. In: *Water, Soil, and Air Pollution* 192:105-116.

O'Shea, J. M. 2002. The archaeology of scattered wreck-sites: formation processes and shallow water archaeology in western Lake Huron. *International Journal of Nautical Archaeology* 31.2:211-227.

Richards, N. 2008. *Ships' Graveyards. Abandoned Watercraft and the Archaeological Site Formation process*. Gainesville: University Press of Florida.

Rönnby, J. 1996. Kronholmskoggen - Om ett skeppsfynd och dess tolkningsmöjligheter. In: H. Ranheden, E. Hyenstrand, M. Jakobsson, J. Rönnby & A. Nilsson (eds), *Metodstudier och tolkningsmöjligheter*. Riksantikvarieämbetet UV Skrifter 20. Stockholm: National Board of Antiquities.

Svenwall, N. 1994. *Ett 1500-talsfartyg med arbetsnamnet Ringaren*. PhD thesis, Stockholm University.

Törnqvist, O. 2003. *Marinens side scan sonar-undersökning i Hovgårdsfjärden och Södra Björkfjärden - Preliminär bedömning efter dyksäsong 2002-2003*. Unpublished report.

- 2009. *Brygginventering och exploateringsindikator för Sveriges kust*. Internal report, Metria Geoanalys.

Varenius, B. 1989. *Båtarna från Helgeandsholmen*. RAÄ UV Rapport 1989: 3. Investigation Report, Stockholm: National Board of Antiquities.

Vuijsters, I. 2004. *Ett osynligt kulturarv. Förslag på åtgärder för bevarande av skeppsvrak runt Gotland*. Seminar paper, Gotland University.

4

Well-preserved Shipwrecks in the Baltic Sea from a Natural Science Perspective

Yvonne Fors & Charlotte Gjelstrup Björdal

The cold brackish water of the Baltic Sea is well known for its unique properties that preserve marine archaeological material. However, the biological activity and chemical mechanisms that take place in such waterlogged wood has consequences for their future conservation and even for their mechanical stability. The most famous example of a wooden shipwreck suffering from the effects of such interactions is the Swedish warship *Vasa* (1628), but similar mechanisms create conservation challenges for shipwrecks world-wide. One of the most recent examples of a seemingly excellently preserved 17th century shipwreck in the Baltic Sea is the so-called Ghost Ship or Ghost wreck (*Spökvraket*) (Fig. 4.1). This article will focus on the biological and chemical action underwater that might be affecting the wood of the Ghost Ship. It is also hoped to explain the potential gains on offer to marine archaeologists, conservators and scientists alike, when undertaking collaborative projects in cultural heritage research at sea.

Introduction: A different perspective on the concept 'well-preserved'

Archaeological finds of organic material underwater, especially Baltic Sea shipwrecks, are often described as being 'in very good condition' or even as 'exceptionally well-preserved'. However, such observations are frequently made before assessment of the actual status of the submerged wood, tending to spring instead from first visual impressions of a more or less intact hull resting on the seabed with intact masts, detailed carvings and artefacts still in place. Such a context

offers the potential of a vast amount of archaeological information. The Baltic Ghost Ship is one of the latest examples of such an exceptionally well-preserved 17th century shipwreck. The enthusiasm created by this find, first located in 2003, is fully understandable.

The Baltic Sea is generally known to have excellent preservation conditions for finds on the seabed due to its cold brackish water and the absence of marine borers such as the 'shipworm' *Teredo navalis*. However, there are more hidden and thus easily overlooked biological and chemical factors that have significant effects on the conditions of timbers. Light-microscope studies often reveal the wood to be in various states of biological degradation and chemical analyses usually indicate contaminations (Fors 2008).

From our knowledge of the nature and origins of these environmental interaction at the seabed there are strong reasons to expect the wood of the Ghost Ship, as well as other shipwrecks in the Baltic, to be affected. Lately, most discussion concerning the famous *Vasa* ship has focused on challenges to preservation. The origin of most of these complex issues has been traced to mechanisms on the seabed. However, it is known that the different conditions at wreck sites determine the varying degree and distribution of both degradation and contamination in wood (Fors 2008). Experience of wooden wrecks at lower depths, such as the Ghost Ship, is limited. It is hoped to reveal here the hidden biological and chemical problems in marine wood in relation to the phrase 'well-preserved', often used for shipwrecks in the Baltic. One also wishes to demonstrate the need and potential of new research involving the collaboration of archaeologists and scientists, who have

Figure 4.1. The Ghost Ship, at 128m depth in the Baltic (Photo courtesy of MMT)

much to gain from one another when new advances are made within this multi-disciplinary field.

Preservation conditions in aquatic environments

The Baltic is famous for its many archaeological wrecks. The busy archipelago fairways with their many reefs are a challenge to navigation, and the Swedish Maritime Museum archive lists over 1,500 wrecks and over 10,000 sinkings along the 3000 km of the eastern Swedish coastline (Djerw & Rönnby 2001:19). Archaeological traces that are no longer visible on land are often preserved under water. The seabed offers many favourable conditions for the survival of organic material, including a wet, dark and cold climate, low oxygen levels, sedimentation and minimum human interference (Pearson 1987; Rönnby 2001). However, these same conditions also initiate long-term conservation problems for sunken wood, as lately described in detail (Sandström et al. 2002, 2005).

The state of a wreck depends on a combination of hydrographical, topographic and biological conditions

at the wreck site (Haasum & Westenberg 1994-95). When buried by sand, silt and mud a relatively stable, protective and anaerobic environment is created. Waterlogged wood has been found to survive for long periods of time and slowly become mineralised through natural sedimentary processes (Florian 1990; Nilsson 2004). Until recently, archaeological remains under water have been relatively well protected from human interference even though mechanical damage from fishing boats and large ferries can cause serious problems. New underwater technology and an increase in the number of amateur divers are additional factors, especially for shipwrecks (Rönnby 2001). Any physical contact with a wreck site alters its stable environment, especially if the sediment layers are disturbed whereby deterioration rapidly increases (Pearson 1987). Natural weather conditions such as waves, currents and winds can also cause changes in the seabed, and the transfer of sand and ice can cause extensive damage (Haasum & Westenberg 1994-95; Rönnby 2001:20).

Environmental effects and climate change have decisive ecological effects, probably not all of which are as yet identified. Contaminating toxins, eutrophication and an increased or changed input of nutrient salts all have significant effects on the chemical balance of the water's composition, its pH, alkalinity, solubility, temperature, oxygen levels, etc. (Stumm & Morgan 1996). In turn, this may have considerable consequences for the aquatic biological environment and in a longer perspective probably also for the marine archaeological material.

Aquatic chemistry in natural waters

Several different micro-climates have been defined in marine environments, but it is the solid-liquid interface of the seabed environment that has the strongest influence on the preservation of organic artefacts of wood (Jones 2003:2,13). Seawater is a solution of rather high concentrations of different inorganic salts, dissolved gases and organic compounds. The composition has remained quite constant over the recent geological past and in an aquatic chemical perspective the ocean can be considered as a steady-state model, where the input and output of compounds is balanced (Stumm & Morgan 1996). The concentrations of the major salt ions are in remarkably constant proportions and therefore directly proportional to the total salt concentration or salinity (in ‰). In over 97% of the seawater in the world, salinity lies between 33‰ and 37‰ (Stumm & Morgan 1996). Increases in salinity may result in increased galvanic corrosion of metals, stone and carbonates (Jones 2003:14). The major ion composition in seawater is $Cl^- > Na^+ > Mg^{2+} > SO_4^{2-} > Ca^{2+} > K^+$.

Generally, elements with low reactivity reside longer in water and consequently occur in higher concentrations there, compared to elements which more quickly convert to an insoluble form, e.g. sedimentation. Also, the relative proportions of the major ions in seawater and river water differ, which means the increases in the concentrations of dissolved salts by evaporation in river water and seawater do not correspond (Stumm & Morgan 1996; Jones 2003). The concentration proportions for other substances are in turn influenced by biological and chemical processes taking place in the sea and in the seabed (Jones 2003: 14).

Gases dissolved in seawater originate from the atmosphere, from biological activity or from degradation of organic debris in the water (Stumm & Morgan 1996). The solubility and consequently also the amount of the two most abundant dissolved gases in the sea, oxygen (O_2) and carbon dioxide (CO_2), decrease as temperature and salinity increases. The concentration of oxygen varies considerably in its many interactions with other chemicals. Biological activity in

the sediment interface involving aerobic degradation of organic compounds, often results in an anoxic seabed. This has an important inhibiting effect on the degradative mechanism in archaeological material, but also initiates other less desirable reactions (Jones 2003:14; Fors 2008).

The oxygen-depleted seabed is a reducing environment, whereas the oxygen-rich water surface is oxidative. Redox reactions involve the transfer of electrons and do not necessarily involve oxygen. An oxidation reaction requires the removal of electrons, while a reduction infers their acceptance (Stumm & Morgan 1996).

Biological wood degradation and chemical mechanisms at the site of a wreck

The reputation of the Baltic Sea as a site for excellent preservation rests mainly on the low salinity of the water (average ~ 6‰). This prohibits the action of the disreputable shipworm, *teredo navalis*, which at salinities of at least 12‰ severely degrades exposed waterlogged wood (Florian 1987). The absence of the *teredo navalis* is essential for the preservation of marine archaeological wood. This mollusc effectively bores tunnels lined with calcium carbonate through wood in saline marine environments. It is capable of totally decomposing a shipwreck within a decade and it is the greatest threat to shoreline historical timbers *in situ*. This physical damage can also impact on subsequent conservation, since the calcium carbonate can prevent conserving chemicals from penetrating the wood (Florian 1987; Jones 2003). There are indications of an increased spread of the *teredo navalis* in the brackish environment of the Baltic Sea as a possible effect of global climate change. Against this background, a novel research project was initiated, aiming to develop strategies for the protection of shipwrecks in the Baltic Sea against increasing attack by wood-degrading marine borers (Björdal 2009).

Unfortunately, the absence of *teredo navalis* does not mean a lack of other wood-decaying organisms. Degradation of waterlogged wood generally occurs in microbial rather than chemical processes and is a part of the biomass cycle in natural ecosystems. In general, a large number of organisms, each specialised to degrade different wood-cell components, are involved. As soon as the wooden object enters the water, the invasion of marine microorganisms begins (Nilsson 2004). The lignin in wood can act as a barrier for microbes, and the polysaccharides (cellulose and hemicellulose) generally degrade first. Microbial attack breaks down or changes the structural components in the wood, which results in disintegration and decreased mechanical strength (Nilsson 2004; Pearson 1987; Jones 2003).

Wood-degrading fungi in marine environments belong to the group of Ascomycetes and *fungi imperfecti*, also called soft rot. Their enzymatic activity leads to softening and darkening of the wood material, followed by a significant reduction in strength (Björdal et al. 1999; Nilsson 2004). Wood degradation by bacteria is a slow process in comparison to deterioration by marine fungi (Nilsson 2004). However, the bacterial colonization of wood increases the permeability and predisposes the wood structure to further microbiological attack (Clausen 1996). The invading bacteria can be distinguished as primary and secondary degraders, with the former attacking intact wood (Blanchette 1995). Based on the specific morphology of the wood decay, as observed by light and electron microscopy, they have been divided into three groups, i.e. tunnelling, erosion and cavitation bacteria (Björdal et al. 1999).

The erosion bacteria are active wood degraders and are prevalent in low oxygen conditions in the sediment (Björdal et al. 1999; Nilsson & Björdal 2008). As primary degraders, erosion bacteria can efficiently break down the lignocellulose structure of the cell walls leaving behind a disintegrated content (Blanchette 1995; Singh & Butcher 1991; Björdal et al. 2000). Since the lignin-rich middle lamella is left relatively unchanged the wood cells remain glued together, which helps the wood to retain its outer physical shape in the swollen waterlogged state, giving the impression of well-preserved wood. However, with the loss of the strength of the cellulose fibres, the physical forces created when water evaporates are enough to collapse the weakened wood cells irreversibly upon drying, with severe shrinkage and distortion as a consequence (Blanchette et al. 1990; Björdal et al. 2005). This explains the biological origin behind the necessity for applying conservation agents to recovered waterlogged wood.

The secondary degrading bacteria include sulphate reducing bacteria which accompany other decaying microorganisms. Scavenging bacteria are not involved in the primary degradation process but can be found in the residual wood material from primary degraders, and are considered the penultimate organism in the degradation process (Singleton 1993; Singh & Butcher 1991; Björdal et al. 2000; Greaves 1971). Laboratory experiments have indicated that sulphate reducing bacteria follow in the tracks of erosion bacteria when degrading wood cellulose and produce hydrogen sulphide *in situ* in the wood. Although the full relationship between sulphate reducing bacteria and erosion bacteria is still largely unknown (Singh & Butcher 1991), these processes are significant for the accumulation of sulphur and iron in marine archaeological wood from the seabed (Fors et al. 2008) (Fig. 4.2). The sulphur, as well as other chemical contaminants in waterlogged wood, originates from

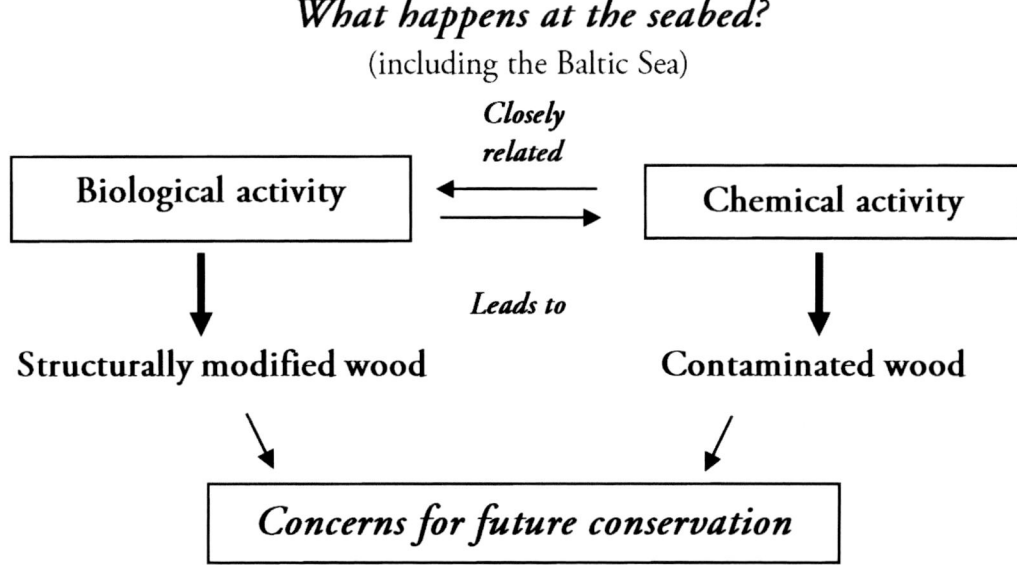

Figure 4.2. Diagram showing some of the many biological and chemical processes taking place at the seabed (of which many are related) having different effects on marine archaeological wood in situ.

the circulation of sulphate, iron, calcium, chlorine, etc. in natural waters. Corroding iron objects at a wreck site contribute additional iron ions (Sandström et al. 2005; Fors 2008).

The sulphur cycle, part I: The site of the Vasa wreck as an example

Several independent records from the 18th to the 20th centuries indicate severe contamination in the water of central Stockholm, where the *Vasa* lay. The breakdown of organic matter in natural waters requires oxygen. An anaerobic environment excludes some biological life. However, it does not discourage the activities of the erosion bacteria or the scavenging sulfate-reducing bacteria (Fors 2008). The mechanisms for sulphur and iron accumulation in the *Vasa* seem to be similar to those in other shipwrecks (Sandström et al. 2005; Fors 2008).

In a low oxygen environment, for example the former contaminated seabed of Stockholm harbour, anaerobic bacteria may continue oxidation processes (Florian 1987). Sulphate-reducing bacteria can utilise the sulphate ions of seawater as an electron acceptor in a process where simple organic molecules, such as organic carbohydrate, simultaneously act as electron donor during the degradation activity (Sørensen et al. 1981). The by-product is hydrogen sulphide, $H_2S(aq)$ according to reaction 1 (Sinninghe Damsté & de Leeuw 1990; Sørensen et al. 1981; Ehrlich 2002).

$$2(CH_2O) + SO_4^{2-} -> H_2S(aq) + 2HCO_3^- \quad (1)$$

The sulphur cycle, part II: conservation problems with sulphur and iron

The bacterially produced hydrogen sulphide reacts with lignin-rich parts of the wood structure to form reduced organosulphur compounds. In the presence of iron, Fe^{2+}, from the seawater or from corroding metal, iron sulphides, such as pyrite, FeS_2, are also formed (Sandström et al. 2005). Similar mechanisms can be traced in the accumulation of reduced sulphur compounds in organic material such as wet humic matter and in anoxic marine sediments (of low iron content), which eventually may end up in fossil fuels, coal and oil (Passier et al. 1999; Thode-Andersen & Jørgensen 1989; Varavamurthy & Mopper 1987). A comparison of shipwrecks preserved under different conditions, indicate that the distribution and amount of sulphur depend on the state of wood degradation, the conditions on the wreck site and the presence of iron (II) ions from corroding iron (Fors & Sandström 2006). Hence, in wood samples from the *Vasa* high sulphur accumulation occurred mainly in the

bacterially degraded surface layer, while for the *Mary Rose* the bacteria had degraded the wood throughout the hull and all analysed cores displayed a fairly uniform concentration of total S (Sandström et al. 2005). High iron and sulphur content has also been established in the hull of the *Batavia* (MacLeod & Kenna 1990) and in several other shipwrecks such as the Viking ships at Skuldelev, the *Kronan*, *Stora Sofia*, *Riksnyckeln*, *Tattran*, *James Matthews*, *Pandora* and *USS Monitor*. So far, the only exception is the Bremen cog (dated to 1380), in Germany, which was preserved in river water with a low sulphate concentration (Fors 2008).

The sulphur compounds, in particular the iron sulphides, oxidize to sulphuric acid in contact with oxygen and high humidity (Figs 4.3a, 4.3b). When sulphate and iron salt precipitates form on the wood surfaces the sulphur cycle is completed (Fors 2008). High acidity sulphate salts have not only been reported from the *Vasa* but on several museum shipwrecks (MacLeod & Kenna 1990; Sandström et al. 2002, 2005). The conservation agent, polyethylene glycol (PEG), used to impregnate and dimensionally stabilise a degraded wood structure, has been found to increase the corrosion rate of metallic iron (Guilminot 2000). Also, additional Fenton type oxidation reactions of the PEG catalysed by iron ions, probably originating from corroding bolts inserted during and after salvage, have been reported to form organic acids in the interior of the hull of the *Vasa* (Almkvist & Persson 2008). The acid hydrolysis and oxidative degradation could eventually reduce the mechanical stability of the wood structure (Fors & Sandström 2006).

The Ghost Ship

The Ghost Ship, or 'Ghost Wreck' is located in the centre of the Baltic Sea, 30 nautical miles east of the small island of Gotska Sandön. It rests upright on the sea floor at a depth of 125m in what is assumed to be an almost anoxic environment. The hull is intact and preliminary evaluations from collected observations of ship type, decoration, exterior and equipment on board date the ship to 1630-50. The most plausible dating from the dendrochronology analysis of a salvaged pine plank with a maximum dating span of 1636-1666, is 1640 ± 4 (Rönnby 2008). The Ghost Ship was first located in 2003 during the search for a Swedish DC-3 airplane lost in 1952. In 2007 and 2008, the ship was surveyed by Deep Sea Productions and MMTAB/ Marin Mätteknik using a Remotely Operated Vehicle (ROV). From that documentation the ship is estimated to be 25m long with a maximum width of about 8 m. The hull sides are concave and curved lengthwise with the stern standing about twice as high as the midship

Figure 4.3a Precipitated acidic sulphate salts from the hold of the Vasa. (Photo courtesy of Magnus Sandström)

Figure 4.3b. Precipitated acidic sulphate salts on a gun shield from the Mary Rose (1545). (Photo courtesy of Magnus Sandström)

41

deck. This tumblehome shape was typical for Dutch fluyts and the ship is built in carvel technique with three gunwales. The fore and main masts are still standing (Rönnby 2008; Eriksson & Rönnby 2012).

According to early observations the sedimentation overlying the Ghost wreck and the surrounding seabed seems to be limited to a thin, white dust layer, reminiscent of limestone, but is more likely the results of the sulphide oxidizing bacteria Beggiatoa spp (Preislet et al. 2007). A thorough investigation concerning the chemical and biological conditions on the seabed and in the water is required. These wreck site conditions differ in many respects from those of the *Vasa* (1628), which went down twenty odd years earlier to a depth of 32m, about 100 m offshore halfway down the entrance to Stockholm harbour. However, the sedimentation over the *Vasa* hull was also relatively limited (Fälting 1961).

In water with higher salinity only the timbers beneath the sediment crust survive, such as the remaining sections of the West Australian *Batavia* (1629) and the English *Mary Rose* (1545). The latter went down outside Portsmouth harbour in 14 m of water and through soft, yielding clays in the anoxic seabed, where about 1/3 of the hull was preserved under the formation of a hard grey shell-filled layer of compacted clay (Marsden 2003; Jones 2003). However, regardless of the different conditions on each unique wreck site, the biological and chemical mechanisms are generally similar (Fors & Sandström 2006; Fors 2008).

The greater depth of the Ghost Ship, the relatively low oxygen content and the undisturbed nature of the wreck site are favourable conditions for a well-preserved hull. However, from our knowledge of the chemical and biological interactions in marine environments and from wooden shipwrecks that have been analysed, it seems very likely that sulphur and iron accumulation will also be found in the timbers, after their 370 years on the seabed. During the expedition down to the ship in November 2008, a piece of wood was salvaged from the wreck site. The plank, which may originate from the stern of the ship (Rönnby 2008), had corrosion-stained nail holes and the outer 2-3 mm of the surface was very soft, degraded and friable.

Biological wood degradation in the Ghost Ship

Preliminary light microscopic studies indicate degradation by erosion bacteria in the plank salvaged from the Ghost Ship in November 2008 (Figure 4.4). A characteristic feature is the non-homogeneous decay patterns with heavily degraded wood cells distributed among sound ones (Blanchette 1990; Björdal et al. 1999; Björdal et al. 2005). The black colour in some cells most likely originates from iron compounds and impurities.

As anticipated, the activity by wood degradation organisms on the seabed is thereby confirmed. There are also reasons to believe that degradation from the erosion bacteria is accompanied by sulphur and iron contamination. Since the penetration of sulphur and iron on the seabed seems to be limited mainly by bacterial activity, the advances of erosion bacteria can be an indication of sulphur penetration in the hull (Fors et al. 2008).

The next step: further analysis of the Ghost Ship

Each wreck site has its unique environment and history that influences the status of its archaeological artefacts, the amount and profile of contamination, subsequent conservation procedures and the long-term stability of the wood (Fors & Sandström 2006). The extent and nature of these contaminations have only recently been discovered and their full consequences have yet to be studied (Fors 2008). Such information should not be seen as a means of preventing future salvaging and conservation of marine archaeological wood, but rather as a step towards improving future conservation techniques. Much can be done at an early stage with the correct methods of sampling and analyses. Many more analyses are required for the Ghost Ship. Some of these are presented below.

Further light microscopy studies of wood samples from the Ghost Ship will be necessary in order to map the biological wood degradation, which seems to be also connected to the sulphur and some of the iron accumulations (Fors et al. 2008). Adequate mechanical testing of the stability of the wood should also be undertaken to evaluate the possible effects of biological and chemical degradation.

The composition and distribution of chemical compounds such as sulphur and iron in the wood of the *Vasa* and *Mary Rose* and other historical shipwrecks have been analysed by combining several different methods (Fors 2008). Much important basic information has been achieved from elemental analyses of total sulphur and iron, combined with x-ray powder diffraction (XRD), x-ray fluorescence (XRF) line scans, electron spectroscopy for chemical analysis (ESCA), scanning electron microscopy (SEM) and elemental analysis (EDS). In XRD analyses true crystalline salts can be identified from precipitates on the dried wood surfaces, providing information about their origin. Iron and sulphate salts that precipitate in combination on a surface pH below 3.5, are strong indications of the production of sulphuric acid in the wood. Elemental analyses offer an insight into the contaminations in the wood. If the analyses are performed at a number of depths down a wood core drilled from the surface directly through the hull, this

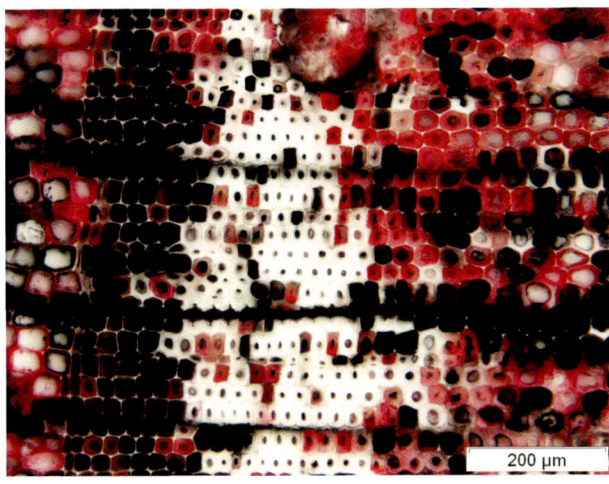 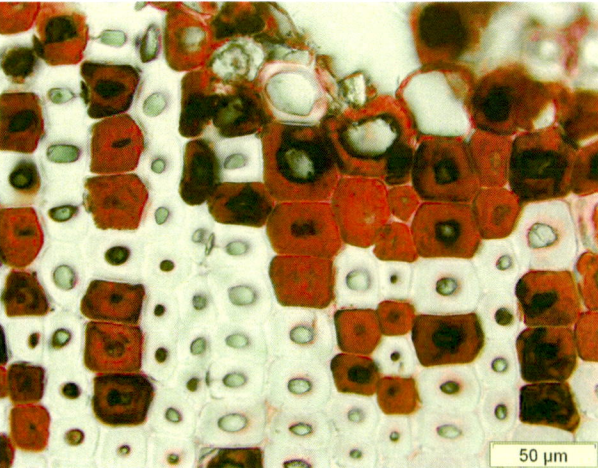

Figure 4.4. Light microscopy images of wood from the Ghost Ship. Cross sections showing fibres adjacent to each other held together by the lignin-rich central lamella. The hollow in each fibre is the lumen. All images show a moderate degradation of the cell wall of the wood by erosion bacteria. A characteristic feature is the heterogeneous pattern with heavily degraded wood fibres (red) distributed among sound ones (white) (Blanchette et al. 1990; Björdal et al. 2005). The blackish appearance of many fibres probably derives from iron, manganese or sulphur contamination.

would allow the distribution of the contaminants in the hull to be estimated. XRF is a valuable and non-destructive technique for analysis at narrow intervals (0.5mm spacing) offering a detailed profile throughout the wood sample. With SEM in combination with EDS the total amount and distribution of most elements over a selected wood surface can be measured on a microscopic level.

Synchrotron-based x-ray absorption near edge structure (XANES) spectroscopy and scanning x-ray spectromicroscopy (SXM) have provided invaluable information but are also expensive and very advanced techniques with restricted access. Advanced sulphur spectroscopy techniques (with a synchrotron as ion source) such as XANES and SXM are necessary for a full speciation and distribution of the different sulphur and iron compounds in the wood; giving the relative amounts of reduced and oxidised species in different cavities of the wood structure. An indication of speciation in reduced and oxidised form can be acquired by ESCA (Fors 2008).

Conclusion

The discovery of the Ghost Ship and other well-preserved Baltic shipwrecks has caused great excitement and led to high expectations. It is not the intention of the present authors to spread disillusionment, but rather instigate preparation for the great challenges that lie ahead. A better understanding of and insight into the conditions at the wreck site and the effect of the environment on the timber, is essential prior to any further excavation and conservation projects.

In many respects the Ghost wreck gives the impression of being extremely well-preserved. Yet, even if the conditions in the Baltic Sea favour the preservation of organic material, previous experience indicates that the Ghost Ship is very likely to be adversely affected by the environment in which it has been resting for over 350 years. The invisible biological and chemical activities inside sub-marine wood result in structural modifications and contaminations, with consequences for its future preservation. The preliminary microscopic analyses of a pinewood plank salvaged from the seabed beside the Ghost Ship indicate degradation patterns in the wood cells that are characteristic of erosion bacteria. This is usually also an indication of chemical contamination, although data about the amount, distribution and chemical speciation is still to be investigated.

Experience of chemical analyses of shipwrecks from such great depths is so far limited and the various chemical contaminants need therefore to be carefully evaluated. It is also important to study the mechanical stability and integrity of the wood in relation to chemical and biological degradation. By so doing, we hopefully can avoid the unpleasant preservation problems experienced with the *Vasa* and the *Mary Rose* from haunting the Ghost wreck should it be salvaged in the future.

Thus marine archaeological material is affected by biological, geological, chemical, physical and environmental interaction. Much more can and should be done to understand these mechanisms and their consequences for the long-term preservation of shipwrecks and other marine archaeological wood.

Collaboration among experts from different fields is essential for obtaining fruitful results. Any 'Ghost wreck project' should involve the collaboration of both archaeologists and natural scientists to open up important new areas of investigation, beneficial to both. Archaeologists and conservators would gain a better understanding of wreck site conditions and the composition of the archaeological material as well as improved methods for preservation and conservation; and the natural scientists (chemists, biologists, physicists, geologists, etc.) would gain access to new applications for and developments in scientific methods and techniques.

References

Almkvist, G. & Persson, I. 2008. Degradation of polyethylene glycol and hemicellulose in the *Vasa*. *Holzforschung* 62: 64-70.

Blanchette, R.A., Nilsson, T., Daniel, G. Fv & Abad, A. 1990. Biological degradation of wood. In: R. M. Rowell, R. J. Barbour (eds) *Archaeological Wood. Properties, Chemistry and Preservation*. Advances in Chemistry Series 225: Chapter 6. Washington DC: American Chemical Society.

Blanchette, R. 1995. Degradation of the lignocellulose complex in wood, *Canadian Journal of Botany* 73 (Suppl. 1): 99-101.

Björdal, C., Nilsson, T. & Daniel, G. 1999. Microbial decay of waterlogged wood found in Sweden. *Int. Biodeterioration and Biodegradation* 43: 63-71.

Björdal, C., Daniel G., & Nilsson T. 2000. Depth of burial, an important factor in controlling bacterial decay of waterlogged archaeological poles. *International Biodegradation and Biodeterioration* 45 (1-2): 15-26.

Björdal, C., Nilsson T. & Bardage S. 2005. Three-dimensional visualisation of bacterial decay in individual tracheids of Pinus sylvestris, *Holzforschung* 59: 178-182.

Björdal, C. 2009. Wreck Protect. An EU/FP7 project led by Dr Charlotte Björdal, SP Trätek, Stockholm. Commencing 2009. http://wreckprotect.eu/fileadmin/site_upload/wreck_protect/pdf/WreckProtect.pdf (accessed 11-07-2013).

Clausen, C.A. 1996. Bacterial associations with decaying wood: A review. *Int. Biodeterioration and Biodegradation* 37: 101-107

Djerw, U. & Rönnby, J. (eds) 2001. *Östersjöns skatter. Det dolda kultur landskapet*. Sjöhistoriska museets rapportserie 14. Stockholm.

Ehrlich, H.L. 2002. *Geomicrobiology of sulfur, Geomicrobiology*, 4th edn Marcel Dekker Incorporated New York.

Eriksson, N. & Rönnby, J. 2012. 'The Ghost Ship'. An Intact *Fluyt* from *c.*1650 in the Middle of the Baltic Sea. *International Journal of Nautical Archaeology* 41: 350–361.

Florian, M-L. E. 1987. The underwater environment. In: C. Pearson (ed.) *Conservation of Marine Archaeological Objects*: 3-32. London: Butterworth.

Florian, M-L. E. 1990. Scope and History of Archaeological Wood. In: R.M. Rowell & R.J. Barbour (eds) *Archaeological Wood. Properties, Chemistry and Preservation*. Advances in Chemistry Series 225: Chapter 1. Washington DC: American Chemical Society.

Fors, Y, & Sandström, M. 2006. Sulfur and Iron in Shipwrecks Create Conservation Concerns. *Chemical Society Reviews* 35: 399-415.

Fors, Y. 2008. *Sulfur-Related Conservation Concerns for Marine Archaeological Wood. The Origin, Speciation and Distribution of Accumulation with some Remedies for the Vasa.* Doctoral thesis. Stockholm University.

Fors, Y., Nilsson, T., & Sandström, M. 2008. Bacterial sulfur accumulation in pine (*Pinus sylvestris*) in simulated seabed environment to elucidate the mechanism in marine archaeological wood. *Int. Biodeterioration and Biodegradation* 62: 336-347.

Fälting, P.E. 1961. *Med Vasa på Strömmens botten*. Stockholm: Almqvist & Wiksell.

Giulminot, E., Dalard, F., & Degigmy, C. 2000. Electrochemical study of iron corrosion in various concentrations of polyethylene glycol (PEG 400) solutions, *Eur. Fed. Corros. Publ.* 28: 300-309.

Greaves, H. 1971. The bacterial factor in wood decay. *Wood Science and Technology* 5: 6-16.

Haasum, S. & Westenberg, B. 1994-1995. Svensk maritime arkeologi igår – idag – imorgon, *Maritim Arkeologi, Sjöhistorik årsbok 1994-1995*.

Jones, M. (ed.) 2003. *For Future Generations, Conservation of a Tudor Maritime Collection.* The Archaeology of the *Mary Rose* 5. Trowbridge Cromwell Press,

MacLeod, I.D. & Kenna, C. 1990. Degradation of archaeological timbers by pyrite: oxidation of iron and sulfur species. In: P. Hoffmann (ed.) *Proceedings of the 4th ICOM Group on Wet Organic Archaeological Materials Conference*. Bremerhaven: 133-142.

Marsden, P. 2003. *Sealed by Time. The Loss and Recovery*

of the Mary Rose. Portsmouth: The Mary Rose Trust.

Nilsson, T. 2004. Biological wood degradation. In: G. Henriksson (ed.) *The Ljungberg textbook; Wood chemistry and Wood Biotechnology 3D1058*. Fibre and Polymer Technology, chapter 9. Stockholm. Kungliga Tekniska högskolan.

Nilsson, T. & Björdal, C. 2008. Culturing wood-degrading erosion bacteria. *International Bioderioration and Biodegradation* 61: 3-10.

Passier, H. F., Böttcher, M.E. & De Lange G.J. 1999. Sulfur Enrichment in organic Matter of Eastern Mediterranean Sapropels: A Study of Sulfur Isotope Partitioning. *Aq. Geochem.* 5: 99-118.

Pearson, C. 1987. On-site storage and conservation. In: C. Pearson (ed.) *Conservation of Marine Archaeological Objects*: Chapter 6. London: Butterworth.

Preisler A., de Beer D., Lichtschlag A., Lavik G., Boetuis A., & Barker Jørgensen B. 2007. Biological and chemical sulfide oxidation in a *Beggiatoa* inhabited marine sediment. *The ISME Journal*, International Society for Microbial Ecology, 1: 341-353.

Rönnby, J. 2001. *Sjunket förflutet. Arkeologiska möjligheter under vatten*. Chapter 6. Stockholm: Runius & Co förlag.

Sandström, M., Jalilehvand, F., Persson, I., Gelius, U., Frank, P. & Hall-Roth, I. 2002. Deterioration of the seventeenth century warship *Vasa* by internal formation of sulfuric acid. *Nature* 415: 893-897.

Sandström, M., Jaliehvand, F., Damian, E., Fors, Y., Gelius, U., Jones, M., & Salomé, M. 2005. Sulfur Accumulation in the Timbers of King Henry VIII's Warship *Mary Rose*: A Pathway in the Sulfur Cycle of Conservation Concern. *Proceedings of the National Academy of Sciences of the United States of America* 102: 14165-70.

Singleton, Jr., R. 1993. The sulfate-reducing bacteria. An overview. In: J.M. Odon & R. Singelton, Jr. (eds.) *The sulfate reducing bacteria: Contemporary perspectives*: Chapter 1. New York: Springer.

Singh, A.P. & Butcher, J.A. 1991. Bacterial degradation of wood cell walls: A review of degradation patterns, *Journal of the Institute of Wood Science* 12: 143-157.

Sinninghe Damsté, J.S. & de Leeuw, J.W. 1990. *Adv. Org. Geochemistry* 16: 1077.

Stumm, W. & Morgan, J. 1996. *Aquatic Chemistry. Chemical Equilibria and Rates in Natural Waters, Environmental Science and Technology*. A Wiley-Interscience Series of Texts and Monographs.

Sørensen, J., Christensen, D. & Jørgensen, B.B. 1981. Volatile fatty acids and hydrogen as substrates for sulfate-reducing bacteria in anaerobic marine sediment. *Applied and Environmental Microbiology* 42: 5-11.

Thode-Andersen, S. & Jørgensen, B.B. 1989. Sulfate reduction and the formation of ^{35}S-labelled FeS, FeS$_2$ and S^0 in coastal marine sediments, *Limnol. Oceanogr.* 34: 793-806.

Varavamurthy, A. & Mopper, K. 1987. Geochemical formation of organosulfur compounds (thiols) by addition of H$_2$S to sedimentary organic matter, *Nature* 329: 623-625.

5

Conceptual Evolution in Ancient Shipbuilding: An Attempt to Reinvigorate a Shunned Theoretical Framework

Daniel Zwick

It has often been noted that archaeologists are adept at borrowing theory but not very good at building it. This applies particularly to evolutionary theory for conceptual lineages; the appropriated use thereof within archaeology is highly contested – particularly in its nautical branch – despite its metaphorical popularity and widespread use. Rejecting evolutionary allusions to the development of water-craft altogether, Thijs Maarleveld conceded that even those who *do* use such terminology *"will promptly deny the suggestion that ships are liable to produce offspring"*, while emphasizing instead *"human decisions regarding continuity or adaptations"* (Maarleveld 1995:4). At first glance, positions in favour of evolutionary analogies are ridiculed by this *reductio ad absurdum*. Upon closer consideration however, one will have to appreciate the extent to which human behaviour is restricted to tradition – i.e. inheritable practice. While things cannot reproduce, ideas can, and the latter become fossilized in the former. Archaeological typologies are intricately interwoven with the taxonomic method from the natural sciences and thus charged with the underlying evolutionary principle of descent with modification. Some critics have conflated the generalised use of evolutionary theory with biological reductionism by primarily associating it with environmental determinism and adaptationalist models. These are considered to adopt *a passive view of human behaviour"* in which *"societies react to external stimuli and do not initiate change for any reasons of their own"* (Preucel & Hodder 1996:207). In many cases, such vaunted criticism appears more like a pledge of fealty to modern post-processual currents, rather than a sincere reflection of what evolutionary principles actually encompass. Irrespective of the underlying profound epistemological question of the extent to which human intentionality is a proximate or an ultimate cause for change (cf. Mayr 1961), evolutionary lineages – whether biological or conceptual – are first and foremost a tool for structuring complex, spatiotemporally diverse yet recurring, phenomena, detached from any claim of full knowledge of the underlying mechanisms. The theory has a biological taint because it was first used purely in a biological rather than a conceptual context, for which reason advocates of the theory's general application have suggested *"to stop using 19th century evolutionary concepts and terms as a basis for the archaeology of the 21st century"* (Clark & Barton 1997:316). In this paper however, the use of this – epistemologically more or less inadequate – terminology is a necessary trade-off, to emphasise the analogies between conceptual and biological evolution in a thought-provoking manner.

Given the complexity of watercraft, there is arguably no better framework through which interpretation and inference could be reconciled with the temporality of the archaeological record. This becomes all the more significant as shipwrecks continue to be encased into "lignified typologies", which – although proven inadequate or outdated – are still being used for convenience or by force of habit. This problem is particularly well manifested in the elusive "cog-type", whose problematic definition shall be evaluated as a case study. This discussion stresses the requirement for a theoretical framework which remains flexible enough to offer interpretative leeway on alternating strands of development, and thereby facilitates a fresh and more objective view on the growing body of differential data from shipwrecks. Or as Charles Darwin noted himself, *"I look at it as absolutely certain that very much in the*

Origin will be proved rubbish; but I expect and hope that the framework will stand" (Gould 2002:2). It did stand. Will it also stand in its appropriated conceptual use within nautical archaeology?

Conceptual evolution: more than a metaphor?

Ironically, Charles Darwin's hypothesis of natural selection was anticipated by several decades in Patrick Matthew's treatise 'On Naval Timber and Arboriculture' (cf. Matthew 1831:364f.), in which the lack of arboricultural practices with regard to timber supply suitable for shipbuilding was primarily stressed (Matthew 1831:106f.). The natural analogy is striking, because shipbuilding was deeply dependent on the availability of suitable compass timber, whose growth was adequately curved and strong. This natural resource dependency affects the selection criteria – quite generally – as *"a cohesive whole with its environment in such a way that this interaction causes replication to be differential"* (Hull 1988:408). Inevitably, this strong dependency will have shaped the concept of universal guiding principles and has therefore quite naturally entered biological metaphors: inspired by the swiftness of fish, the English shipwright Mathew Baker likened the hull shape of the 'race-built galleon' to the slender shape of a *cod's head and mackerel's tail* (Fig. 5.1). It conveyed not only the concept of a novel ship design, but also the underlying idea of hydrodynamics (Adams 2003:106). Although no treatise on shipbuilding before William Froude could be regarded as incorporating

naval architecture in the scientific sense, the importance of hydrodynamics must have been intuitively perceived and employed; as it turned out, to a noticeable effect: The commander of the Portuguese galleons of the 1588 Spanish Armada reportedly noted that the English race-built galleons could tack 4-5 times in the same time as it took his ships to tack just once (Parker 1996:281). While critics of evolutionary allusions reject the notion of an undirected development process, the "invention" of the race-built galleon appears to be more by "differential replication" rather than by intent. It originated from an experimental naval programme initially developing galleasses, which had to have distinctly long slender hulls in order to be capable of manoeuvring under oars (cf. Phillips 1994:102). While the success of the galleass programme was limited, the actual novelty consisted of the crossing of the slender galleass hull with the full-rig and other characteristics of carracks, thereby forming a sharp contrast to the 'medieval' naval tactics of floating fortresses involving grappling and fighting at close quarters, – still prevalent in other parts of Europe –and replacing it with an emphasis on manoeuvrability and long-range artillery. Although Mathew Baker was preeminent among shipwrights in England who began to explore hull design on a conceptual level in the 16th century, the correlation between waterline length and hull speed – as later captured by the formula

$$V_{hull} \approx 1.34 \times \sqrt{L_{wl}} \text{ (metres)}$$

was not known at that time. Thus the advantageous qualities of hull design resulting from a blend of constructional principles occurred more by coincidence than intent – by trial and error – emphasising the

Fig. 5.1. The long and narrow "race-built" hull of an Elizabethan galleon, inspired by the shape of a cod's head and a mackerel's tail. From the Fragments of Ancient English Shipwrightry, by Mathew Baker and others (1586) (Pepysian Library, Magdalene College, Cambridge).

undirected nature of differential replication in this particular instance. But can this be also formulated as a more general principle?

While this example was laid out as bait for the reader's imagination to demonstrate that the genuine nature of "inventions" is far from being an uncontested matter, there is another analogous aspect that deserves attention – the linguistics.

Naturally familiar with the taxonomical principle, the marine biologist James Hornell coined the way ethnographically studied watercraft were classified and – unsurprisingly – made blatant use of biological terminology by attesting a *"genetic relationship"* between the bark canoes, dugouts and plank-built boats, for instance (Hornell 1946:181). Similar allusions to striking genetic connotations also became popular whenever hereditary patterns in the development of shipbuilding traditions were implied, using terms like *"extended family"* (Eldjarn & Godal 1988:68), *"archetype"* (Crumlin-Pedersen 1965:82; Fliedner 1969), *"cross-fertilization"* (Hocker 1999:22) or *"hybrid type"* (Crumlin-Pedersen 2000:240, 2003:266), to name a few. They stress lineages as though they constitute phyletic relationships. This underlying evolutionary principle also marked the debate on whether planked craft originated from an expanded and extended dugout or a skin-boat with overlapping seams (cf. Crumlin-Pedersen 1970a; Hasslöff 1972:28; Johnstone 1980:115; McGrail 1981:22) (Fig. 5.2). It is taken for granted that such changes are not inventions from scratch, but that new features were gradually incorporated, developed further in small steps from pre-existing designs that were conceptually not vastly distinctive from their predecessors.

The late Ole Crumlin-Pedersen (1997:11) aptly observed that

"...within a particular "school of boat-building", a traditionally conditioned regularity is to be found in all vessels, which makes it possible for the ship-archaeologist to sort parts of ships and boats in much the same way as that in which the zoologist sorts a mixed bag of bones so that the "species" and the "family" as well as individual variations in size can be identified".

In fact, the most insightful method of "dissecting" a shipwreck is by cutting it into cross-sections like an animal, in order to reveal constructional elements that could be indicative or even diagnostic of a spatiotemporally determinable tradition, such as *meginhufrs* and *bitis* are for Scandinavian Viking Age vessels. The biological analogy is enforced by the use of organic terms for certain constructional elements, such as ribs, skeleton and skin. In the widest sense the linguistic atavism is a constructional one: the aforementioned components were the actual building

materials of hunter-gatherer craft, like skins in Inuit *umiaks* for instance (Petersen 1986:29ff.). This is not necessarily just an accidental linguistic correlation, but may relate to a principle dubbed 'heritage constraint', in which original concepts coin long-lasting ways an element or its function is perceived, even when the original use has been rendered obsolete. Such atavisms indicate the possible origin with regards to a shared ancestral character (cf. O'Brien & Lyman 2009:234); they could also be highlighted by the differential use of technical terms in different regions and dialects, which are indicative of origin (Eldjarn & Godal 1988:24f.)

Undoubtedly, hereditary relationships in organisms can be traced in biological lineages. This paper argues that in the case of the 'evolution of boat- and shipbuilding' there is also more substance behind the metaphorical veil, in that conceptual lineages are as meaningfully constituted as biological lineages. Obviously, the inheritability of cultural phenomena differs from biological mechanisms, but selection processes within the field of biology itself are also vastly different and only conceivable by drawing analogies (Aldrich et al. 2008:579). Therefore, there is no reason to believe that traditions – as a consequence of social learning and replication – are exempt from this holistic principle. In the following, the three main principles of a Darwinian framework (variation, selection and

Fig. 5.2. Descent with modification? A smooth conceptual transition from the expanded and extended dugout to the plank-boat: Haapio/esping before and after expansion (above) and the smaller of the Kvalsund boats from ca. 700 (below) (after Crumlin-Pedersen 1970b).

retention) are translated into nautical archaeological case studies and supported in several cases with new insights from the cognitive sciences.

Variation

The source value of shipwrecks is unparalleled due to the great variation in constructional properties. It was fittingly observed that *"in any preindustrial society … a boat or a ship was the largest and most complex machine produced"* (Muckelroy 1978:3). In spite of the unique potential for modular complexity, it often seems that the scientific value of shipwrecks cannot be fully unleashed, as the study of shipwrecks is regarded as too disparate and too technical to be meaningfully integrated into the general field of archaeology; a problem of which maritime archaeologists are well aware (cf. Cederlund 1995:103ff.; Gibbins & Adams 2001:283ff.; Maarleveld 1995:3). Nonetheless, there is a general sentiment that the only way to get intrinsic insights into shipbuilding traditions – and thus indirectly into societal developments – is by recording and comparing mundane constructional details. Apart from the cultural and social background of the shipbuilder, it can reveal something about the availability of timber and other materials, the prestige of the vessel and owner in terms of the quality of the material, workmanship and decorations, its purpose and destined maritime or fluvial environment, the cultural zones the vessel frequented as potentially indicated by repairs carried out in a 'foreign' technique or built of imported timber. So the study of the ship-structure could be rewarding in itself, let alone the information gained from contextual information such as accompanying archaeological finds. One potential of the study of shipwrecks clearly lies in the differential constructional features, captured in this section in terms of variation. Due to varied access to resources, skills, rights and – above all – the lack of blueprints, shipwrights could not implement a similar degree of standardisation as is possible in modern times. Even ships built in essentially the same tradition will have different features. Nevertheless, the analytical process of inferring these differences has often been cut short by the malpractice of simply dubbing shipwrecks as 'types' known from historical sources, as though such "identification" constitutes the ultimate purpose of a study, as Thijs Maarleveld (1995:5) points out.

Apart from the problem that a historical 'type' is unlikely to correlate specifically to a type in the constructional sense – as archaeologists would prefer it – there is a temptation to think in terms of a 'standard type', representing a state of equilibrium in the development process before it became obsolete with the next innovation. Therefore, shipwrecks featuring a greater modular variety are often seen as imperfect approximations of a standard set of characteristics, particularly those labelled as 'hybrid types' in the belief that they are just intermediate or transient forms undergoing a temporary transformational phase. This underlying conceptual problem is deeply embedded within the rationale of evolutionary theory; but without being caused by it, as has been often unjustly implied.

This raises the question of how variation manifests in the maritime archaeological record and what significance the scale of variety has with regard to continuity and change in shipbuilding and contemporary societal circumstances. While the following sub-sections will deal with some observable phenomena of variation in shipwrecks, the anthropogenic and environmental mechanisms causing or limiting variation are expanded upon further in the section on selection and retention.

Confluence of influences: greater variation in estuarine regions?

A recent ethnographic study from India attested an overwhelming variety of boat-types in the estuarine region of the Ganges Delta, which were *"not technically adapted to the polymorphic fluvial environments"* (Palmer & Blue 2009:483). At first glance, this appears counter-intuitive to evolutionary theory, but only if taken in its most reductionist sense in applying a latent environmental determinism. However, the selective pressures are different from region to region. Particularly with regard to freshwater environments, it has been observed that archaic details *"stem from a milieu where boats are not absolutely necessary for survival"* (Christensen 2000:167). Therefore, boatbuilding traditions tend to survive much longer further inland, due to the lack of stimuli for change, as Christer Westerdahl similarly observed (1995:213f.). Noting the prevalence of certain types of water-craft in certain riverine regions, and their sometimes surprisingly great distinctions to types from neighbouring river valleys in southeast Norway, Arne Emil Christensen proclaimed *"as a general rule that each valley or lake/river system has, or had its own boat type"* (Christensen 2000:165). Similar observations were made elsewhere, where very pronounced differences between respective river-systems also became manifest in the material culture (cf. Filgueiras 1979:45; 1988:382; Westerdahl 1995:214). Correspondingly, river-systems were regarded as a self-contained zone of transport geography (Westerdahl 1995:214ff.). While river-systems as self-contained transport zones condition a surprising regional regularity in inland water-craft, variations become observable wherever these zones overlap. This is not only the case in delta regions, but also at pivotal points of transhipment. A case study from Denmark has highlighted that mercantile towns tend not to be located directly at an anchorage at the river mouth, but a bit further upstream where the water is just broad enough to be reached by seagoing vessels, and at a point that articulates with road transport (Crumlin-Pedersen 1990:95). Thus, great variation in watercraft could be also anticipated in urban centres of transhipment where seagoing and inland vessel meet, even some 50 km upstream, as in the case of Bremen (cf. Zwick 2012a). In contrast to their seagoing counterparts, inland and other regional vessels would have been exposed to totally different and generally lower selection pressures, which tend to abet the retention of some ancient modular features. As such the L-shaped chine girder at the turn of the bilge could be described, which is a continuous feature with only modest changes in riverine watercraft spanning over a millennium in the Rhine area (cf. Vlierman 1996:104f.) and at least 650 years in the Weser (Zwick 2012a:287). One might ask whether – as a rule of thumb – less well adapted solutions in boatbuilding would have been considered negligible, possibly weighted in terms of a distinctive expression of identity at the expense of solely functional aspects.

'Hybrid' types: intermediate forms or variants in their own right?

As stressed above, the term 'hybrid' is used somewhat generically to indicate that a mixture of modular features is believed to stem from different traditions. Such deviations are primarily – somewhat one-sidedly – associated with differential influences on a cultural level. Other aspects which affect variation, such as the social role and purpose of a vessel, have only recently been more explicitly addressed with regard to small vernacular watercraft (cf. Bill 1997). Still, the 'cultural lens' seems often to be the guiding principle in evaluating a shipwreck.

In the case of the Kronholm wreck from the first half of the 13th century, a gradual amalgamation of shipbuilding between Scandinavians and northern Germans has been asserted with regard to a set of mixed features: the carvel-laid bottom, straight stem and fastening method was attributed to a German influence, while the slenderness of the frames and the use of pine instead of oak for the floor timbers was thought reminiscent of Scandinavian influence (Rönnby 1996:70). If seen through a 'cultural lens' the interpretation does not seem too far-fetched given that the wreck-site is located in a silted-up former anchorage site in Paviken on Gotland near the provincial capital Visby, with its strong local presence of an influential German mercantile community.

However, there are other possible explanations for modular variation in this case. If the find location is

taken as indicator for the building location – for which no provenance has yet been ascertained – then one could also argue that the availability of oak in this region was limited or more costly, given that the timberline for oak is further south than for pine. The slender frames might be explained by the fact that pine woods would not have provided as strong and ample compass timber as oak woods. Thus the shortage of a key resource might have affected the appropriation with a more slender frame-system; the tradition was not essentially changed but just adapted to the local circumstances, which would have conditioned some analogous features in two dissimilar conceptual lineages. Through the limitation of a key resource, here oak, this would have effected – if translated into Darwinian terms – an 'evolutionary convergence' between two traditions in a particular environmental 'niche'. Aside from the importance of distinguishing between homologous and analogous features in similar phenomena, it is worth noting that the underlying mechanisms of such convergence are not caused by environmental factors alone, but also by anthropogenic factors, as will be demonstrated further below with regard to the *Grâce Dieu* case study.

Not unlike the Kronholm wreck, the Gedesby wreck is also considered an unusual find which has been dubbed as 'hybrid construction' (Crumlin-Pedersen 2003:266). At first glance, it appears to be a vernacular vessel, perhaps a ferry, wide and spaciously built, to carry cattle as indicated by a layer of dung (Bill 1997:83). It was found in a rural harbour near Gedesby, on the Danish Island of Falster, and was dated by dendrochronology to ca. 1320 (Bill 2003:14). In considering its vernacular purpose, one would not expect to find any innovative constructional details, especially in regard to the present connotation of the word 'innovation'; implying a technological cutting edge. Thus the excavators were surprised to find novel construction, such as *"stem- and sternhook,…. protruding beams and massive beam knees, the occasional use of moss as luting and the use of sawn planks in the construction, with a broad margin the oldest example of this technique in a clinkerbuilt vessel in Scandinavia"* (Bill 1997:78). The only remaining details considered to be Scandinavian are the T-shaped keel and the entirely clinker-planked hull, yet even the long plank scarfs are still quite distinct from the short Scandinavian ones (Bill 1997:14f.). Also absent were the mouldings which normally decorated the visible edges of planks in Scandinavian watercraft at that time (Bill 1997:66). Were these later changes affected by an external influence, or was this a development within the local tradition, merely inspired by external influences? In fact, are there any unmistakably Scandinavian features left in the Gedesby wreck at all? If not, can it be viewed through a 'cultural lens'? Again, with no ascertained provenance of the timber, one may only speculate how this vessel ended up in a small rural Danish harbour. Incidentally, a few years before the Gedesby ship was built, the Danish King Eric Menved ordered in 1304 that only cogs should be included in the *leding* - the Danish naval defence system (Lund 1996:282f.). Amongst other things, this was arguably owing to the advantage of raised fighting platforms on these high-sided and large ships. This decision must have marked a great turning point, as Denmark's *leding* still relied on 1100 longships in the 13th-century (Crumlin-Pedersen 1972:190). Whether these new cogs were of foreign design or adapted Danish versions is not clear. The Gedesby wreck is neither high-sided nor large and certainly not a cog, but its very presence in a Danish harbour could be seen – through the 'cultural lens' – as a harbinger of a process through which Denmark gradually opened up to a foreign shipbuilding tradition. Alternatively, the possibility of similar vessels plying Danish waters long before the basic components of this tradition were appropriated for royal service cannot be excluded. The fact that the earliest wrecks of the elusive "cog-tradition" are to be found in Denmark shows that such "un-Scandinavian" vessels were not an uncommon sight and perhaps even preferred by some Danes. After all, these types were less elaborately built than Scandinavian vessels and would have been cheaper to construct (Dokkedal 1996:62). When even a king could dispense with longships built in the local prestigious tradition, a peasant or ferryman would have probably cared little about sailing a less prestigious ship than his forefathers, especially one that smelled of dung.

While it is not entirely clear if – or to what degree – the alleged 'modular hybridism' of the Gedesby wreck reflects a transformational phase in shipbuilding, the Kalmar I wreck from the second half of the 13th century is built in an astonishingly similar way (Fig. 5.3). It has a comparable length-to-beam ratio of roughly 2:1, a T-shaped keel, and was fully clinker-planked, in which the planks were connected with iron rivets, the hood-ends of the planks overlapped the sternpost, but were notched into the stempost, and the hull was strengthened by protruding cross-beams (Åkerlund, 1951:27ff.). One may even question whether the strong curvature of Kalmar I's stem – as originally reconstructed by Åkerlund – is actually correct or guided by his contemporary bias on how stems of historical vessels should look (cf. Åkerlund 1951:62f.). Only the lowermost portion was preserved, from which a more moderately raking stem - similar to the one from the Gedesby wreck - is very feasible. Given the number of shared features, one may wonder whether both wrecks really represent some kind of transient hybrid type, or

whether they constitute a class in their own right; a class of vernacular watercraft that is obviously not as prominent a ship-type as a 'cog' or 'longship' in written sources due to its mundane purpose. One might also question whether innovation was imposed from above and could be only found in state-of-the-art vessels intended for warfare and royal service, or if actually the greatest impetus for innovation and change evolved at a local scale by trial and error.

Although it is not possible yet to answer all these questions on the basis of the number of shipwrecks from this period known today, one thing is clear: an explanation aligned to the conventional "lignified typology" in which mixed features are merely interpreted in light of an *"interchange of constructional features between Nordic ships and cogs"* (Crumlin-Pedersen 2000:241) would do no justice to the breadth of variation and would be only employable in the most holistic sense, which would discourage further debate.

A telling 'freak' feature

An interesting case study on variation in a shipbuilding tradition is showcased by the wreck of the *Grâce Dieu* in the Hamble River. Its *raison d'être* was an attempt by King Henry V to build a ship as large as Genoese mercenary carracks in French service, which were admired by the English during the siege of Harfleur of 1415; in 1436 retrospectively described as *"orrible, grete and stoute"* (Warner 1926:51). They had a deadweight capacity of between 400 and 600 tons, whilst few contemporary English ships exceeded 300 tons (Friel 1994:85). These carracks were fitted with a mizzen mast, which must have been a striking feature at a time when only single-masted vessels plied the waters of northern Europe. The term *mesan maste* (mizzen mast) was not in use before 1420 (Friel 1994:80; Hutchinson 1994:44). With the capture of two of those carracks in 1410 and Henry's plans to build up a navy of such 'great ships' one would have imagined that a technology transfer would have been straightforward, in that the carracks' construction just needed to be replicated. Interestingly, this was not the case. Built in 1418, *Grâce Dieu* had great dimensions and was multi-masted, thus having an analogous outer appearance to the Genoese carracks, but the English appropriations happened within the boundaries of their own shipbuilding tradition, i.e. of the shell-first clinker technique. What Seán McGrail (2001:244) has termed the *"final phase of the Nordic tradition"* is the visual manifestation of the clinker-technique reaching its limitation; an evolutionary *cul-de-sac*, so to speak. This is reflected by the triple-planking (Fig. 5.4-2), a unique 'freak' feature which was the English adaptation necessary to build such large ships within the limitation of shell-

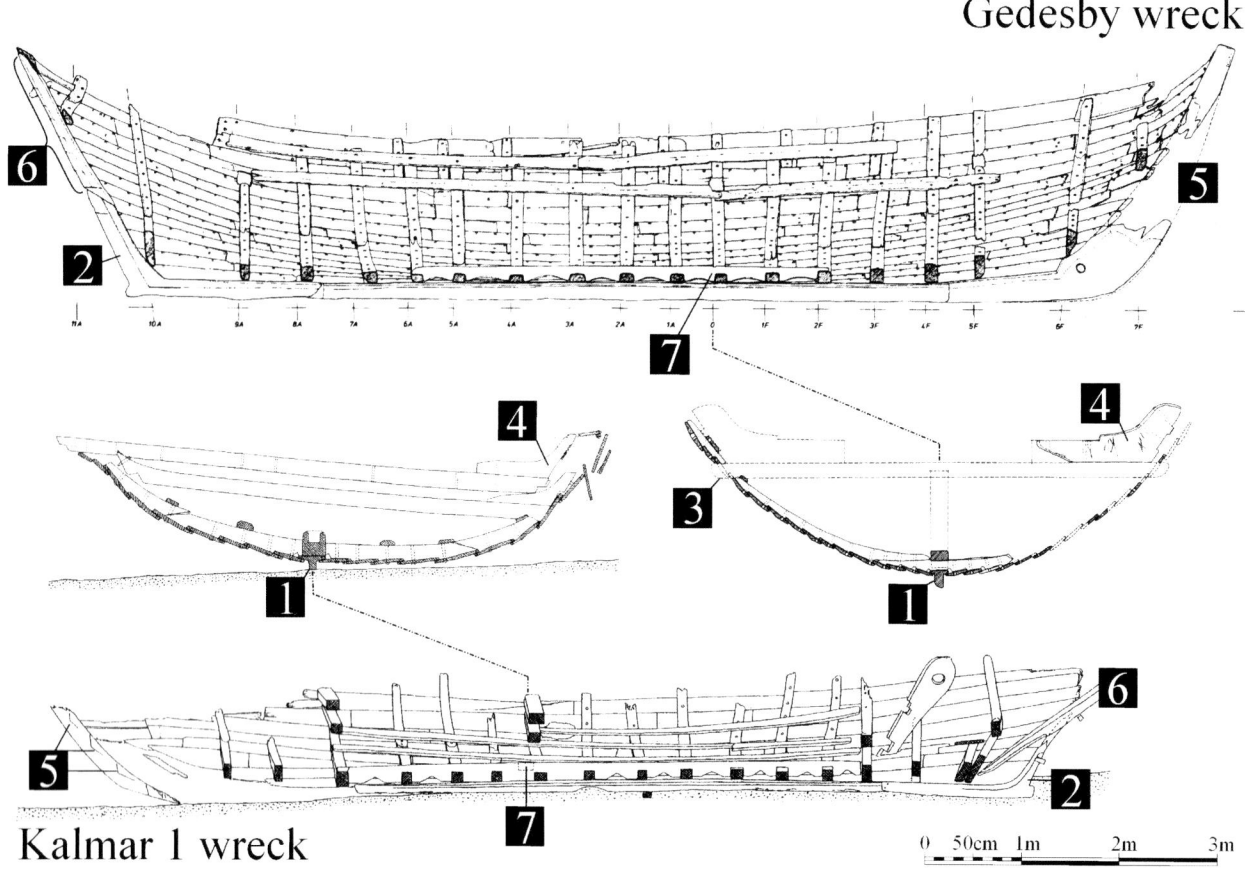

Fig. 5.3. Hybrid-type or a class of vernacular craft in its own right? Comparative constructional analysis of the Kalmar I wreck and the Gedesby wreck, displayed here in opposite orientations: 1) T-shaped keel, 2) stem- and sternhook, 3) protruding beam (not visible on this cross-section of Kalmar I but detected by the excavator), 4) massive beam knee, 5) hood-ends notched into stempost, 6) hood-ends overlapping stern-post, 7) mast-stem integrated in keelson (after Bill 1997, fig. 36.1 and Åkerlund 1951, pl. 5c, 6e, modified by the author).

first construction. In evolutionary terms, this could be described as 'evolutionary convergence', in which two unrelated conceptual lineages (two distinctive shipbuilding traditions) started to display analogous features (in terms of size and rigging of the vessel) due to extra-somatic pressures (competition amongst conspecifics). Thus, the inspiration from another type caused new variation in the form of analogous appropriation, but within the boundaries of their own tradition, rather than by a true adaptation of an aspect of a "foreign" homological conceptual lineage.

Selection

It is remarkable that *Grâce Dieu* retained entirely the "DNA" of the Nordic clinker shipbuilding tradition, since no apparent effort was undertaken to copy the carracks' construction on a conceptual level. This notion is very important in light of the central critique that evolutionary theory would act upon the

presumption that variation is a random rather than a deliberate selection process of the shipbuilder (cf. Hocker 2004a:8; Maarleveld 1995:4). Admittedly, the choice of using triple-clinker is a conscious act, but the necessity of adopting this particular solution for building larger vessels in the shell-first technique was accidental, as 'selection' would have had no direct influence on the formation of new traits and the successfulness of its outcome. Selection in the Darwinian sense implies an undirected rather than deterministic process (cf. Cullen 2000:102; Rindos 1985:65). Therefore evolutionists would readily agree that variation is by no means random, but undirected, which is particularly well manifested in the outcome of the triple-clinker solution.

'Maladaptive traits' as indicators of a biased transmission?

Whether *Grâce Dieu* was considered a successful ship by contemporaries will probably never be known. The

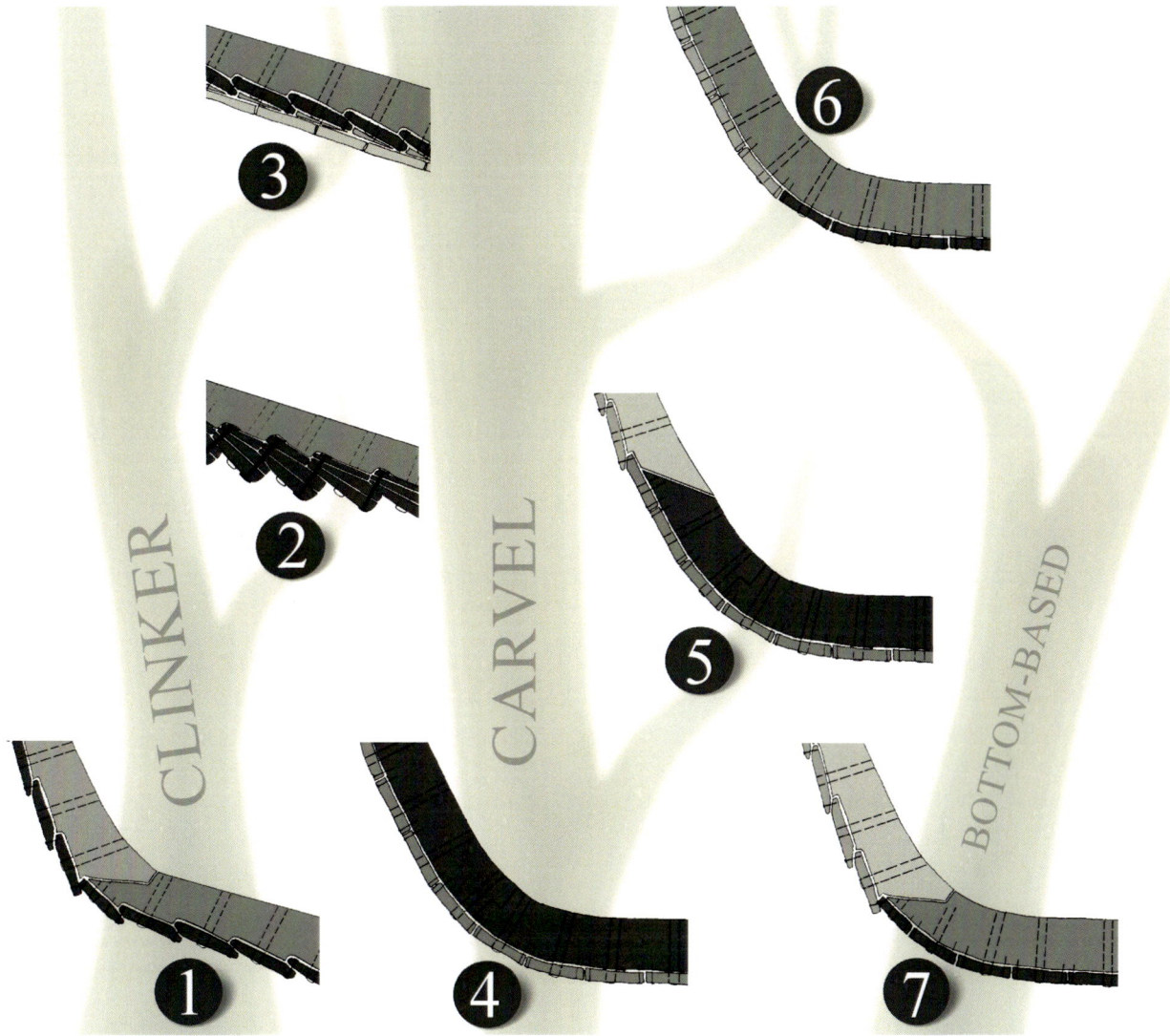

Fig. 5.4. Simplified model in which conceptual lineages of shipbuilding traditions are represented as a phyletic tree. The triple-clinker method (2) as hitherto unique in the GRÂCE DIEU stems from a clinker tradition (1), but prompted by the aspiration to reach a ship-size analogous to carvel-built carracks (4). Later analogies also include converted clinker constructions amended with a second layer of flush-laid planking (3), carvel-clinker hybrids (5) or a "cross-fertilization" between carvel (4) and bottom-based technology (7), leading to the (6) Dutch-flush method. The building sequence is indicated by the darkness of a shaded area, i.e. the darker the earlier (the author).

fact that she made only one voyage on which a near mutiny occurred and was then permanently moored near Bursledon in River Hamble for subsequent use as a representational ship could be possibly ascribed to her unseaworthiness, but also to the ending of the war with France which removed the need to keep large warships in active service (cf. Carpenter Turner 1954:68; Friel 1993:10; Rose 1977:5). In any case, the great waste of resources – in particular of iron needed for the massive bolts to hold five layers of planking together and the fact that the triple-planking method was not applied in later constructions, indicates that this method did not stand the test of time. In the meantime problems also emerged with attempts to maintain the captured

Genoese carracks when the keeper of the king's carracks begged in a petition for permission to hire *"carpenters and caulkers of foreign country[s]…for in this country we shall find few people who know how to renew and amend the same carracks"* (Friel 1995:173f.). In fact, the conceptual gap between craft built in the shell-first and skeleton-first methods can be perceived to be as large as the gap between vertebrates and crustaceans, as it incorporates an entirely distinctive concept of how shape and stability is given to the vessel, which affects the work processes and sequences accordingly.

As such, the maladaptive appropriation leading to the triple-clinker solution is a prime example for what cognitive scientists have termed *transmission bias*. In inaccurate replications such as this, *"We assume that cognitive processes generate strong attractors, but that inferences, based on the available public representations, are highly inaccurate. We use discrete-representations to show that, even when transmission fidelity is very low, cultural transmission can still create cultural inertia and adaptive cultural evolution"* (Henrich & Boyd 2002:97). Translated into plain English, the 'attractors' would be the size and general appearance of the Genoese carracks, which were deemed worth replicating, but no inference could be made due to the lack of 'public representations', i.e. the lack of instances in which Genoese shipbuilders practised their craft in front of the eyes of English shipbuilders that would have provided a chance to emulate their techniques and methods through social learning. Consequently, the transmission fidelity is very low due to the lack of visual examples, while at the same time there is no doubt of an inertia which spawned some analogous features. This phenomenon has been described as *prestige-biased transmission* or *cues of success*; an indirectly influenced transmission of observable phenomena deemed to be advantageous but difficult to replicate (Henrich & McElrath 2007:559). This kind of cultural transmission is a very noisy process which leads to high inaccuracy, primarily because representations are not really replicated but rather reconstructed. The evidence suggests that the process of adoption of the carvel-technique in northern Europe was long-winded. In the case of another English ship built 1419 in Bayonne, documentary evidence suggests that although the hull was clinker-built, the skeleton-first concept of how tailframes were used permeated the building sequence, arguably breaking the strict shell-first into an alternating building sequence (cf. Loewen 1997:328ff.). This raises the question of whether high fidelity replication of certain modular features occurred on the basis of a successful inference or whether they were actually mediated by persons acquainted with the 'foreign' method. In any case, the free choice of construction technique would have been very much constrained by the *conformist bias* of the local shipbuilding tradition, the *transmission bias* of details inferred from other traditions and, last but not least, the dependence on individuals well-versed in 'foreign' concepts. As we shall see in the next section, even with the influx of foreign shipwrights and the due appreciation of their knowledge and skill, transmission remained a tenacious process, although it undoubtedly led to fresh and sustainable impulses in shipbuilding. Given the fact that shipwrights were at that time illiterate practitioners and that the free flow of ideas was consequently restricted to the aforementioned parameters, it can be concluded that Thijs Maarleveld's (1995:4) emphasis on *"human decisions regarding continuity or adaptations"* implies an unrealistic level of consciousness and choice than can be advocated in this paper.

Analogous change: 'evolutionary convergence' during the carvel revolution

A century after the *Grâce Dieu*, carvel planking had become a more common feature in northern European waters, but even then it often remained an analogous rather than a homologous feature.

In the Noorderquartier – the northern Netherlands – an aspect of the bottom-based method prevalent in the Hanseatic sphere was retained, i.e. bottom planks were laid out first, held together temporarily by cleats until floor-timbers were inserted later (cf. Maarleveld 1994:155ff). Dutch shipwrights were more prone to implement the carvel technique quicker than elsewhere, because they would have been partially familiar with flush-laid planks due to the predominant locally-employed bottom-based tradition, in which the bottom planking was flush-laid too (cf. Bill & Hocker 2004; Bill 2009:259; Hocker 2004b; Maarleveld 1992:169, 1994:155ff). Nevertheless, it was not a complete transition to the skeleton-first technique, as it mainly encompassed an entirely carvel-planked hull, leading to the aforementioned "cross-fertilization" known as *Dutch flush* (Fig. 5.4-6). With the increase of ship sizes, Dutch shipbuilders circumspectly doubled the carvel-planking, thus going to great lengths to retain the inherent shell-first character in a carvel planked hull. This way of construction became known as *double-Dutch* (cf. Lemée 2006:233ff.; Maanders 2003:320; Maarleveld 1994) but did not last long however, as it was proven to be redundant for its imagined purpose (Thijs Maarleveld, pers. comm.). Thus the innovative *double-Dutch* solution was a maladaptive feature, but in a fairly neutral sense in that it was simply superfluous rather than fatal. Cognitive psychologists who study creativity in evolutionary terms would probably refer to the *double-Dutch* solution as a 'perceptual set', which describes a phenomenon in which a subject with a history of solving problems in a particular way or tradition *"will continue to apply this strategy even when a simpler method would succeed"* (Morgan et al. 1992:130). The fact that in the southern region of Maaskant, which had belonged to the Spanish Netherlands since the mid 16th century, a moulding system existed that adhered exactly to the Iberian method (Probst 1994:143), suggests that the political circumstances were a decisive factor in which techniques would amalgamate at a local level, abetted by the mobility of foreign shipwrights.

While in these cases the clinker planking was replaced by carvel, there is an increasing number of finds in which an additional layer of carvel planking was fastened on top of the clinker-built shell (Fig. 5.4-3). The frequency and chronological range of such finds suggests that it was not merely a transient 'freak feature' within a gradual development process towards carvel, but probably a more established standard. These ships belonged only by outer appearance – i.e. by analogy – to the new generation of carvel-built ships, whilst inherently still embedded in the old Nordic tradition of shell-first clinker construction. There is not enough data yet to identify a clear pattern whether the second flush-laid planking shell was added during later rebuilding (cf. Auer 2009; Gøthche 1991; Hasslöff 1972; Ossowski 2006; Probst 1994), but it was claimed at least in one case that this two-layer system was incorporated from the very start before launching (cf. Mäss 1994). Apart from protecting a worn out hull or strengthening it against ice pressures, which might explain why this type of construction occurs only in the Baltic Sea, the analogous carvel planking could be also explained in terms of a *prestige-biased transmission* (cf. Henrich & Gil-White 2001). This is highlighted by so-called 'half-carvels' from the 16th century onwards, which are clinker-built below the water-line, but carvel-planked above the water-line – i.e. at the visible portion of the hull, where fashionable analogous features mattered. These vessels are essentially still built in the old clinker method, which was then associated with vernacular craft of peasants, so it is essentially a make-believe construction to increase the owner's prestige (Eriksson 2010:78f.)

Environmental determinism: a reductionist implication?

As demonstrated above, the genesis of watercraft is by no means determined by environmental factors alone. In fact, it is determined to a great extent by cultural contact in general and *prestige-biased transmission* in particular. However, it would be short-sighted to take practical necessity out of the equation of adapting watercraft to the respective environment. Although some like to stress that it is – in theory – possible to cross an ocean with a raft, such aberrant behaviour would have had – as a common practice – wider implications for the successfulness of the parent society.

Universally-shared constructional solutions in discrete shipbuilding traditions can be observed in comparable environmental conditions, particularly with regard to differential requirements in sea-going and inland craft (cf. Hornell 1920:69; Greenhill & Mannering 1997; Steffy 1994). Although great diversity is to be found in beaching craft in all parts of the world, fishermen independently adopted similar solutions in order to cross the surf, i.e. flat bottoms and high-ended prows (Palmer, forthcoming). Apart from the maritime

environment itself, terrestrial parameters come into play with regard to the availability of resources, which affect analogies in discrete conceptual lineages. It has been observed, for instance, that the large paddled craft of the Maori in New Zealand, the Haida on the northwest coast of America and – as an anachronistic analogy – the depictions of Aegean Cycladic ships all looked very similar. While there was undoubtedly no cultural contact whatsoever between the three, the occurrence of giant trees was seen as the determining factor for the peculiar construction and appearance (Guttandin, forthcoming).

Adaptability to environmental conditions should not be perceived as a gradual subconscious process of 'natural selection' through trial and error. On the contrary, the suitability of different classes of watercraft in their respective environments was even formally recognized. This is reflected in a 13th century Danish itinerary, describing a route along the Swedish and Finnish coast to Estonia. The route was split into an inner and outer route in the Stockholm archipelago, in which only the inner route continued to be measured in *ukæsio* units. The etymological origin of this unit strongly suggests that it was not a distance measure *per se*, but related to the shifting of rowers, thus only relevant to vessels propelled under oars. Apart from this indication, the winding inner archipelago and the likely presence of portages on the inner route (cf. Zwick 2012b:109f.) all indicate that those recording the itinerary were well aware of the necessity of using a distinctive class of water-craft for the inner route; moderately sized vessels, small enough for traversing portages and suited to navigating in these narrow waters under oars and sails, perhaps similar to the Helgeandsholmen V wreck from around 1300 (cf. Varenius 1989, 38ff.). Half a millennium later, in the 'Age of Sail', the galley appears somewhat outdated, but the implied anachronism is unjust. When the Russo-Swedish struggle for maritime supremacy reached its peak, Fredrik Henrik Chapman was ordered to develop hull designs for a new archipelago fleet – *skärgårdsflottan* – where a class of hybrids propelled under oars and sails was "re-invented" in order to safeguard the waters of the Swedish and Finnish archipelago. Significantly, this fleet was most of the time under the command of the army rather than the navy, as an amphibious arm of a primarily terrestrial strategy to exert rule on the dispersed islands (cf. Norman 2000). Thus, the environmental factor is mirrored in the differential participation of sections of the parent society, which determines a distinctive premise under which a particular shipbuilding practise can flourish. This diachronic perspective demonstrates that environmentally conditioned regularity, manifested in analogous technical solutions, can be found irrespective of the conceptual basis of a shipbuilding tradition or the period. Similar types of environments and resources encourage similar solutions to meet natural requirements, comparable perhaps to an ecological niche which affects evolutionary convergence amongst different species.

Shipwreck as the ultimate selection process?

Although a majority of watercraft that survive in the archaeological record were scrapped, reused or intentionally deposited, the popular image of shipwrecks is associated with the foundering of a vessel. This is a recurrent allegory for the struggle for survival, touching on the primal evolutionary impulse most famously captured in Lucretius' words: *"Pleasant it is, when over a great sea the winds trouble the waters, to gaze from shore upon another's tribulation: not because any man's troubles are a delectable joy, but because to perceive from what ills you are free yourself is pleasant"* (Lucretius, De Rerum Natura, Book II, line 1, transl. Leonard 1943). This excerpt describes the dark fascination of a spectator witnessing a distress at sea, who gains his relative fortune in the knowledge to be eluded from the maelstrom of atoms of the treacherous and hostile maritime element (cf. Blumenberg 1997:31ff.). This recurrent maritime allegory must have captured the minds of many generations and might be seen as the ultimate selection process and, indeed, punishment for failing to live up to the challenge of conquering the sea. How does the failure to meet this challenge reflect on the parent society? And is the database of shipwrecks consequentially biased towards failures, "in that it inevitably accounts for bad designs, for poorly maintained, old and rotten vessels, or for aberrant behaviour"? This question, posed as 'Devil's advocate' by Adams (2003:19) is twofold, in that – firstly – the possibility is addressed that failures could be overrepresented in the archaeological record. Its implication would be that constructional properties observed in shipwrecks should not be seen as typical examples of a shipbuilding tradition. And secondly, it raises the question whether the wrecks of communities and cultures which encourage aberrant behaviour in maintaining and crewing their ships are overrepresented too. The latter issue touches upon the cultural transmission of maladaptive social norms, which has been addressed by proponents of the Dual Inheritance Theory, which stresses culture-gene, co-evolutionary tendencies. This theory emphasises that the success of a population (and thus their genetic legacy) depends on whether their culture abets adaptive or maladaptive behaviour (cf. Henrich & McElreath 2007:567ff.). Admittedly, this framework sounds very academic and its real life impact is questionable, but

with respect to the example of the Spanish Armada it is very thought-provoking: aside from the constructional favourability of the English 'race-built' galleons, the chances of success of the Spaniards were also decreased considerably by a societal malpractice of rating social rank higher than nautical experience: the 'landlubber' Duke of Medina Sidonia was appointed admiral of the Spanish Armada, which indeed appears to have been – amongst other aspects – a determining ingredient for its defeat and the gradual decline of Habsburg supremacy.

While conceding that some shipwrecks may have occurred because of an erroneous construction, the vast majority occurred due to a combination of forces, which included human error. (Adams 2001:294). This is illustrated vividly in Adam Olearius's travelogue from 1635, describing a dreadful tempest, which *"...continu'd all night, during which, we discover'd, that our Mariners were as raw as the Ship was new ...'* and a master's mate with a false sense of security, who exclaimed *"there was no danger, since we had Sea-room enough"*, until the ship eventually hit a rock, causing the crew to panic and pray, the master to weep, and the eventual loss of the vessel off the island of Öland (Olearius et al. 1662:34).

A scenario in which societal norms had an aberrant effect is often drawn in the case of the Swedish warship *Vasa*, which capsized on her maiden voyage in 1628. According to a popular myth this is a direct consequence of subsequent alterations of specifications at the high-handed behest of the king, which deviated from the shipwright's original design. While this particular point has been refuted (Cederlund & Hocker 2006:44f.) the Admiral Klas Fleming was apparently not granted enough authority to object to the comissioning of an unseaworthy ship. One month before the ship sailed he conducted stability tests but when heeled over the ship showed such a weak righting moment he had to abort, so he must have been well aware of the imminent danger. Nonetheless he was pressurized by the king's express request to send the ship to sea in support of his war with Poland (Cederlund & Hocker 2006:53). Although this could be merely attributed to a lack of character on the admiral's part, it could nevertheless be argued that insubordination to an absolutist ruler - even if well-founded - might have brought about dire consequences for the admiral and thus prompted abberant behaviour out of fear to fail the king, with disastrous effect.

A similar case has been made with regard to the *Mary Rose*, which was deemed not worthwhile studying because of her technological failures (cf. Mudie 1996). Admittedly, the latter remark was made by a naval architect commissioned with the reconstruction of John Cabot's ship *Matthew*, who searched for a "default blueprint" of a contemporary successful ship. For the study of the dynamics of change and innovation in past human societies, however, *Mary Rose* is a prime case study; not in spite of, but *because* of her constructional error – just like *Vasa*. While the hull itself was not badly designed and had completed numerous successful voyages since her launch in 1511, the rebuilding measures of 1536 to accommodate heavier artillery decreased stability considerably, which was the main reason why she capsized. A dendrological study confirmed that it was specifically the structure to support a gun-deck – i.e. riders, diagonal and vertical braces, heavy transom knees and deck beams – that was added around that date (Dobbs & Bridge 2000:258). So the transmission mechanism was, firstly, of modular nature from the evolutionary perspective in analytically discrete variants (cf. O'Brien & Lyman 2009:229), and secondly of undirected – hence indeterminate – nature, because the rebuilding measures were not designed by the original builders, as Adams (2001:294) points out. Here the error was fossilized in the wreck, exposing the lack of knowledge about how the centre of gravity would be affected by additional heavy guns placed along a flush deck, itself of considerable mass. It was therefore not a determinist process – which would have effected an adequate adaptation – but in fact a selective process of undirected nature. The catalyst that affected a precipitous adoption of a novel ballistic strategy was a societal one; the competition with France for maritime supremacy.

Although modular change was of course affected by a number of intentional acts, it was effectively an undirected transformation process in its outcome. Thus trial and error are indicative of change, as it reflects experimentation with innovative forms. As a natural consequence, errors in particular tend to survive archaeologically in shipwrecks that sank as whole assemblages – a time capsule – whose fate it was to escape scrapping or intentional grounding. In retrospect, the assumption that the database is somewhat biased towards failure does not undermine the archaeological potential of those wrecks, but rather increases it, since they are likely to contain innovations that have not been excessively tested and thus might indicate a transformational phase in ship construction.

'Intelligent design' or not: 'memes' as units for cognitive selection?

It would be beyond the scope of this paper to make an in-depth assessment of the findings of the neurological, psychological or social sciences on the exact nature of human decision-making. Although one is naturally inclined to regard one's own actions to be wholly conscious and one's own thoughts to be genuinely original, human cognitive behaviour is to a large extent conditioned by subliminal factors resulting from imitative social learning, which shape dialects, gestures, skills, behaviour, ethics and even opinions. Nonetheless, the question of the finer-grained processes for the transmission of knowledge and skills is central for understanding the significance of continuity and change within shipbuilding traditions. Therefore, some basic issues of this intricate question shall be briefly explored.

A pattern of inheritability in anthropogenic products has long been recognized. The Swedish antiquarian Oscar Montelius rhetorically asked whether human latitude is really so constricted that no discrete form could be created and concluded: *"Before examining the circumstances one feels inveigled to answer suchlike questions with "no". Since the strange history of human manufacture has been studied closer, one will find that the answer has to be "yes". Development can occur slow or fast, while new forms are always bound to the same laws of development, which also apply for nature"* (Montelius 1903:20). Indeed, in view of the overwhelming evidence for material culture in which some cultural 'phenotypes' lasted throughout the centuries, it has been hypothesised that there must be a unit through which cultural inheritance is replicated. As recently stressed by certain social scientists, *"the existence of social replicators cannot be denied simply because DNA-like mechanisms are absent"* (Aldrich et al. 2008:586). Despite such a replicating unit being neither visible nor measurable, Richard Dawkins famously promoted the 'meme' as the replicator of units of cultural inheritance, in equivalence to the gene as archetypal replicator (Dawkins 1976). The extra-somatic consequence of a meme, which becomes manifest in behavioural patterns among others, has been duly addressed with the notion that a *"meme is the least unit of sociocultural information relative to a selection process that has favourable or unfavourable selection bias that exceeds its endogenous tendency to change"* (Wilkins 1998:8). This is a very important point, because it highlights that the size of the unit is not fixed but can vary, depending on the context, while the fidelity – i.e. the degree to which an object is replicated – is conditioned by the selection bias, which basically *is* the context. This striking ambivalence, which makes 'memes' even less tangible, has sparked some criticism and prompted some to abandon the meme-theory altogether. It was stressed that cultural transmission processes are – unlike genetic systems – usually incomplete and imperfect, in which high fidelity replication is the exception rather than the rule. Moreover *"cultural representations are rarely discrete units, suggesting that the idea of a 'replicator' (or meme) makes little sense for most types of cultural representations"*, giving rise to the idea of *mutation-like* processes being more relevant than *selection-like* processes (Henrich & Boyd 2002:88, see also Henrich & McElreath 2003:131). Although the essence appears to be correct, there does not necessarily appear to be a contradiction to meme-theory, for Dawkins principally agreed that cultural copying processes are less precise than genetic ones, and also conceded that they contain a mutational element (Dawkins 1999:112). Besides, genes are not discrete units either, because *"selection at any one locus is not independent of selection at other loci"* Dawkins (1999:111) continues, *"Once a lineage begins evolving in a particular direction, many loci will fall into step, and the resulting positive feedbacks will tend to propel the lineage in the same direction, in spite of pressures from the outside world. An important aspect of the environment which selects between alleles[1] at any one locus will be the genes that already dominate the gene-pool at other loci."* Also, in a cultural context, there seem to be alleles in terms of a predisposition to adopt certain new concepts if the locus is dominated by a set of similar memes. Dutch shipbuilders were therefore arguably more prone to adopt carvel technology than practitioners of the Nordic clinker tradition, because they were already familiar with a "meme" of carvel technology, i.e. flush-laid bottom planking, as a prevalent feature in the local bottom-based tradition (for definition see Hocker 2004b). Therefore, they had a common denominator with the carvel technology, although it also encompassed the "alien" meme of skeleton-first construction. Despite the Dutch being arguably more open to this technology due to similarities within their own conceptual inheritance in naval architecture, the transmission of carvel technology still remained biased, leading to a low fidelity replication in the initial stage of construction: The bottom planking was held together by temporary cleats and thus retained an aspect of shell-first technology, leading to the *"Dutch-flush"* method (Fig. 5.4-6), which has been so aptly framed as *"cross-fertilization"* by Fred Hocker (1999:22).

However, how could the causality of this conceptual deviation – which spawns new variation – be envisioned? With regards to the proposed 'mutation-like' process, the aforementioned 'freak feature' of the triple-clinker solution comes to mind. Would it really be apt to refer to it in analogy as 'mutation-like'? This is highly questionable, even if one is willing to accept the Darwinian premise that mutations are – although seemingly random –always according to laws, without displaying any specific tendency towards adaptive

qualities. The underlying idea that innovations are merely random would appear – very understandably – alienating to many at first glance, but maybe less so when the units are broken down to trial and error on a cognitive micro-scale, which could be perhaps quintessentially perceived as *"Lamarckian causal arrows leading from phenotype to replicator"* (Dawkins 1999:112; see also Cullen 2000:32ff.). Nevertheless, the main reason why the analogy to a mutation-like process appears to be controversial is because 'freak features' seem to occur predominantly during transitional phases; as side products of a noisy replication process, conditioned by the cognitive filter of the transmission bias. Although – in contrast to Darwinian gradualism – extrinsic factors are thought to have an influence on the frequency with which new variants are spawned by mutations, a notion promoted by the theory of punctuated equilibrium (cf. Gould 2002:870ff.), it remains questionable whether it would be apt to speak of mutation-like processes in cultural analogies. Until this issue is solved, it is perhaps better to speak more neutrally in terms of an "undirected process", in order to highlight the non-deterministic outcome of cultural transmission (cf. Cullen 2000:102; Rindos 1985:65).

Ironically, in the same year that Richard Dawkins aimed to deconstruct the replicating mechanisms behind phenomena of cultural inheritance, Wendell Oswalt published a paper where he similarly made an attempt at deconstruction; however, not of the causality of replication mechanisms, but of their visible outcomes. He divided the modular structure of hunting gear into *techno-units* in order to make a cost-benefit assessment. Highly complex gear, for example, is not necessarily seen as the expression of a more advanced concept, but may just as well reflect the scarcity of a key resource; necessitating an alternative solution with a higher investment in *techno-units* to achieve the same goal (cf. Oswalt 1976). It has been suggested that we speak of a 'cultural selection pressure', in which the device which fulfils its purpose best with the lowest investment in materials continues to be used, whereas other devices *"die out"* (Kunst 1982:13). This may tend to be true, but has to be regarded nevertheless as gross simplification, rooted in the misapprehension of a 'cultural selection' being a genuinely conscious process; "selection" used in the vernacular sense of the word implying free choice. As has been previously pointed out, replication processes are distorted by a transmission bias and yield a differential outcome and rarely lead directly to the wholesale adoption of the favoured design with the lowest investment of material and work – quite the contrary, as has been exemplified by the cumbersome adaptation of the carvel technology in northern Europe.

---

1   As defined by Dawkins: *"Each gene is able to occupy only a particular region of a chromosome, its locus. At any given locus there may exist, in the population, alternative forms of the gene. These alternatives are called alleles of one another"* (Dawkins 1999:283).

Retention

Evolutionary theory is often reduced to being merely a gradual and progressive framework, in that – allegedly – the struggle for survival imposes a permanent competitive situation, through which maladaptive traits are sieved out. This reductionist application of evolutionary theory for explaining technological change in shipbuilding has been rightly scrutinized; amongst others this critique is reflected in the sentiment that *"in nautical archaeology the idea of an unfailing evolution from raft to ocean-liner has not stopped since Hornell"* (Maarleveld 1995:4), or that attempts to rationalise the linear evolutionary development of watercraft *"have created a series of problems that apparently defy explanation"* in that the social, economic, political and religious preconditions comprising the context within which change was generated were ignored (Adams 2001:307). Even Ole Crumlin-Pedersen, who frequently used evolutionary concepts, noted that *"today, the focus of interest has moved from evolution-based typologies to the study of ancient boats in their societal context"* (Crumlin-Pedersen 2004:42) as though evolutionary development occurs detached from societal influences. These views reflect the notion that the "irrational" factor of culture and society is *not* seen as an inherent part of evolutionary processes.

As demonstrated above however, evolutionary theory neither implies a permanent competitive situation, nor is it streamlined to the best possible designs. On the contrary, evolutionary theory provides explanations for some striking retention in modular features at the expense of adaptability.

Social learning, apprenticeship and 'conformist bias'

Gunnar Eldjarn and Jon Godal made it very clear in their famous ethnographic study on Norse vernacular watercraft, in which they opposed the ritualised way of doing things in historical times to our contemporary popular culture, which has cultivated individualism in spawning a mind-set of feeling free of norms and rules; a gap that is filled by the slavish following of fashion to attain identity by conformity. This present-day bias might have given rise to the strong emphasis on individual agency in the post-processualist agenda. In former times, however, boatbuilding was essentially a ritual, in which deviation from the norm was despised and boat-types were defined to such a degree that a local identity was evident through a common form and its associated work processes: *"Båt-typane vart svært så veldefinerte. Identiteten var tydeleg gjennom lokal, felles form. Dette galdt også sjølve arbeidsprosessen; måten ein gjorde ting på."* (Eldjarn & Godal 1988:32). But

what exactly causes this strong conservatism which discourages change or even downright suffocates deviation? The answer might lie in a new swathe of cognitive science, which has rediscovered evolutionary models and translated them into conceptual terms.

In this context the notions of neo-Darwinian cultural evolutionists with regard to conservative traits in selection is noteworthy; referring to concepts like the *conformist bias* as a form of imitative social learning (Richerson & Boyd 2005:162), to *path dependency* in which antecedent conditions define and delimit agency (Spencer 1997), or *heritage constraint* as the habitual cultural phenotype (Cullen 2000:100ff.). All of these concepts describe more or less the same phenomena, which tend to preserve a tradition. These subliminal forces became manifest in ethnographic studies, in that *"boats are a central part of the identities of the peoples who use them and they are artefacts that are deeply embedded in the history and culture of the societies. Quite simply, the local shape constitutes a 'proper boat' in the eyes of the local people"* (Palmer & Blue 2009:484). When ethnographers asked Indian boatbuilders why they constructed their boats the way they did, the only answer they could give was *"tradition"* (Blue 1997:341), or more specifically, *"because that is what we do around here"*, *"because we always do it that way"* or *"because that is how my father taught me to do it"* (Palmer, forthcoming). This shows that the possibility of selection from a range of alternatives is not even considered. Here, the notion of the underlying principle is important; that no selection in the evolutionary sense has taken place in merely reproducing a homologous feature and thus, continuing a conceptual lineage.

While ethnographic studies already provide a hint for the rigidity of cultural transmission in pre-industrial societies, a more immediate glimpse of the manifestation of a heritage constraint in an actual event is described in Snorri Sturlson's Heimskringla written around 1230.

Early next morning the king returns again to the ship, and Thorberg with him. The carpenters were there before them, but all were standing idle with their arms across. The king asked "what was the matter?" They said the ship was destroyed; for somebody had gone from stem to stern, and cut one deep notch after the other down the one side of the planking. When the king came nearer he saw it was so, and said, with an oath, "The man shall die who has thus destroyed the vessel out of envy, if he can be discovered, and I shall bestow a great reward on whoever finds him out." "I can tell you, king," said Thorberg, "who has done this piece of work." "I don't think," replies the king, "that any one is so likely to find it out as thou art." Thorberg says, "I will tell you, king, who did it. I did it myself." The king says, "Thou must restore it all to the same condition as before, or thy life shall pay for it." Then Thorberg went and chipped the planks until the deep notches were all smoothed and made even with the rest; and the king and all present declared that the ship was much handsomer on the side of the hull which Thorberg had chipped, and bade him shape the other side in the same way, and gave him great thanks for the improvement (Laing 1844:457).

Although, in this case, an inventive individual has liberated himself from his 'conformist bias' by thinking outside the box – actually a great example of individual agency – this nevertheless shows how deeply ingrained the idea about the shape of a *proper ship* must have been in the collective mind-set. This societal pressure would have made it hard for any individual to deviate from the norm, the way it was taught by the forefathers. Moreover, this particular ship was apparently seen within a lineage of royal ships and thus obtained a certain identity not unlike that of a creature's, with which we touch once more upon the "absurd" idea of ships with offspring, which is maybe not *that* absurd after all. King Ólafr Tryggvason's new ship was called *"Orm hinn langa"* (the long serpent), while its predecessor – also called *Orm* – was thence re-named *"Orm hinn skammi"* (the short serpent) (Falk 1912:32). Apart from the obvious faunal allusion, there appears an explicit hereditary line as the same "species", in which the new orm replaces the old orm as royal flagship.

Homology as continuity: 'atavisms' in shipbuilding

Evolutionary development does not consist of continuous smooth change, but also periods of equilibrium. The absence of conceptual change is no less interesting, as it gives an idea of the depth of an ingrained practice for doing and manufacturing things in the ritualized social landscape. It is particularly 'atavisms' – archaic constructional details with no function in the utilitarian sense – which indicate a stasis in a specific environmental, social or cultural context.

Although atavisms – in the biological sense – are the functionally obsolete phenotypes within lineages, they remain identifiable characteristics of a species and thereby – translated into the cultural sense – may have acquired symbolic value, as a unique cultural expression of a certain shape or form. One good example is the late medieval version of the *Oberländer*-type; a planked river-craft of the Rhine area, based on a trapezoidal substructure. This peculiar shape had been initially determined by halved logs, used to their maximum width, i.e. the base of the log having a larger diameter than its upper part. Detlev Ellmers (2002:102) points out that the shortage of adequately thick logs in late medieval times led to a shift to wholly planked versions of the *Oberländer*-type, whilst the peculiar shape –

despite having become obsolete – was retained. A similar scenario was suggested for the Utrecht-type in that the depletion of a large oak tree population would have prompted *"boat builders to replace the logboats with fully planked bottoms while retaining the characteristically deep curvature typical of Utrecht-type hulls"* (Van de Moortel 2009:333). Surely, in the first case, and probably also in the latter, change occurred due to the paucity of a resource. However, instead of reassessing the construction as a whole, a makeshift strategy was adopted to overcome the most imminent problem – a short term solution. This is a good example for homology, both in its static and transient sense. While the use of logs corresponds to what has been called an 'ancestral trait', the log-shaped planked version would consequently be a 'derived trait' (cf. O'Brien & Lyman 2009:234). Particularly in the first case, the disproportionately cumbersome implementation of a conventional solution may be yet again identified as a 'perceptual set', which generates anachronistic modular features that make little functional sense.

There are scholars, however, ascribing little diagnostic value to homologous features. Timm Weski (1999a: 97) criticised the tracing of shipbuilding traditions through hereditary constructional features, such as clamps for lashed plank-to-frame fastenings, as shared by the Hjortspring, Oseberg and Gokstad ships. He argued that this cannot be seen as a diagnostic feature through which a tradition could be identified, because the same building method could be also found on the Solomon Islands. Here Timm Weski categorically rules out the potential of homologous features for reconstructing a hereditary relationship, by merely opposing the possibility of an independent development of similar solutions elsewhere. The error of this thought lies in the conflation of the concepts of homology and analogy, irrespective of the spatiotemporal context.

The type-fallacy: illusive conceptual lineages

While retention is well-reflected in certain characteristics in the form of atavisms, homologous features, and other traces indicating continuity, it becomes a contested issue when the attempt is made to cast it into a typology and to bundle lineages with historically-derived type tags. The problem of classifying shipwrecks was summarized by Seán McGrail (1995:139f) as follows: *"If classification schemes are too complex, they run the risk of obscuring patterns; if too simple, the classifier may be tempted to drive them too far and draw unwarranted conclusion".* The underlying problem has also been discussed as a dichotomy between essentialist and materialist perspectives (cf. O'Brien & Lyman 2009:229), which shall be demonstrated as a case study in the following section. Obviously, the perception of the tradition will be distorted by various shortcomings, such as an unbalanced representation of certain types of wrecks in the database or the mix up between analogous and homologous features, blurring the understanding of conceptual lineages within shipbuilding traditions. Therefore, archaeologists will always have to keep in mind that they are essentially dealing with a fictitious typology (cf. Kunst 1982:3), which – of course – should ideally match up with the real typology. Fictitious typologies ought therefore to be seen as transient approximations and remain flexible enough to maintain an objective view as the database grows, or in McGrail's words, *"The aim of establishing such a classification scheme is not to fossilise types, for any scheme must be capable of responding to newly acquired data; nor is the aim to demonstrate any 'evolution' or 'development' of one type from another in a hierarchy of classes (cladogram)"* (McGrail 1998:4). While there cannot be any doubt of the validity of his first point, McGrail's later advice ought to be viewed with caution, because a detachment from hereditary lineages would undermine the study of traditions. Restrictively, one has to see McGrail's criticism of evolutionary concepts in light of how James Hornell employed them, i.e. as direct biological analogies, somewhat awkwardly superimposed on watercraft and not conditioned to conceptual lineages.

The actual problem is constituted by the challenge to align the fictitious typology as close to the real one as possible. In the case of watercraft from the recent past and the late post-medieval period the type-concept can be used with little bias, due to the wealth of written records. It is often possible to link a wreck not only to a type, but to even reveal the vessel's identity. The decisive hint is seldom found in the construction itself, but in the artefact assemblage, such as a ship's bell bearing the vessel's name (Ossowski 2008:50), gauge marks (Auer & Belasus 2008:136), and stone ballast with a petrologically-determined provenance (Adams 1985) as indication for the origin of the ship, or the emblem of the guns, revealing the maker, owner, date, and place of origin (Martin 2001:384). These hints are traced through contemporary records, so that light may be shed on concomitants and individuals, as in the case of the *Amsterdam*, where astonishingly many details emerged through a historical-archaeological approach (cf. Gawronski 1987:31ff.). It becomes clear that the main emphases in post-medieval shipwreck studies lie more on the artefact assemblage on the one side and archival studies on the other, while the construction itself is of relatively minor importance; in spite of the fact that theoretical treatises on shipbuilding accounted little for how the work had been actually conducted, as Colin Martin (2001:394) points out. Whenever no

contemporary records or meaningful find assemblages could be found, it is not only impossible to identify the vessel by its name, but often even by its type, since the type in early modern times referred to the way the vessel was rigged rather than how it was constructed. Moreover, nautical terminology has never been static, so the same type name might also have been employed for a totally differently constructed vessel (cf. Baker 1998:18; McGrail 1998:3).

The study of medieval shipwrecks is even more problematic, especially when it often follows a similar approach. The strong reliance on historical sources has prevailed, despite that specific written evidence is almost totally lacking for the medieval case, such as registers of ship-losses, payrolls, construction drawings and ship models which would allow detailed structural insights; with the only exceptions being the renowned models of Ebersdorf (Steusloff 1983) and Mataró (Culver & Nance 1929; van Nouhuys 1931; Winter 1956). The use of methods to classify medieval wrecks in a similar way as modern wrecks, has encouraged the malpractice of taking vague sources at face value, in order to link a shipwreck's construction to a historical type. This has led to the erroneous impression that the identification of a defined "type" should constitute the ultimate purpose of a study, as has been rightly critiqued by Thijs Maarleveld (1995:5).

The way typologies are built reveals that the large conceptual gap between the study of post-medieval and medieval shipwrecks is often hugely underestimated. Application of the same standards is attempted, due to a preoccupation with the ethnic or cultural affiliation of the wreck and its historical type; as though this would present a shortcut in the classification process, through which the painstaking examination of homologous and analogous modular features could be circumvented. Both concepts rise and fall with the predominant historical theory of the day and hence form no independent analytical tool (cf. Indruszewski 2004: 20ff).

The cog delusion

There is arguably no better case to demonstrate the type-fallacy than the example of the alleged 'cog-type'; particularly because the constructional properties, as currently defined, are widely taken for granted today and have ossified the narrative. This section highlights how the failure to formulate a consistent theoretical framework for mechanisms of cultural inheritance and technological transmission in shipbuilding technology has resulted in an arbitrary "cog-typology", which was strongly biased by the sequence of wreck discoveries. Although Thijs Maarleveld's strict antagonism towards

Darwinian processes in cultural development is opposed here, his critique that archaeological interpretation tends to be too dependent on historical type-concepts (cf. Maarleveld 1995:5f.) can be endorsed, as archaeologists have effectively stolen the thunder of their own discipline's interpretative potential.

This unwholesome dependency can be observed with regard to the 'Bremen Cog' of 1380, which became a paradigm for the "cog-type". Discovered in 1962 during dredging works in the River Weser, approximately 4 km downstream of the City of Bremen, Germany, the hitherto unfamiliar construction and visually distinctive appearance of the wreck was noted and led to the identification as a "cog" (Fliedner 1964). This identification was based on Paul Heinsius' (1956:55ff.) inference of the term cog, mainly from historical sources, in a study that suggested that regional variation of ship design is reflected in iconographic representations. The decisive hint is often seen in a documentary reference from 1483 to the Stralsund seal of 1329 *"vnser Stad Sigel ghenomed den kogghen"* (our seal reproduced from the cog) (Fliedner & Pohl-Weber 1968:24); in spite of the fact that the cog had been superseded in the late 15th century written sources by the hulk. So the 'cog' reference could have been a generic reference for an 'old ship'. Moreover, the two ship depictions on the seals of Lübeck and La Rochelle were also referred to as cogs by contemporary sources and look different from the Stralsund seal, which casts further doubt upon the reliability of the respective references (cf. Crumlin-Pedersen 2000:233; Weski 1999b:366ff.). Admittedly, it cannot be denied that there is a striking similarity between the Stralsund seal and the great majority of ship-depicting seals from the Hanseatic sphere, which coincided spatiotemporally with the heyday of the cog. So let us accept the premise – for the sake of brevity– that from these three seals most contemporaries would have chosen the Stralsund seal as the most truthful representation of a 'cog' and that cogs could be – consequently – identified by a flat bottom, a sharp transition to the stem- and sternposts, the straightness of the same, a stern-rudder and the exceptionally high hull sides. So far so good, but what followed next was an exactly inversed process of inference. Subsequently further criteria were inferred archaeologically from the 'Bremen Cog' and fed back to the defining criteria of the "cog-type", i.e. all criteria that could be neither deduced from written sources nor pictorial representations. These encompassed a 'keel-plank' replacing a proper keel, hooks that connected the plank-keel and the stem- and sternposts, flush-laid ('carvel') bottom planking gradually becoming lapstrake towards the hood-ends, clinkered side-planking, the use of double-bent nails in plank-to-plank fastening and, last but not least, the

use of moss as caulking material, held in the groove by laths stapled with *sintel* cramps (cf. Crumlin-Pedersen 2000:232f.; Hocker 2004b:75). While there can be no doubt that the criteria were distinctive enough to form an independent shipbuilding tradition, the additional criteria were simply added to the type definition as though the Bremen Cog was a blueprint – a perfect representation of its own tradition. *"Considering that the Bremen ship was beyond doubt called a cog by those who built and sailed her, why should this term not be used for that ship and for other seagoing Late-Medieval vessels with the same basic characteristics? We have described precisely the complex of features which we take as a definition of a cog in archaeological terms"* (Crumlin-Pedersen 2000:239) (Fig. 5.5). The complex features of a singular specimen – a paradigm – were apparently thought adequate for a universally applicable set of defining criteria, through which – perhaps inadvertently – a high degree of standardization was implied. The underlying problem presented here is typical for studies that entail evolutionary concepts, touching on the central issue of the dichotomy between a materialistic or essentialistic bias, prompting an inclusive or exclusive rationale in deducing a typology. For the essentialist, the type is real and variation an illusion, while for the materialist the average type is an abstraction and variation is real (O'Brien & Lyman 2009:229). Ole Crumlin-Pedersen thus follows a very essentialist approach in that sense, since he is concerned with tying a type down to a precise set of construction details inferred from the archaeology, yet unwarranted by historical sources. He evidently did not fail to notice himself the fragile basis of his claim and continued – somewhat apologetically – that if a vessel fulfils *"our criteria, it is a cog in our archaeological terminology"* (Crumlin-Pedersen 2000:239). The emphasis on *our* suggests that he foresaw the conflict of 'cog-type definition' between historians and archaeologists. His belief in the continuity in this set of deduced features was indeed so strong that he expected the same characteristics also in the ancestral character of wrecks of the same tradition, making the revealing remark of hoping to find more *"proto-cogs"* in order to *"guide further discussions on the pre-12th-century history of vessels with this particular set of constructional characteristics"* (Crumlin-Pedersen 2000: 239f.). The belief in such proto-cogs probably stems from over-interpretation of the 9th century reference to *cogscult* – often translated as cog tax – which *"confirms the existence before 1150 of ships called by a term equivalent to the present term cog"* (Crumlin-Pedersen 2000:238). 'Confirm' is a strong word, given that this is an equation with two unknowns. Firstly, there is no positive evidence to suggest that people used the term "cog" to describe a similar type of ship in 900 and 1150,

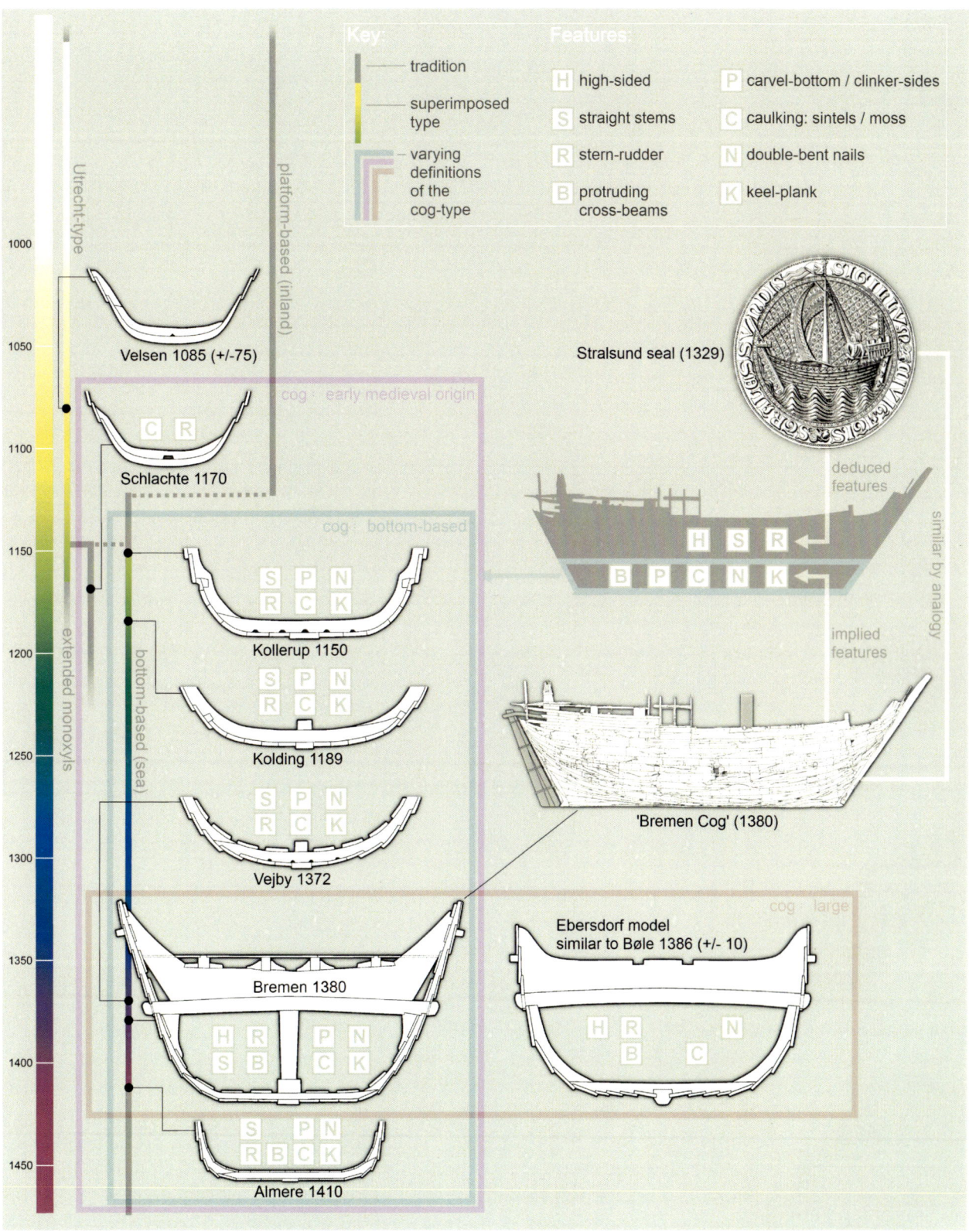

Figure 5.5. This graph highlights the conflicting deduction and definition of the cog-type. The graph schematically demonstrates the problem of superimposing the concept of a cog-type on traditions, as the boundaries between traditions are floating and thus any attempt to establish a standard-type would exclude forms that clearly belonged to the same tradition, or shared at least ancestral links. With the exception of rare cases like the 'Bremen Cog', most shipwrecks tend to be only preserved at the bottom construction and thus there is virtually no overlap with pictorial representations. Thus the cog-type definition rises and falls with the frail analogy between the ship depicted on the Stralsund seal and the Bremen Cog. While having some analogous features in common, most features that are currently associated with cogs are actually derived from the 'Bremen Cog' itself and fed back into the general cog type-concept, thus artificially elevating it to a paradigm (Graph: Daniel Zwick).

let alone employed the same guiding principles in its construction. Secondly, the term *cog* in this particular case seems to relate rather to a *Koke* in a regional Frisian dialect, i.e. a legal person (Fliedner 1969:44; Heinsius 1956:70). Also *Koggenland* in West Frisia has nothing to do with cogs, since a *kogge* was also a term to denote a judicial district consisting of four to five villages, which has not, however, stopped the authorities adopting a historicised image of a "cog" on the province's new coat-of-arms. The assumption that cogs plied the water in early medieval times has also induced the assumption that half of the Hedeby and Birka coins depict cogs. Despite Crumlin-Pedersen (1965:122ff.) convincingly arguing that the angular appearance can be in some cases ascribed to a *barð*, a piece of deadwood added to the stem and sternpost to enhance lateral stability, he over-interprets those depictions where the sheer of the planks is less pronounced and therefore lacks the deadwood at the keel transition thought to represent these "stem beards". Is the proto-cog a phantom?

In a nutshell, medieval sources are mute on constructional peculiarities, only rendering the general impression that cogs were large transport ships suited for long voyages (cf. Jahnke & Englert, forthcoming; Paulsen 2010). There is, for instance, no way of knowing whether the four Danish cogs that approached Tallinn in 1220 (cf. *Heinrici Chronicon Livoniae* XXIV:7, see Bauer 1975:266) were constructed similarly to the *"duas magnas naves, que koggen appellantur"* (UHdL 91, acc. to Jahnke & Englert, forthcoming), which were granted to Wismar in 1209 by the emperor. The four Danish ships that Henry of Livonia – a German missionary – perceived as cogs were maybe even called something different by the Danes. Admittedly, the general appearance and operational capabilities of cogs could be inferred indirectly, so there is at least a slight contextual intersection between historical and archaeological sources: Henry of Livonia's description of kedge anchors being brought out by smaller boats in order to kedge nine German cogs out of a narrow inlet (*Heinrici Chronicon Livoniae* XIX:5; Bauer 1975:189ff.), suggests that cogs could not be propelled under oars of their own accord; an impression that is congruent with the impressions gained from seal depictions on which alleged cogs are represented as high sided and bulky vessels. In spite of some hints that seem to support the conventional way in which cogs are defined today, it seems nevertheless questionable whether the cog-type constituted a type in the strict constructional sense as currently endorsed by a majority of scholars.

Essentialist properties define an idea, or archetype, to which objects are only imperfect approximations (cf. O'Brien & Lyman 2009:229). Several smaller

wrecks from the Ijsselmeer are perceived in this way. Despite them sharing many constructional features with the 'Bremen Cog' and evidently being descended from the same shipbuilding tradition, they could not, by definition, be cogs due to their modest sizes. For this reason they were called – somewhat awkwardly – "cog-like" vessels (van de Moortel 1991; Reinders 1985a:400ff., 1985b:7ff.). Another imperfect approximation would be the atypical deep keel in the 'Bossholmen Cog', which Fred Hocker called an exception (2004b:75). The latter restrictively admits that the *"identification of the diagnostic characteristics largely depends on whether the author has an inclusive or exclusive orientation"*. Now the question arises, of how the number of possible exceptions to the rule could be objectively fixed in order to determine whether the wreck is still part of a certain tradition or not. Merely by the number of deviating components, or through a modular hierarchy, in which some constructional features are thought to be more integral to the conceptual lineage than other more subsidiary criteria?

The exclusive orientation of the essentialist approach artificially divides a congruent tradition by means of a superimposed idealised type-concept. Inversely, a type in the historical sense may encompass various strands of archaeologically verifiable traditions.

This type-travesty was noted by several authors who were concerned with establishing a more objective typology; in the case of the "cog" most notably spearheaded by Timm Weski's proposition to call it the *Ijsselmeer type* instead, with regard to its assumed origin (Weski 1999b). Weski's critique in itself is absolutely justified, but his alternative proposition would have spawned another bias regarding the type's assumed origin, as Crumlin-Pedersen convincingly pointed out (2000:26ff.). Anton Englert suggested referring to the tradition in the archaeologically correct sense as the *Kollerup-Bremen type* (Englert 2000:44). Although this would foreclose the historical type bias, it would suffer the drawback of implying a preconceived linearity in the development from the Kollerup wreck of 1150 to the Bremen wreck of 1380. The *bottom-based shipbuilding tradition* (Hocker 2004b) appears to be the most objective typological concept, but it has weaknesses too, as it is arguably too exclusive. Bottom-based ships have, strictly speaking, structurally a lot in common with a group of entirely clinker-built ships that are commonly associated with the Nordic tradition. Both have in common shell-first construction and the bottom strakes of bottom-based ships – albeit carvel-laid – gradually overlap at their hood-ends too (cf. Lahn 1992:34). It could be therefore argued that these are conceptually not as distinctive from fully clinker-built ships as has often been implied. The claim that the bottom-based tradition has in effect a 'monopoly' – paraphrasing here – on cogs (cf. Hocker 2004b:72ff.) has to be seen critically, since there is no evidence to suggest that entirely clinker-built vessels, such as the kind of ship after which the Ebersdorf Ship was modelled in all possible detail (cf. Steusloff 1983:189), or the Bøle wreck (Daly & Nymoen 2008), were not referred to as cogs by contemporaries, despite also featuring a great visual similarity to the "cog-depicting seals". Although a certain similarity in appearance can be taken for granted, it seems highly questionable whether the term cog denominated a type of ship in a strict constructional sense. As argued above, analogous criteria can be treacherous, as they suggest a conceptual coherency, but may entail totally different conceptual solutions in the construction.

The type of medieval source that makes most frequent mention of ship types are customs and tax registers, in which types would have been classified in relative terms since capacities fluctuated over time (Wolf 1986:28). What mattered primarily to the customs officer was an estimate of the loadbearing capacity, according to which the toll could be fixed. He would have neither crept into the hold to ascertain whether the bottom planking was carvel or clinker, nor would he have measured the curvature of the stem in order to determine whether the ship was a cog or not.

In opposition to the essentialist approach stands the materialist approach, in which the ideal type becomes an abstraction of reality and variation regarded as the regular case. Although Detlev Ellmers has a similar take on the justification of identifying shipwrecks by their historical type (Ellmers 1972:14, 1979:493f.), he contrasts the essentialist approach by conceding great constructional variety within a type. This manifests particularly well in the case of what he called the 'Schlachte Cog'; a late 12th century wreck from Bremen with a unique construction, consisting of an extended log-based stern section, which finishes in a carved out skeg with fittings for a stern-rudder (cf. Wesemann & von Fick 1993; Zwick 2012a:287ff.). The reason for calling it a cog was based on Ellmers' conviction that the cog evolved gradually from an extended log-boat to a planked sea-going ship (Ellmers 2005:69). There are two problems with this. Firstly, a log-based "cog" would have been anachronistic when planked versions of allegedly the same type had emerged some decades earlier. Secondly, the underlying evolutionary concept is stripped of its analytical potential and reduced to a hypothesis, which was simply superimposed upon the wreck. Not for a moment was the possibility of a different ancestry considered, such as the local tradition of river-craft which employed to some degree concepts from extended log-boats, tentatively associated with

the *eke* or "oaks". The conceptual gap to extended log-boats would have been much smaller, yet the unusual 'freak feature' of a stern-rudder was apparently seen as the decisive factor for drawing a link to cogs, rather than addressing it as an analogous feature, which the builder apparently took great lengths to include, given that the whole stern had to be carved out from the trunk to obtain an analogous shape to planked vessels. Notwithstanding, the wreck entered the literature as the 'Schlachte Cog' (or 'Schlachte Kogge' in German), so as not to leave any interpretative leeway or – heaven forbid – allow a re-evaluation of its type (cf. Rech 1991, 1993, 2004: 243ff.; Wesemann & von Fick 1993). In general, the establishment of a presupposed type as an epithet has to be condemned as unscientific practice, since it precludes a serious inquiry into the phenomenon itself. This should even extend to the 'Bremen Cog', as Timm Weski (2006) more recently stressed.

Neither Crumlin-Pedersen's nor Ellmers' approach is fundamentally wrong; the first simply believed that a type is characterised more by continuity and the latter favours more variation within a type over time. Contradictions are mainly due to the urge to harmonise the essentialist historical perspective with the materialistic archaeological perspective. The over-interpretation of details at this contested interface has arguably multiplied the error in interpretation.

Conclusion

It could be concluded that the arbitrary use of type concepts distorts typologies which ought to be based on traditions. Therefore, to speak of cog-like vessels whenever wrecks with flush-laid bottom planks and clinkered sides held together with double-bent nails are excavated would make as much sense as for future archaeologists to refer to a 19th century river barge as an ocean-liner-like vessel, because its hull is – similar to the *Titanic's* – clad by riveted steel plates. Type and tradition are entirely different concepts, therefore the use of the term "cog-tradition" reflects a redundant concept. Historical type-concepts seldom relate to a typology in the archaeological sense, i.e. tradition, and should therefore be treated as discrete entities. This puts more emphasis on a discrete tool for developing typologies more independent from the prevalent historical narrative. As advocated in this paper, such a tool could be gained by following an evolutionary approach, or at least, by becoming more aware of the mechanisms behind inheritable cultural phenomena that form a tradition.

As was stated a decade ago, however, there *"can be little doubt that a serious engagement with the problems raised by a scientific evolutionary archaeology will require* practitioners to work outside the norms of contemporary social theory" (Murray 2002:56). While the body of work on scientific evolutionary archaeology and other relevant work that examines hereditary patterns in culture and behaviour has grown, not much has changed in terms of wider acceptance. The implementation of this new perspective with concrete nautical archaeological case studies – as done in this paper – should not be regarded as an effort to install a universally applicable framework for interpretation, but should be seen as an attempt to understand the finer-grained causes and mechanisms through which continuity is preserved, or innovation and change effected. It is hoped that this contribution will rekindle the debate on the significance and scope of hereditary patterns within shipbuilding traditions and, thereby, lead to the development of more sensible, truly archaeological typologies, through which genuine traditions could be reconstructed. Whether this goal

can be achieved by an evolutionary approach has yet to be shown – the gauntlet has been thrown. Who will pick it up?

Acknowledgements

I am particularly indebted to Jon Adams for reviewing this paper, challenging me on several points in a thought-provoking manner and for providing numerous amendments. I also thank Nicole Taylor for cross-reading and Anton Englert, Thomas Guttandin, Thijs Maarleveld, Oliver Nelle, Colin Palmer, Johan Rönnby, Timm Weski and Christer Westerdahl for kind comments on the first draft of this paper, access to unpublished manuscripts or further literature recommendations. The views presented in this article do not necessarily reflect those of the aforementioned.

References

Åkerlund, H. 1951. *Fartygsfynden i den Forna Hamnen i Kalmar*, Stockholm: Sjöhistoriska Samfundet.

Adams, J. 1985. Sea Venture: A second interim report, part 1. *International Journal of Nautical Archaeology* 14.4: 275–99.

Adams, J. 2001. Ships and boats as archaeological source material. *World Archaeology* 32.3: 292-310.

Adams, J. 2003. *Ships, Innovation and Social Change. Aspects of Carvel Shipbuilding in Northern Europe 1450-1850*, Stockholm: Stockholm University.

Aldrich, H. E., Hodgson, G.M., Hull, D.L., Knudsen, T., Mokyr, J. & Vanberg, V.J. 2008. In Defence of Generalized Darwinism. *Journal of Evolutionary Economics* 18.5: 577-96.

Auer, J. 2009. Fieldwork report. Ostsee Bereich IV, Fischland, FPL 7. *Esbjerg Maritime Archaeology Reports 2*. Esbjerg: University of Southern Denmark.

Auer, J. & Belasus, M. 2008. The British Brig Water Nymph or ... even an Englishman cannot take the liberty to deride a civil servant on German soil. *International Journal of Nautical Archaeology* 37.1: 130-141.

Baker, W.A. 1998. The technical importance of shipwreck archaeology. In: L. E. Babits & H. van Tilburg (eds) *Maritime Archaeology. A Reader of Substantive and Theoretical Contributions*: 17-21. New York & London: Plenum Press.

Bauer, A. 1959 (repr. 1975). *Heinrich von Lettland – Livländische Chronik*. Ausgewählte Quellen zur deutschen Geschichte des Mittelalters - Freiherr vom Stein-Gedächtnisausgabe 24, Darmstadt.

Bill, J. 1997. *Small Scale Seafaring in Danish Waters AD 1000-1600*. Ph.D. thesis. University of Copenhagen.

Bill, J. 2003. Schiffe als Transportmittel im nordeuropäischen Raum. In: *Warentransport im Mittelalter und in der Frühen Neuzeit. Transportwege – Transportmittel – Infrastruktur* (= Mitteilungsblatt der Deutschen Gesellschaft für Archäologie des Mittelalters und der Neuzeit 14), 2003.

Bill, J. 2009. Zwischen Kogge und Kraweel. Traditioneller Kleinschiffbau in Südskandinavien in einer Zeit der Wende. In: B. Scholkmann, S. Frommer, C. Vossler (eds) *Zwischen Tradition und Wandel- Archäologie des 15. und 16. Jahrhunderts*. Tübinger Forschungen zur historischen Archäologie 3: 251-260. Büchenbach: Faustus.

Bill, J. & Hocker, F. 2004. Haithabu 4 seen in the context of contemporary shipbuilding in Southern Scandinavia. In K. Brandt and H.J. Kühn (eds) *Der Prahm aus dem Hafen von Haithabu. Beiträge zu antiken und mittelalterlichen Flachbodenschiffen*. Schriften des Archäologischen Landesmuseums – Ergänzungsreihe 2: 43-53. Neumünster: Wachholz.

Blue, L. 1997. Boats of South Asia. *International Journal of Nautical Archaeology* 26.4: 339-343.

Blumenberg, H. 1997. *Schiffbruch mit Zuschauer. Paradigma einer Daseinsmetapher*, Frankfurt am Main: Suhrkamp.

Carpenter Turner, W.J. 1954. The building of the Gracedieu, Valentine and Falconer at Southampton, 1416-1420. *Mariner's Mirror* 40.1: 55-75.

Cederlund, C.O. 1995. Ship archaeology - "communications archaeology", In: C. O. Cederlund (ed.) *Medieval ship archaeology.* Stockholm Marine Archaeology Reports 1:103-106. Stockholm: University of Stockholm.

Cederlund, C.O. & Hocker, F. 2006. *Vasa I: The Archaeology of a Swedish Warship of 1628.* Stockholm: Statens Maritima Museer.

Christensen, A.E. 2000. Some archaic details of Norwegian fresh-water boats. In: J. Litwin (ed.) *Down the River to the Sea.* Proceedings of the Eighth International Symposium on Boat and Ship Archaeology, Gdańsk 1997: 163-168. Gdańsk: Polish Maritime Museum.

Clark, G.A. & Barton, C. M. 1997. Rediscovering Darwin. In: C.M. Barton and G.A. Clark (eds) *Rediscovering Darwin: Evolutionary Theory and Archaeological Explanation.* Archaeological Papers 7: 309-319. Arlington, VA: American Anthropological Association.

Crumlin-Pedersen, O. 1965. Cog – Kogge - Kaag. Træk af en frisisk skibstypes historie. In: *Handels- og Søfartsmuseet på Kronborg Årbog* 1965: 81-144.

Crumlin-Pedersen, O. 1970a Skin or wood? A Study of the Scandinavian Plank Boat. In: O. Hasslöf, H. Henningsen & A.E. Christensen (eds) *Ships and Shipyards, Sailors and Fishermen:* 213-239. Copenhagen: Rosenkilde & Bagger.

Crumlin-Pedersen, O. 1970b. The Viking Ships of Roskilde. In: B. Greenhill (ed.) *Aspects of the History of Wooden Shipbuilding.* Maritime Monographs and Reports 1: 7-23. Greenwich: National Maritime Museum.

Crumlin-Pedersen, O. 1972. Die Wikinger und die hansischen Kaufleute: 900-1400. In G.F. Bass (ed.) *Taucher in der Vergangenheit. Unterwasser-Archäologen schreiben die Geschichte der Seefahrt,* Luzern: Bucher.

Crumlin-Pedersen, O. 1990. Sejle op ad åen. Skibsfund og sejlspærringer i danske indvande. In: *Vandløb og kulturhistorie.* Skrifter fra Historisk Institut 39: 93-104. Odense: Odense University.

Crumlin-Pedersen, O. 1997. *Viking Age Ships and Shipbuilding in Hedeby/Haithabu and Schleswig.* Ships and Boats of the North 2. Schleswig & Roskilde: Archaeology State Museum of the Christian-Albrecht University, Viking Museum Haithabu, National Museum of Denmark, Viking Ship Museum Roskilde.

Crumlin-Pedersen, O. 2000. To be or not to be a cog: the Bremen cog in perspective. *International Journal of Nautical Archaeology* 29.1: 230-246.

Crumlin-Pedersen, O. 2003. Die Bremer Kogge – ein Schlüssel zur Geschichte des Schiffbaus im Mittelalter. In: G. Hoffmann & U. Schnall (eds) *Die Kogge - Sternstunde der deutschen Schiffsarchäologie.* Schriften des Deutschen Schiffahrtsmuseum 60: 256-271. Hamburg: Convent.

Crumlin-Pedersen, O. 2004. Nordic clinker construction. In: F. M. Hocker & C. A. Ward (eds) *The Philosophy of Shipbuilding. Conceptual approaches to the study of wooden ships:* 37-63. College Station: Texas A&M University.

Cullen, B. S. 2000. *Contagious ideas: On evolution, culture, archaeology and cultural virus theory.* Oxford: Oxbow Books.

Culver, H. B. & Nance, M. 1929. A contemporary Fifteenth Century Ship. *The Mariner's Mirror* 15.3: 213-221.

Dawkins, R. 1976. *The Selfish Gene.* Oxford: Oxford University Press.

Dawkins, R. 1999. *The Extended Phenotype: The Long Reach of the Gene,* Oxford: Oxford University Press.

Dobbs, C.T.C. & Bridge. M. 2000. Preliminary Results from Dendrochronological studies on the Mary Rose. In: J. Litwin (ed.) *Down the River to the Sea.* Proceedings of the Eighth International Symposium on Boat and Ship Archaeology, Gdańsk 1997: 257-262. Gdańsk: Polish Maritime Museum.

Dokkedal, L. 1996. *Koggen i Nordeuropa fra 1150-1450 e. Kr. – Definition af skibstypen og diskussion af en mulig årsag til dens anvendelse i nordeuropæisk skibsfart,* (University of Copenhagen Ph.D. dissertation).

Eldjarn, G. & Godal, J. 1988. *Nordlandsbåten og Åfjordsbåten I: Båten i bruk.* Lesja: A. Kjellands.

Ellmers, D. 1972. *Frühmittelalterliche Handelsschiffahrt in Mittel- und Nordeuropa,* Neumünster: Wachholtz.

Ellmers, D. 1979. Schiffsarchäologie. In: H. Jankuhn & R. Wenskus (eds) *Geschichtswissenschaft und Archäologie. Untersuchungen zur Siedlungs-, Wirtschafts- und Kirchengeschicht*: 485-518. Siegmaringen: Thorbecke.

Ellmers, D. 2002. Baumschiff und Oberländer. Archäologie, Ikonografie und Typenbezeichnungen einer mittelalterlichen Binnenschiffsfamilie. In: K. Elmshäuser (ed.) *Häfen, Schiffe, Wasserwege: zur Schiffahrt des Mittelalters.* Schriften des Deutschen Schiffahrtsmuseums 58: 97-106. Hamburg: Convent.

Ellmers, D. 2005. The Hanseatic Cog of Bremen AD 1380. *Drassana* 13: 58-72.

Englert, A. 2000. *Large cargo vessels in Danish water AD 1000 - 1250.* Ph.D. thesis. University of Kiel.

Eriksson, N. 2010. Between clinker and carvel: aspects of hulls built with mixed planking in Scandinavia between 1550 and 1900. In: A. Girininkas (ed.) *Underwater Archaeology in the Baltic Region*. Archaeologia Baltica 14: 77-84. Klaipėda: Klaipėda University Press.

Falk, H. 1912. Altnordisches Seewesen. In: *Wörter und Sachen* 4, Heidelberg: C. Winther.

Filgueiras, O. L 1979. A presumptive Germanic heritage for a Portuguese boat-building tradition. In: S. McGrail (ed.) *The Archaeology of Medieval Ships and Harbours in Northern Europe*. Second International Symposium on Boat and Ship Archaeology, Bremerhaven 1979. British Archaeological Reports – International Series 66: 17-34. Oxford: British Archaeology Reports.

Filgueiras, O.L. (ed.) 1988. *Local Boats* 2. Fourth International Symposium on Boat and Ship Archaeology, Porto 1985. British Archaeological Reports – International Series 438.2: 275-528. Oxford: British Archaeology Reports.

Fliedner, S. 1964. Der Fund einer Kogge bei Bremen im Oktober 1962. In: *Bremer Jahrbuch* 49: 7-10.

Fliedner, S. 1969. 'Kogge' und 'Hulk'. Ein Beitrag zur Schiffstypengeschichte. In: *Die Bremer Hanse-Kogge*: 39-121. Bremen: Focke Museum.

Fliedner, S. & Pohl-Weber, R. 1968. *Die Bremer Kogge*. Hefte des Focke-Museums 19. Bremen: Focke Museum.

Friel, I. 1993. Henry V's Grace Dieu and the wreck in the R. Hamble near Bursledon, Hampshire. *International Journal of Nautical Archaeology* 22.1: 3-19.

Friel, I. 1994. The Carrack: The Advent of the Full Rigged Ship. In: R. W. Unger (ed.) *Cogs, Caravels and Galleons. The Sailing Ship 1000-1650*: 77-90, London: Conway Maritime Press.

Friel, I. 1995. *The Good Ship. Ships, Shipbuilding and Technology in England 1200-1520*. London: British Museum Press.

Gawronski, J. H. G. (ed.) 1987. *V.O.C. Schip Amsterdam*. Annual Report of the VOC-Ship "Amsterdam" Foundation. Amsterdam: VOC Schip Amsterdam.

Gibbins, D. & Adams, J. 2001. Shipwrecks and maritime archaeology. In: *World Archaeology* 32.3: 279-291.

Gould, S.J. 2002. *The Structure of Evolutionary Theory*. Cambridge MA: Belknap Press of Harvard University Press.

Gøthche, M. 1991. Three Danish 17th - 19th century wrecks as examples of clinker building techniques versus carvel building techniques in local shipwrightry. In: R. Reinders and K. Paul (eds) *Carvel Construction Technique*: 85-88. Oxford: Oxbow Books.

Greenhill, B. & Mannering, J. (eds) 1997. *The Chatham directory* of *Inshore Craft: Traditional working vessels of the British Isles*. London: Chatham.

Guttandin, T. Seagoing Paddled Ships. In: H. Tzalas (ed.) *Tropis IX. 9th International Symposium on Ship Construction in Antiquity, Agia Napa 2005*. Athens. (forthcoming)

Hasslöff, O. 1972. Main principles in the technology of shipbuilding. In: O. Hasslöff, H. Henningsen, & A.E. Christensen (eds) *Ships and Shipyards, Sailors and Fishermen*: 27-72. Copenhagen: Copenhagen University Press, Rosenkilde & Bagger.

Heinsius, P. 1956 (reprinted 1986). *Das Schiff der hansischen Frühzeit*. Weimar: Böhlau.

Henrich, J. & Boyd, R. 2002. On Modeling Cognition and Culture. Why cultural evolution does not require replication of representations. *Journal of Cognition and Culture* 2.2: 87-112.

Henrich, J. & Gil-White, F. 2001. The Evolution of Prestige: freely conferred deference as a mechanism for enhancing the benefits of cultural transmission. In: *Evolution and Human Behavior* 22.3: 165-196.

Henrich, J. & McElreath, R. 2003. The Evolution of Cultural Evolution. In: *Evolutionary Anthropology* 12: 123–135.

Henrich, J. & McElreath, R. 2007. Dual inheritance theory: the evolution of human cultural capacities and cultural evolution. In: R. Dunbar and L. Barrett, (eds) *Oxford Handbook of Evolutionary Psychology Oxford*: 555-570. Oxford: Oxford University Press.

Hocker, F. M. 1999. Technical and organizational development in European shipyards 1400 – 1600. In: J. Bill & B.L. Clausen (eds) *Maritime Topography and the Medieval Town*. Papers from the 5th International Conference on Waterfront Archaeology in Copenhagen, 14-16 May, 1998: 95-108. Copenhagen: National Museum of Denmark.

Hocker, F. M. 2004a. Shipbuilding: Philosophy, Practice, and Research. In: F. M. Hocker & C. A. Ward (eds) *The Philosophy of Shipbuilding. Conceptual approaches to the study of wooden ships*: 1-11. College Station: Texas A&M University.

Hocker, F. M. 2004b. Bottom-based shipbuilding in northwestern Europe. In: F. M. Hocker & C. A. Ward (eds) *The Philosophy of Shipbuilding. Conceptual approaches to the study of wooden ships*: 65-93. College Station: Texas A&M University.

Hornell, J. 1920. Origins and ethnographical significance of Indian boat design. *Memoirs of the Asiatic Society of Bengal* 7: 139-256.

Hornell, J. 1946. *Water transport. Origins and Early Evolution*. Cambridge: Cambridge University Press.

Hull, D.L. 1988. *Science as a Process: An Evolutionary Account of the Social and Conceptual Development of Science*. Chicago: University of Chicago Press.

Hutchinson, G. 1994. *Medieval ships and shipping*, London: Leicester University Press.

Indruszewski, G. 2004. *Man, Ship, Landscape. Ships and seafaring in the Oder Mouth Area AD 400-1400. A case study of an ideological context.* Copenhagen: National Museum of Denmark.

Jahnke, C. & Englert, A. The state of historical research on merchant seafaring in Danish waters and in the western Baltic Sea 1000-1250. In: A. Englert (ed.) *Large Cargo Ships in Danish Waters 1000-1250.* Ships & Boats of the North. Roskilde: Viking Ship Museum. (Forthcoming)

Johnstone, P. 1980. *The Sea-Craft of Prehistory*, London & New York: Routledge.

Kunst, M. 1982. Intellektuelle Information – Genetische Information. In: *Acta praehistorica et archaeologica* 13/14: 1-26.

Lahn, W. 1992. *Die Kogge von Bremen =the Hanse Cog of Bremen. Bd. 1: Bauteile und Bauablauf = Structural members and construction process.* Schriften des Deutschen Schiffahrtsmuseums 30. Hamburg: Convent.

Lemée, C.P. 2006. *The Renaissance Shipwrecks from Christianshavn.* Ships and Boats of the North. 6. Roskilde: Viking Ship Museum.

Leonard, W. E. 1943. *On the Nature of Things.* London: Dent.

Laing, S. 1844. *Heimskringla: A History of the Norse Kings.* London: Longman, Brown, Green, and Longmans.

Loewen, B. 1997. Bayonne 1419. Lapstraking and moulded frames in the same hull? *The Mariner's Mirror* 83.3: 328-330.

Lund, N. 1996. *Lid, leding og landeværn.* Roskilde: Vikingeskibshallen.

Maanders, M.R. 2003. The Mysteries of a Baltic Trader, in: C. Beltrame (ed.) *Boats, Ships and Shipyards.* Proceedings of the Ninth International Symposium on Boat and Ship Archaeology, Venice 2000: 320-328. Oxford: Oxbow.

Maarleveld, T. J. 1992. Archaeology and early modern merchant ships. Building sequence and consequences. An introductory review. In: A. Carmiggelt (ed.) *Rotterdam Papers VII: a contribution to medieval archaeology*: 155-174. Rotterdam: A. Carmiggelt.

Maarleveld, T.J. 1994. Double Dutch Solutions in Flush-Planked Shipbuilding: Continuity and Adaptations at the Start of Modern History. In: C. Westerdahl (ed.) *Crossroads in Ancient Shipbuilding.* Proceedings of the International Symposium on Boat and Ship Archaeology 6, 1991 Roskilde: 153-163. Oxford: Oxbow.

Maarleveld, T. 1995. Type or technique. Some thoughts on boat and ship finds as indicative of cultural traditions. *International Journal of Nautical Archaeology* 24.1: 3-7.

Mäss, V. 1994. A unique 16th-century Estonian ship find. In: C. Westerdahl (ed.) *Crossroads in Ancient Shipbuilding.* Proceedings of the International Symposium on Boat and Ship Archaeology 6, 1991 Roskilde: 189-194. Oxford: Oxbow.

Martin, C. 2001. De-particularizing the particular: approaches to the investigation of well-documented post-medieval shipwrecks. *World Archaeology* 32.3: 383-399.

Matthew, P. 1831. *On Naval Timber and Arboriculture.* London: Longman, Rees, Orme, Brown, and Green.

Mayr, E. 1961. Cause and Effect in Biology. *Science* 134: 1501-1506.

McGrail, S. 1981. *The Ship: Rafts, Boats, and Ships.* Greenwich: National Maritime Museum.

McGrail, S. 1995. Romano-Celtic boats and ships: characteristic features. *International Journal of Nautical Archaeology* 24.2: 139–145.

McGrail. S. 1998. *Ancient Boats in North-West Europe. The Archaeology of Water Transport to AD 1500.* London & New York: Longman.

McGrail, S. 2001. *Boats of the World.* Oxford: Oxford University Press.

van de Moortel, A. 1991. *A Cog-like Vessel from the Netherlands.* Flevobericht 331. Lelystad: Rijkswaterstaat Directie Flevoland.

van de Moortel, A. 2009. The Utrecht Ship Type: an Expanded Logboat Tradition in its Historical Context. In: R. Bockius (ed.) *Between the Seas. Transfer and Exchange in Nautical Technology.* Proceedings of the Eleventh International Symposium on Boat and Ship Archaeology, Mainz, 2006: 329-336. Mainz: Römisch-Germanisches Zentralmuseum.

Montelius, O. 1903. *Die älteren Kulturperioden im Orient und in Europa I. Die Methode.* Stockholm: Asher.

Morgan, D.L., Morgan, R.K. & Toth, J.M. 1992. Variation and Selection: The Evolutionary Analogy and the Convergence of Cognitive and Behavioral Psychology. *The Behavior Analyst* 15: 129-138.

Muckelroy, K. 1978. *Maritime Archaeology.* Cambridge: Cambridge University Press.

Mudie, C. 1996. Matthew and Naval Architecture. In: *Historic Ships: Design, Restoration & Maintenance.* London: The Royal Institution of Naval Architects.

Murray, T. 2002. Evaluating evolutionary archaeology. *World Archaeology* 34.1: 47-59.

Norman, H. 2000. *Skärgårdsflottan: Uppbyggnad, militär användning och förankring i det svenska samhället 1700-1824.* Lund: Historiska Media.

van Nouhuys, J.W. 1931. The model of a Spanish caravel of the beginning of the 15th century.

Mariner's Mirror 17: 327-346.

O'Brien, M.J. & Lyman, R.L. 2009. Darwinism and Historical Archaeology. In: T. Majewski & D. Gaimster (eds) *International Handbook of Historical Archaeology*: 227-252. New York: Springer.

Olearius, A., Davies, J. & von Mandelslo, J.A. 1662. *The Voyages & Travels of the Ambassadors from the Duke of Holstein, to the Great Duke of Muscovy, and the King of Persia*. London: Dring & Starkey.

Ossowski, W. 2006. Two double-planked wrecks from Poland. In: L. Blue, F. Hocker & A. Englert (eds) *Connected by the Sea*. Proceedings of the Tenth International Symposium on Boat and Ship Archaeology, Roskilde 2003: 257-265. Oxford: Oxbow.

Ossowski, W. 2008. *The General Carleton shipwreck, 1785*. Gdańsk: Polish Maritime Museum.

Oswalt, W.H. 1976. *An Anthropological Analysis of Food-Getting Technology*. New York: John Wiley & Sons.

Palmer, C. The Diversity of Traditional Boats: What causes it and why does it persist? In: *Proceedings of the 10th TAG conference, Exeter 2006*. (Forthcoming)

Palmer, C. & Blue, L. 2009. The country boats of the Ganges delta. An ethnographic study of inland navigation. In: R. Bockius (ed.) *Between the Seas. Transfer and Exchange in Nautical Technology*. Proceedings of the 11th International Symposium on Boat and Ship Archaeology, Mainz 2006: 479-488. Mainz: Römisch-Germanisches Zentralmuseum.

Parker, G. 1996. The Dreadnought Revolution in Tudor England. *Mariner's Mirror* 82.3: 269-300.

Paulsen, R. 2010. Die Koggendiskussion in der Forschung. Methodische Probleme und ideologische Verzerrungen. *Hansische Geschichtsblätter* 128: 19-112.

Petersen, H.C. 1986. *Skinboats of Greenland*. Ships and Boats of the North 1. Roskilde: Viking Ship Museum.

Phillips, C. R. 1994. The Caravel and the Galleon. In: R. W. Unger (ed.) *Cogs, Caravels and Galleons. The Sailing Ship 1000-1650*: 91-114. London: Conway Maritime Press.

Preucel, R.W. & Hodder, I. 1996. *Contemporary archaeology in theory: a reader*. Oxford: Wiley-Blackwell.

Probst, N.M. 1994. The Introduction of Flush-Planked Skin in Northern Europe and the Elsinore Wrecks. In: C. Westerdahl (ed.) *Crossroads in Ancient Shipbuilding*. Proceedings of the Sixth International Symposium on Boat and Ship Archaeology, Roskilde 1991: 143-152. Oxford: Oxbow.

Rech, M. 1991. Übersicht der Schiffsfunde auf Bremer Gebiet. In: *Bremer Archäologische Blätter - Neue Folge*

1: 25-32.

Rech, M. 1993. Neufund einer Kogge: Fundgeschichte und Datierung. *Bremer Archäologische Blätter - Neue Folge* 2: 31-35.

Rech, M. 2004. *Gefundene Vergangenheit - Archäologie des Mittelalters in Bremen*. Bremer Archäologische Blätter, Beiheft 3. Bonn: Habelt.

Reinders, R. 1985a. Recent developments in ship and boat archaeology in the Netherlands. In: C. O. Cederlund (ed.) *Postmedieval Boat and Ship Archaeology*. British Archaeological Reports - International Series 256: 399-412. Oxford: British Archaeology Reports.

Reinders, R. 1985b. *Cog finds from the Ijsselmeerpolders*. Flevobericht 248. Lelystad: Rijkswaterstaat Directie Flevoland.

Richerson, P.J. & Boyd, R. 2005. *Not by genes alone: how culture transformed human evolution*. Chicago: University of Chicago Press.

Rindos, D. 1985. Darwinian selection, symbolic variation, and the evolution of culture. *Current Anthropology* 26: 65-88.

Salisbury, W. 1961. The Woolwich Ship. *The Mariner's Mirror* 47.2: 81-90.

Spencer, C. 1997. Evolutionary approaches in archaeology. *Journal of Archaeological Research* 5.3: 209-264.

Rönnby, J. 1996. Kronholmskoggen – Om ett skeppsfynd och tolkningsmöjligheter. In: H. Ranheden, E. Hyenstrand, M. Jacobsson, J. Rönnby & A Nilsson (eds) *Metodstudier & tolkningsmöjligheter*. Arkeologiska Undersökningar 20: 65-75. Stockholm: Riksantikvarieämbetet.

Rose, S. 1977. Henry V's Grace Dieu and Mutiny at Sea: Some new evidence. In: *The Mariner's Mirror* 63.1: 3-6.

Steffy, J.R. 1994. *Wooden ship building and the interpretation of shipwrecks*. College Station: Texas A&M University.

Steusloff, W. 1983. Das Ebersdorfer Koggenmodell von 1400. *Deutsches Schiffahrtsarchiv* 6: 189-207.

Varenius, B. 1989. *Båtarna från Helgeandsholmen*. Stockholm: Riksantikvarieämbetet.

Vlierman, K. 1996. *Kleine bootjes en middeleeuws scheepshout met constructiedetails*. Scheepsarcheologie II. Flevobericht 404. Lelystad: Rijkswaterstaat Directie Flevoland.

Warner, G.F. 1926. *The libelle of Englyshe polycye: a poem on the use of sea-power 1436*. Oxford: Clarendon.

Wesemann, S. & von Fick, C. C. 1993. Die neue Kogge - Ausgrabung und Bautyp (Vorbericht). *Bremer Archäologische Blätter – Neue Folge* 2: 36-45.

Weski, T. 1999a. Fiktion oder Realität? Anmerkungen zum archäologischen Nachweis spätmittelalterlicher

Schiffsbezeichnungen. *Skyllis* 2.2: 96-106.

Weski, T. 1999b. The IJsselmeer type: some thoughts on Hanseatic cogs. *International Journal of Nautical Archaeology* 28: 360-379.

Weski, T. 2006. Wurde wirklich eine Kogge gefunden? Spätmittelalterliche Funde der Schiffsarchäologie in Nord- und Ostsee. *Antike Welt. Zeitschrift für Archäologie und Kulturgeschichte* 1: 91-96.

Westerdahl, C. 1995. Traditional zones of transport geography in relation to ship types. In: O. Olsen, J.S. Madsen and F. Rieck (eds) *Shipshape: Essays for Ole Crumlin-Pedersen*. Roskilde: Viking Ship Museum.

Wilkins, J.S. 1998. What's in a meme? Reflections from the perspective of the history and philosophy of evolutionary biology. *Journal of Memetics - Evolutionary Models of Information Transmission* 2.1: 2-33.

Winter, H. 1956. *Die Katalanische Nao von 1450*.

Magdeburg: Loef.

Wolf, T. 1986. *Tragfähigkeiten, Ladungen und Maße im Schiffsverkehr der Hanse vornehmlich im Spiegel Revaler Quellen*. Cologne & Vienna: Böhlau.

Zwick, D. 2012a. Variationen in der mittelalterlichen Schiffbautechnik anhand von Wrackfunden in Bremen. In: *Holzbau in Mittelalter und Neuzeit*. Mitteilungen der Deutschen Gesellschaft für Archäologie des Mittelalters und der Neuzeit 24: 283-298.

Zwick, D. 2012b. Lineare nautische Netzwerke im Ostseeraum des Mittelalters? In: S. Kleingärtner & G. Zeilinger (eds) *Raumbildung durch Netzwerke? Der Ostseeraum zwischen Wikingerzeit und Spätmittelalter aus archäologischer und geschichtswissenschaftlicher Perspektive*. Zeitschrift für Archäologie des Mittelalters. Beiheft 23: 95-115. Bonn: R. Habelt.

6

In Details Remembered: Interpreting the Human Component in Shipbuilding

Fred Hocker

Much of the scholarship devoted to the historical, archaeological or anthropological interpretation of ships and wrecks has focused on teasing out the conceptual background to the design process, to a large extent by examination of the construction process. From Olof Hasslöf's initial characterization of "shell" and "skeleton" methods of construction (1958, 1972), through the classic work of Basch (1972), Pomey (1988, 1994, 2004), Steffy (1985, 1994), Rieth (1981), and Crumlin-Pedersen (1972, 2004) to the analysis of "mixed" construction methods and transitions (Rieth 1984; Maarleveld 1994; Hocker 2004; see especially the recent summary analysis of Pomey et al. 2012) to the race to find the "first" frame-first hull (Jézégou, M.-P. 1985; Kahanov et al. 2004; Beltrame and Bondioli 2006), the emphasis has often been on the thoughts in the ancient shipwright's mind more than the tools and materials in his hands. In effect, we have sought platonic ideals, the creative spark behind the conceptualization of different traditions of shipbuilding. Shipwrecks and surviving vernacular traditions have been the vehicle for reaching this superlunary sphere, in line with conventional anthropological-archaeological theoretical thinking, which favors the discovery of general rules applicable to communities over exploring the idiosyncrasies of the individual.

In fact, for many years, theoretical writing on maritime archaeology effectively deplored the analysis of individual sites and specific events, adding a disparaging tone to the phrase "historical particularism", for example in the writings of Richard Gould and contemporaries (Gould 1983). The view was that a concern with the particular was a limited approach, inherently inferior to the grand thoughts

of more inclusive, overtly anthropological theoretical approaches. In spite of the inevitable swing in the theoretical pendulum in the 1980s where, particularly in Europe, there was a rehabilitation of connections with history and the specific event, 'theory', whether it could be confirmed by the evidence found in the mud or not, was nevertheless portrayed as the higher calling. Perhaps this is why, in falling victim to the temptation to indulge in theory for theory's sake, many a graduate student has wasted half of an 80-page thesis attempting to demonstrate mastery of a large body of arcane and somewhat vague epistemological literature when he or she should have spent more time testing the theory against some real world data. The small details we see in ship remains, the variations in tool technique and problem solving, are a vital clue in trying to understand the behavior of specific individuals and small groups engaged in a complex process which is both technological and intellectual. By understanding the meaning of unique features of individual ships, one shipwreck at a time, we can create a much richer and more comprehensive tapestry of this corner of human behavior, while generating the real data needed for grander, more synthetic studies of broader trends and conceptual ideals. It is nice to keep an eye on the horizon, but useful to watch where you are putting your feet as well.

A few scholars have investigated the technical process of converting concept into reality, notably Eric Rieth (2008), and a large group of boatbuilder-scholars working at the Viking Ship Museum in Roskilde, Denmark (for example, Nielsen 2006), and some have looked at the materials of shipbuilding from economic, ecological or environmental perspectives (Loewen and

Delhaye 2006; Loewen 2007; Goodburn 2009), and there have been occasional studies of tool usage and technique (Finderup 2006 and Goodburn 2009), but hardly anyone has addressed the human element in the messy reality of building wooden ships. No real ship corresponds exactly to the platonic ideal on which it is based, and many do not even come close. What we find in the ground or under the water is the product not only of ideology, tradition, society, environment or whatever the theoretical focus happens to be, but also of the decisions and actions of individuals and small groups.

Individuals do not always follow the rules or do things logically, they make mistakes and lose concentration at critical points, and they react to the immediate stimuli around them as well as the larger cultural and environmental forces beloved of anthropologists. These departures from the ideal are sometimes seen as factors obscuring the original design, or the result of substandard workmanship. In other cases, we interpret them as deliberate choices made by the shipbuilder based on careful reasoning, when they may just as easily be the product of too much mead the night before. As a third-generation boatbuilder I know says, reasoned decision-making often falls victim to the economic imperative to Get [Stuff] Done (Evelyn Ansel, pers. comm.). These irregularities are worth investigating for their own sake, since the immediate motivations behind them are just as much a part of the process of shipbuilding or any other human activity as larger cultural forces and deliberate reasoning. In many cases, they may provide the essential clue to deciphering the human process behind the artefact.

They also illuminate a key part of the shipbuilding process, the communication and dynamics within the groups who build ships. Very few vessels of any size were built by one person working alone. The size of the component timbers of even small vessels is unwieldy for one person to handle, and the conversion of raw material into planks and frames is rarely practical alone. Once the workforce is greater than one, communication and organization become an integral part of process. Two people cannot share the same idea with perfect correspondence (the core principal of deconstructionist theory), and the natural differences in perception and execution of basic concepts creates an inescapable tension which has to be resolved or managed in order for progress to occur. The larger the group, the more important these become. Effective communication or the lack of it can be seen in the results.

From 2007-2011, the National Maritime Museums of Sweden carried out a highly detailed documentation of the warship *Vasa*, a very large and complex vessel built 1626-1628 by a workforce of over 300 men from at least four different countries, speaking at least three different languages, trained in two different shipbuilding traditions and using at least two different systems of measurement. Over 98 per cent of the original wooden hull structure survives, from the keel up to the fiferails, as well as two lower masts and most of the wooden parts of the rigging. This level of preservation provides a largely complete picture of the shipbuilding process as practiced at one navy yard in the 1620s, and one of the most interesting discoveries has been the degree to which the ship does not conform to consistent rules or practice, not in the overall form and structure nor the fine details. While it is dangerous to extrapolate general trends from a single shipwreck (not that it discourages most of us from doing so), many of the idiosyncrasies seen in *Vasa* are present in other wrecks if one looks carefully. They provide a telling clue to shipyard organization, cultural contact and the social tensions in a large workforce.

The myths of symmetry and regularity

We tend to assume that ships are symmetrical about a central vertical plane, with a few notable exceptions such as the Venetian gondola, which is deliberately built with asymmetry to compensate for the offset position of the gondolier, or Viking ships, which have the rudder, and thus hull resistance, offset to one side. In reconstructing ships, which are usually better preserved on one side than the other, we usually base the reconstruction of the missing side on the surviving remains of the opposite side, but sometimes we go too far. Peter Marsden, in his attempt to reconstruct the missing port side of *Mary Rose*, based his work on the principle of perfect symmetry of form, construction and internal arrangement to mirror the surviving starboard side, and expended a great deal of effort to identify the plane of symmetry (Marsden 2009:20-31). The result included some decidedly odd features, such as deck beams with a knuckle in the middle (rather than accepting that the beams were not perpendicular to the center plane), and did not reconcile certain components of the hull structure, particularly at the stern. Marsden based this approach on an assumption that ships are fundamentally and perfectly symmetrical, and cited as evidence several wrecks, including *Vasa*.

Although Marsden's reconstruction of *Mary Rose* is an extreme case and few others working with ship remains would argue for perfect symmetry, there is a focus on regularity, the even repetition of scantlings and intervals as a sign of quality or care in construction, which pervades much of the research, just as there are assumptions that modern rules regarding timber spacing, scarf arrangement, and other features reflect the sum of historic wisdom. For example, it is common to note that having a line of frame ends along a single strake creates a weakness in the hull, or that placing plank scarfs close together rather than staggering them over wide intervals results in a weaker planking shell.

The flaw in this reasoning is the messy reality of ship construction by humans in wood: a species prone to inconsistent behavior working with a material of inconsistent properties. Most ships are certainly symmetrical in concept, since common sense suggests that an asymmetrical ship is unlikely to hold a straight course, but the process of construction introduces asymmetry and irregularity to a greater or lesser degree. Even when efforts are made to build the hull from symmetrically converted wood, using one half of a tree for a plank on the port side and the other half for the corresponding plank on the starboard side (seen in several cog wrecks, such as the Almere, Kolding and Doel 1 vessels - Hocker and Vlierman 1997; Hocker and Daly 2006 and Haneca and Daly in press), the material is not perfectly symmetrical and the process of working it cannot be symmetrical. Whether a person is right-handed or left-handed, he or she will have a bias towards one direction in using tools, so that the port plank will not be worked the same way as the starboard one. In the absence of modern measuring tools, it is also impossible for the craftsmen to determine if the two planks are in fact mirror images of each other at anything other than a very coarse level of accuracy. Regular scantlings and rule-driven construction are equally illusive. Viking shipwrights routinely grouped the plank scarfs together near the ends of the ship, yet it did not seem to cause them to sink.

Assymmetry and irregularity are thus not matters of fact, but of degree; the closer one looks, the less alike the port and starboard sides are, and some ships are more inconsistent than others. Richard Steffy noted that the two sides of the Kyrenia ship of c. 300 BC were noticeably different in shape below the waterline (Steffy 1985), and measurement of the surviving 1841 American whaleship *Charles W. Morgan* during its restoration in the 1980s showed that there was more hull on one side of the keel than the other, and that this had been part of the original construction (Roger Hambidge, pers. comm.).

One question to ask here is how much asymmetry or irregularity is significant, in terms of ship performance? The Viking Ship Museum in Roskilde, Denmark, routinely tests its new replicas, some of the most accurate and carefully built in the world, for symmetry in performance. What they have discovered is that while it is impossible to build a wooden hull in which the port and starboard sides agree to within less than about 20mm, the resulting divergence is rarely a

problem in sailing, although some subtle peculiarities may appear once the crew is familiar with the vessel. The difference may be so small as not to be noticed, but it is a commonplace among sailors to remember boats which would perform better on one tack than the other, or tack better in one direction. It might need correction, but it may simply become part of the boat's character. These kinds of quirks are among the features which allow us to anthropomorphize inanimate objects, to think of a boat or car as "she."

From an archaeological perspective, a more useful question to ask of asymmetry is where does it come from and what does it mean? Is it simply the result of inevitable small variations in materials and hand craftsmanship, or might it have more complex causes and more significant meaning? In the case of *Vasa*, where asymmetry is a noticeable feature, it is a clue to a number of cultural phenomena with relevance far beyond one Swedish shipyard.

Vasa and the lack of symmetry and uniformity

In *Vasa*, there is marked asymmetry and irregularity in form, construction and internal configuration. Some of this is intentional, such as the location and arrangement of compartments in the stern, but much of it is the unintended consequence of human factors and the social structure of the Swedish navy yard in the 1620s. It is also a product of the design and construction methodology, which did not rely on drawings, and a vital clue to the very different concepts of quality appreciated by different maritime traditions in northern Europe.

Deliberate or functional asymmetry

Much of the internal volume of the ship is essentially the same on both sides. In the gundecks, there is an effort to concentrate hatches and other potential obstructions along the centerline, largely in order to assure clear space for the operation of the guns. Paired features, such as the bilge pumps on the lower gundeck or the hatches either side of the pump on the upper gundeck, are located more or less symmetrically. The same is true of most of the belaying points for the rigging on the weather decks. This is not simply an aesthetic consideration, but part of the functional reality of operating the ship. It is more efficient in teaching the conscripts who made up most of the crew if functional features are located in the same place – the port main brace should belay directly across the quarterdeck from the starboard main brace. Less confusion results and it is easier to find things in a hurry or in the dark.

In some cases, functional requirements dictate asymmetrical placement. The fore halliard and main topsail halliard knightheads are single bitts, but located offset from the centerline to starboard (Fig. 6.1). Their position is dictated by potential interference with other lines. The fore halliard cannot come down to the deck on the centerline because it would foul the mainstay, and the main topsail halliard would foul the mizzen stay. The mizzen stay itself is offset slightly to port in order to clear the main halliard. The rigging of the topropes, which is inherently asymmetrical, brings the fall down on one side of the deck but not both and not on the centerline.

In the interior of the ship, further asymmetry is created by functional as well as symbolic requirements. The great cabin, at the after end of the upper gundeck (Fig. 6.2) is accessible through a single door. It cannot be placed on the centerline, as it would interfere with the steersman and the mizzenmast, so it has to be offset, in this case to port. It would be possible to achieve symmetry through a matching door to starboard, but this would violate part of the door's symbolic function. The single entrance to the great cabin, which was the symbolic seat of the king's authority, emphasizes the power behind the door. A single door offers greater security and more restricted access; in the otherwise largely common or communal space of the ship, it creates a separate, private area for the most powerful person on board, reinforcing his status. Functionally, the single door also maximizes the interior deck space which can be used for seating and furniture, rather than traffic, a further advantage for the powerful. At the other end of the great cabin, there is a stern gallery, accessible through a single door offset to starboard. This minimizes traffic flow in this small area, leaves the central part of the bulkhead uninterrupted for a large, leaded glass window (an expensive status symbol). Despite the asymmetry, the two doors offset to opposite sides achieve a harmonic balance in internal arrangement, as aesthetic standards for elite buildings encouraged.

Unintentional asymmetry

The deliberate offsetting of rigging hardware and doors is easy to see and relatively straightforward to interpret. In many ways, the non-deliberate asymmetry in construction and form seen throughout the ship is more interesting, as it reveals much less obvious aspects of the culture which produced them. The hull shows quite significant differences in form, port and starboard sides differing in places by up to 100 mm. The most noticeable area is in the bow, where the greater fullness

Figure 6.1. The halliard knighthead and topsail sheet bitts at the foremast, as seen from aft. (Photo: the author).

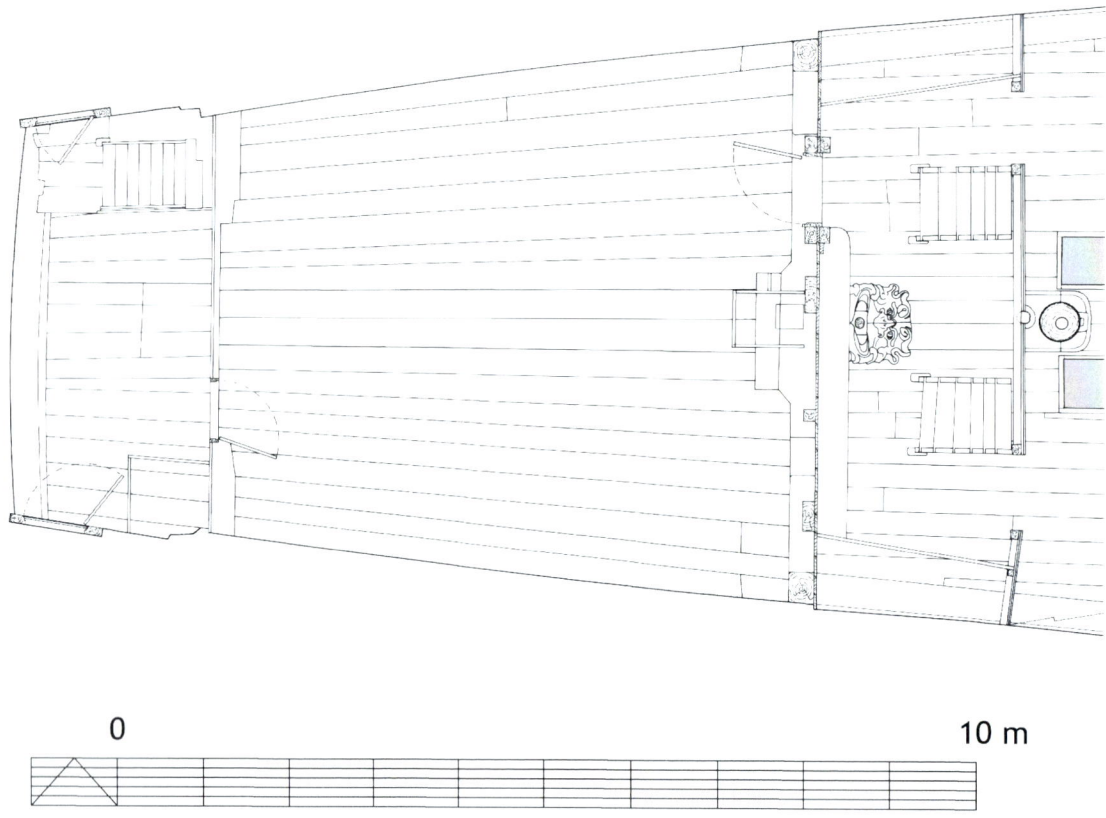

Fig. 6.2. Plan of the steerage and great cabin on the upper gundeck of Vasa (drawing: the author).

of the port side is readily visible to the naked eye. In theory, this should have made the port bow more buoyant than the starboard bow, and may have required some trimming with offset ballast. We cannot know, as the ballast all shifted into the port bilge when the ship sank.

Major features are not symmetrically disposed in the ship. The most readily visible irregularity is in the location of the gunports (Fig. 6.3). In some cases, the port and starboard ports at one position may be the same distance aft of the stem, and thus symmetrically disposed, but most pairs on both gundecks and the upper deck show some difference, with the offset varying from a few centimeters up the full width of a port. The reason for the difference is not immediately obvious, although it may be related to the deck structure. The gunports are located more or less equidistant between deck beams, but the beams vary in the angle at which they cross the centerline, and none are actually square. Thus the rooms between them are not symmetrically disposed. Other deck and bulwark features, such as the location of breaks in the railings to accommodate the rising decks of the sterncastle and the forward edges of the decks, are not symmetrical either. The forward edge of the quarterdeck is 18cm farther forward on

the port side than the starboard side, which results in a different shape to the stairway cutout and the end of the waterway where it joins the side.

The most jarring lack of symmetry is in the beakhead. One would think that it would be centered and point forward along the central axis of the hull, but it skews substantially off to port. At its forward end, 9.9 metres before the stem, the centerline of the figurehead is 0.78 metres offline. The bowsprit also points off towards the port side, although not as much, only about 0.66 metres. Some of the skew is the result of settling in the museum, but most is a feature of the original construction (Fig. 6.4).

At a structural level, there is even more difference. The framing on the port side is not laid out as its counterpart to starboard. For example, there are 103 top timbers to port, but only 100 to starboard. Kroum Batchvarov's analysis of the framing behind the ceiling shows that while there is a general system in use, port and starboard sides do not match and there is no consistent location for the upper or lower ends of individual framing elements. Even more interesting are cases where it can be seen that the same structural problem was solved in different ways in different places. For example, the port and starboard clamps supporting

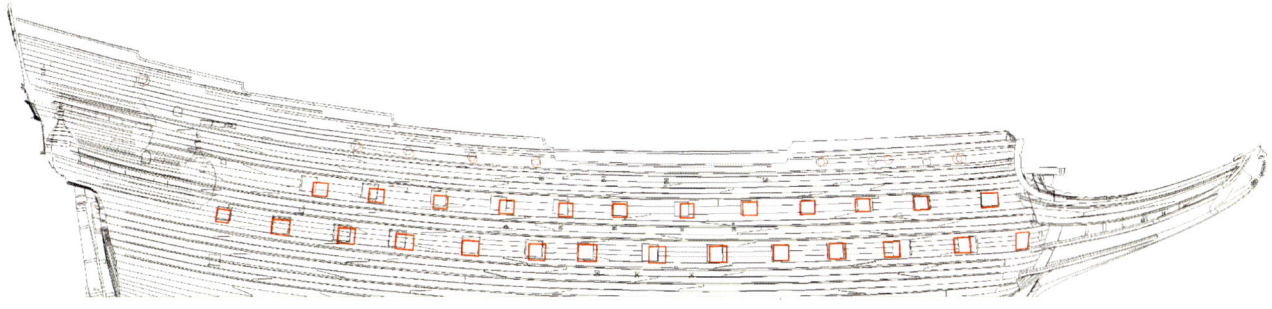

Figure 6.3. The starboard side of Vasa, with the corresponding gunports of the port side in red to show the lack of consistent alignment (drawing: the author).

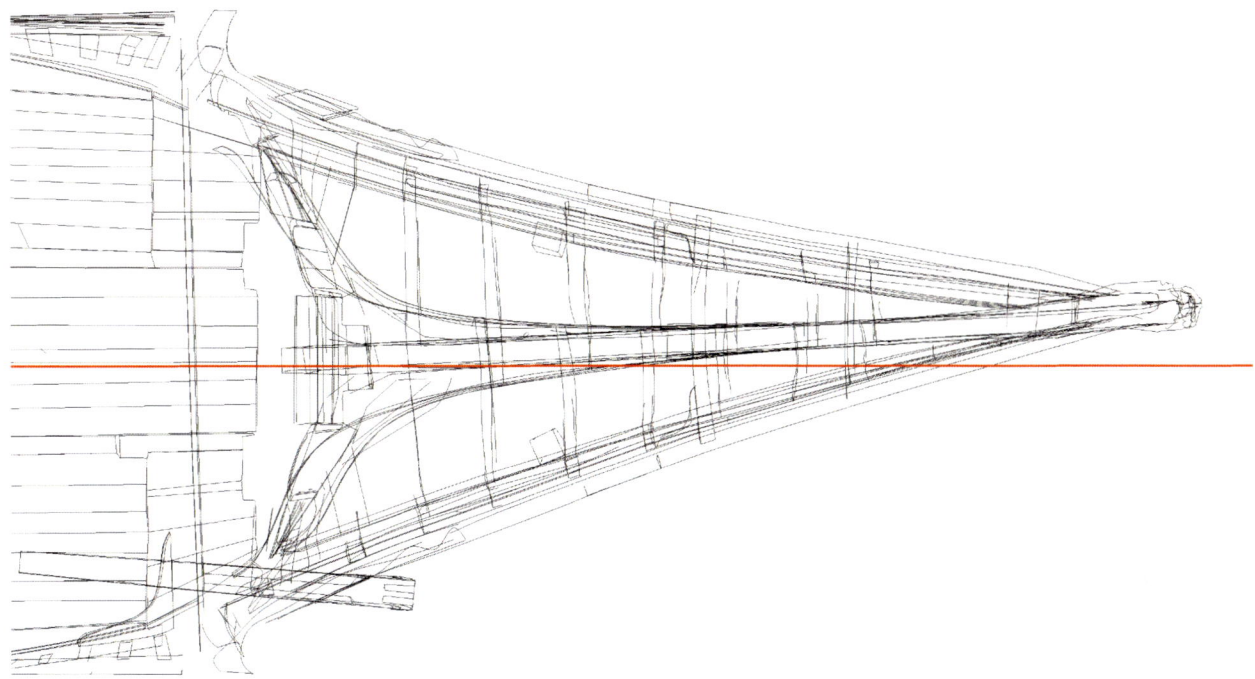

Figure 6.4. Raw total station plot of the beakhead of Vasa, with the hull centerline in red (drawing: the author).

the orlop beams are not laid out or scarfed together in the same way. Two different scarf types are used, and the scarfs do not face in the same direction, suggesting that the port clamp was assembled in a different order than the starboard. The planking plan on the outside of the frames, while nominally symmetrical amidships and towards the stern, is distinctly different at the bow. Although the number of hooding ends on the port and starboard sides of the stem are the same, they do not align and the arrangement of drop strakes to reduce the planking girth is very different (Fig. 6.5).

At a metrological level, there is no standard system of measurement used in the construction of the ship. To begin with, there is no adherence to consistent scantlings except where it is necessary for timbers to fit together. Frames vary in sided width over a wide range, and deck beams vary in both width and depth. In many cases, nominally straight timbers taper from one end to the

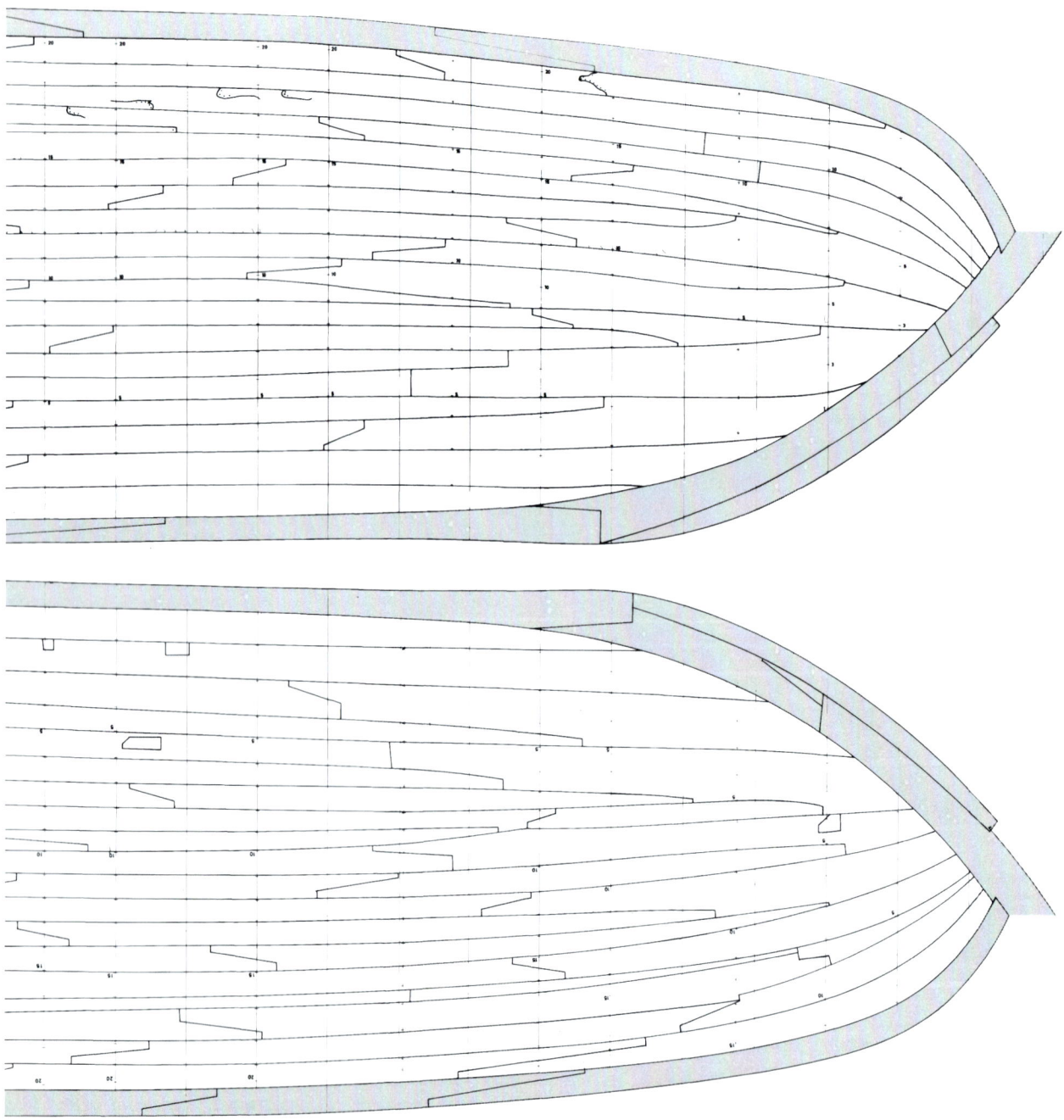

Figure 6.5. The bottom planking at the bow of Vasa. (Drawing by Eva Marie Stolt and the author).

other and wind. Large timbers often have waney edges, and packing pieces and shims are used to fill out spaces under frames and on top of beams. Where dimensions might matter for fitting and assembly, there is still no reliance on a single standard. Five carpenter's rules, wooden sticks a foot long and divided into inches, have been found in the ship, some in contexts that make it clear that they were lost during construction and some belonging to the carpenters serving onboard the ship. Some of the rules are divided into twelve inches, which was typical of the Swedish foot (among others), while some are divided into eleven inches, which was typical of the Amsterdam foot and other Dutch measures (Fig. 6.6). If this were not confusing enough, no two rules are the same length. It appears that either the carpenters came from a wide range of places with different standards, or that each man made his own rule with no great concern if it matched any official standard. There is some evidence that standard measures were used for some features, but not the same standards. The draft marks cut into the stem and sternpost are at one foot intervals which average out very close to the Swedish foot, officially established at 297 mm in the early 17th century. On the other hand, the diameters of the fore and main tops work out more or less exactly to 12 and 13 Amsterdam feet (283 mm) respectively.

Do these differences and irregularities make a difference in the hull's strength or performance? Probably not in a physically significant way, although it is possible that the unballasted hull was heavier on one side than the other - a timber cut to six Dutch inches square would be about 8 percent heavier than a timber cut to six Swedish inches - and thus required some care in ballasting. But they do tell us something of the philosophy behind the construction of the ship, and emphasize some underlying tensions in the shipyard's organization. It is precisely because these differences do not make a difference in the final product that they are instructive regarding the construction process.

An international workforce

Historical sources show that the carpenters employed at the Stockholm navy yard in the 1620s were about evenly split between permanent employees recruited in Sweden, and thus most likely (but not exclusively) of Swedish or Finnish heritage, and carpenters recruited for seasonal labor in the Low Countries, and thus

Fig. 6.6. Four of the carpenter's rules found on Vasa, all different lengths. (Photo by Anneli Karlsson, courtesy Vasa Museum).

mostly of Dutch or German extraction. The seasonal labourers were paid at more than twice the rate that the native carpenters received (Table 6.1), and they also received travel expenses and beer as part of their compensation, as the account books for the shipyard show (Riksarkivet Skeppsgårdshandlingar 1625-1626). It is hard to imagine that this did not create some tensions between the two groups. The language difference probably also meant that the men were divided into gangs on the basis of heritage for the sake of communication efficiency, and so the effect of the different craft traditions in which they had been trained might be reinforced rather than blended.

The need for clear communication was thus at a premium, and if some sort of *lingua franca* had not developed, the managers of the shipyard needed to be able to communicate in at least both Swedish and Dutch. Dutch terms did become common in Swedish shipbuilding in the 1620s, and survive today, but this process was only beginning when *Vasa* was built. We know that the original master shipwright, Henrik Hybertsson, came from Holland but had lived in

Sweden since about 1602, and his papers show that he could write both Dutch and Swedish (his personal notes are in Dutch, but the accounts are kept in Swedish). The master shipwright who took over from him once he became too ill to continue direct supervision in 1626, Henrik "Hein" Jakobsson, was also from Holland, and had moved to Sweden around 1620, so he probably also spoke passable Swedish, although his papers do not survive to confirm this. The large number of Dutch craftsmen recruited to jump-start Swedish industries under Gustav II Adolf (r. 1611-1632) and his father Karl IX (1599-1611) meant there may well have been a large enough ex-patriot community in Stockholm that it was not absolutely essential for every immigrant to learn Swedish, and there was a strong German presence in the town as well dating back to the later Middle Ages. German was a common second language in the capital, and some administrative documents used it. Still, men of business seem to have used Swedish in their local dealings as a matter of necessity. In any case, communicating in both languages, or all three, and possibly in terms understandable in both craft

Cost	Dalers
Salary to Dutch carpenters	10,400
Swedish carpenters	5,300
Sawyers and borers	2,400
Sculptors and joiners	4,600
All types of iron bolts	8,700
Other iron fittings with anchors	2,300
All types of nails, 14-, 15-, 16-, 17-, 13-, 12-, 11-, 10-, 9-, 8-, 7-, 6-, 5-, 4-, 3-inch together with two-brads, one-brads, finish nails bulkhead nails with roves counted together	5,500
Oak planks 1500 pieces at 3 dalers	4,500
All types of oak timber	9,600
There remain as exceptions freight on the timber, arming cloths, equipment together with other items that may be added	
	53,300

Table 6.1. Accounting of the costs associated with the construction of Vasa, as compiled by the son of the master shipright after completion. The numbers of Swedish and Dutch carpenters were about even, but the Dutch were seasonal and only worked about 7 months of the year (Riksarkivet, Kammarkollegiet M1779; translation by author).

traditions, was probably a necessity for the master shipwrights.

On a larger scale, the asymmetry and irregularity reveal a fundamental difference in the understanding of the concept of quality between shipwrights working largely in the Dutch tradition and those working in other countries, such as England or France. Partly this is a result of the different design and construction methods employed in the Low Countries and elsewhere. In a construction tradition tied to the use of drawings and geometric design methods, as was common in English yards, evenly finished and spaced frames square to the keel were an essential part of the construction process, in order to make sure that the finished ship came close to the design. In the Dutch tradition, no drawings were used, and each timber added to the structure only had to fit the timber already in place. In this system, there was less waste if frames were set square to the interior face of the planking rather than the keel, and it did not matter if they were skewed or had significant wind.

On a less functional level, or in what Björn Varenius (1992) characterized as "supra-functional" characteristics, the evenness of finish and scantling was seen as a sign of quality in English yards and by English customers. Even surfaces and regular scantlings are not in fact necessary for the performance or durability of a ship, but in some cultures they are perceived as essential features in order for the ship to be considered acceptable or of high quality. Varenius worked mostly with the decorative features which appeared on Viking ships and which disappeared around 1200, but the issue is the same: some aspects of construction are worth investment by the owner even if they contribute nothing to physical function. In the modern world, we tend to see regularity in appearance and construction as a sign of quality. Each new BMW coming off the assembly line should be built to an identical standard, the panel shut lines should be of even width, the metal surface and paint finish should be smooth. Higher price means better fit and finish, because it costs more to achieve but is also worth more in the market. We thus tend to identify more closely with English shipwrights of the 17th century, who were more likely to cut their frames to even scantlings, squared up on all faces and smoothly chamfered on the upper edges before fastening them to the keel at right angles and even intervals. It is easy in this world view to see Dutch construction, with its waney edges and irregular scantlings, as shoddy or lower quality, but there is nothing in the construction of *Vasa* or the other excavated Dutch-built ships of the early 17th century (for example, see Lemée 2006) to suggest that they are badly built. Structural joints fit tightly, fastenings are cleanly drilled and driven, and scantlings are appropriate for the loads they are to bear.

In fact, in Dutch eyes, the irregularities deplored by an English shipwright are a sign of value. Dutch culture in the Golden Age valued beauty and quality no less than English or French, but the wealth of the Low Countries was based on efficiency and organizational skill, and there was a certain reluctance to indulge too much in ostentation (Schama 1987). In Dutch shipbuilding, efficient use of resources was a sign of quality, or at least value for money. Cutting larger timbers down to evenly squared scantlings was wasteful of time and materials, adding cost without adding value. Setting timbers perfectly square to the centerline did not add strength to the structure. The timbers in a vessel built in this tradition make the most of the trees available. Planks are not cut to widths based on the aesthetics of smooth, faired curves and arbitrarily determined seams, or the dictates of a rigidly symmetrical layout, but are made as wide as the raw material and hull form will allow. Where an English shipwright would discard a piece of wood with rot in it, his Dutch counterpart would be more likely to cut out the bad bit and let in a graving piece, if the flaw was small enough and it would not affect the structural strength. *Vasa*, although a brand new ship, is covered with these graving pieces in planking, ceiling and deck planking as well as heavier timbers (Fig. 6.7). These are not repairs in the conventional sense, but part of the process of converting the raw timber into ship elements. In American shipbuilding, such pieces are still called "Dutchmen." The term may be disparaging, but it is a lasting testimony to a different way of thinking about the physical process of shipbuilding.

Conclusions

The pursuit of the conceptual ideals behind ship design and construction is an important path in maritime archaeology, but it is not the only path and it does not realize all of the archaeological potential of ship remains. Understanding the messy reality of how ideals are translated into timber and iron reveals as much about a culture as the abstract mathematical principles in the shipwright's mind. With the emergence of scientific ship design in the Renaissance, abstract concept and messy reality were physically divorced. Ship design became a separate endeavor, and its best practitioners achieved high status as gentlemen and academics, while construction was a matter for mechanics and tradesmen. Designers strove for this new status, and the treatises they produced in the 16th and 17th centuries, unlike those of the 15th century, were written to demonstrate their brilliance and worthiness, while the status of men who put axe to wood declined. Even Samuel Pepys, who probably respected the competence of practicing shipwrights more than

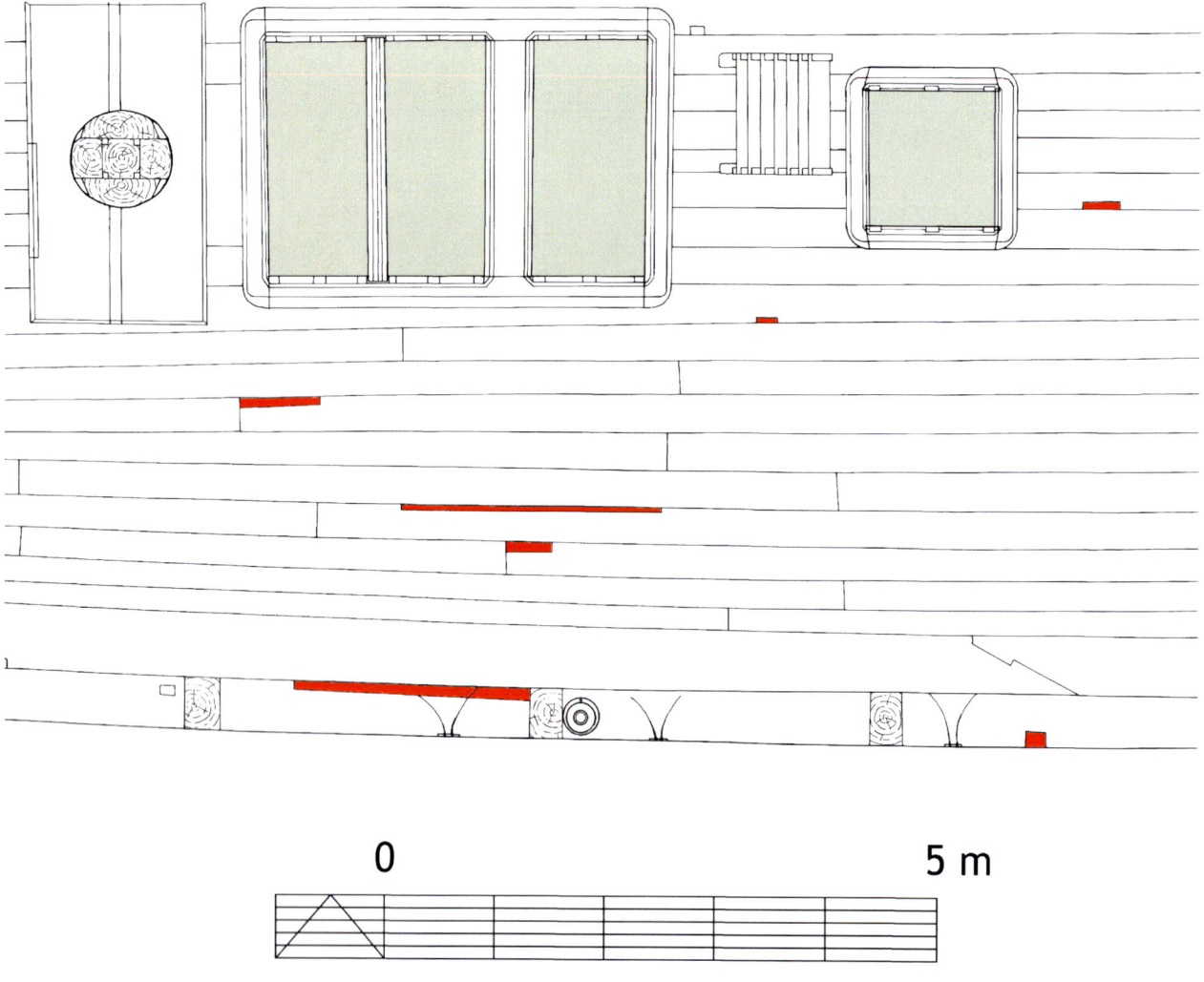

Fig. 6.7. A group of "Dutchman" (highlighted in red) let into the lower gundeck planking to starboard of the mainmast, mostly filling out flaws in the edges of the planks. Note also the companionway offset to port (drawing: the author).

many of his social class, still spoke of "their knowledge lying in their hands confusedly" (Ollard 1991:270). Perhaps modern academics studying ancient ships feel a greater attraction for the more intellectual side of the process, just as modern society is more likely to recognize the designer of a great building than the engineers, masons and the men on the high steel who turned the architect's vision into concrete and glass. Perhaps the emphasis on archaeological theory rewards the thinkers of great thoughts more than those who get mud under their fingernails and know which end of a hammer to hold on to, today as much as three centuries ago.

But the truths revealed by both paths are equally valid, as they address different sides of the human character, the thinker and the maker. Both approaches are necessary, and their integration an essential part of constructing a comprehensive understanding of a technical process like shipbuilding as well as its social context and consequences. Ship remains reveal more about a culture than its technical problem-solving framework, they illuminate broader questions of resource utilization, social organization, and mind. As I hope the above has shown, the idiosyncratic physical features of a single ship can point the way to larger ideas and forces at work in society. I would like to think that the man with the axe can achieve equal dignity in the modern academic consciousness and that he will be remembered as well as the man at the drafting table. If we pay attention to the small details, he will be.

References

Basch, L. 1972. Ancient wrecks and the archaeology of ships. *International Journal of Nautical Archaeology* 1: 1-58.

Beltrame, C. and Bondioli M. 2006. A hypothesis on the development of Mediterranean ship construction from Antiquity to the Late Middle Ages. In L. Blue, F. Hocker and A. Englert (eds) *Connected by the Sea: Proceedings of the Tenth International Symposium on Boat and Ship Archaeology Roskilde 2003*: 89-94. Oxford: Oxbow Books.

Crumlin-Pedersen, O. 1972. Skin or wood? A study of the origin of the Scandinavian plank-boat. In O. Hasslöf, H. Henningsen and A.e. Christensen (eds) *Ships and Shipyards, Sailors and Fishermen: Introduction to Maritime Ethnology*: 208-234. Copenhagen: National Museum of Denmark.

Crumlin-Pedersen, O. 2004. Nordic clinker construction. In F.M. Hocker and C. Ward (eds) *The Philosophy of Shipbuilding: Conceptual Approaches to the study of Wooden Ships*: 37-64. College Station: Texas A & M University Press.

Finderup, T. 2006. History written in tool marks. In L. Blue, F. Hocker and A. Englert (eds) *Connected by the Sea: Proceedings of the Tenth International Symposium on Boat and Ship Archaeology Roskilde 2003*: 21-26. Oxford: Oxbow Books.

Goodburn, D. 2009. Woodworking aspects of the *Mary Rose*. In P. Marsden (ed.) Mary Rose *Your Noblest Shippe: Anatomy of a Tudor Warship*: 66-80. Archaeology of the *Mary Rose* 2. Portsmouth: Mary Rose Trust.

Gould, R. (ed.) 1983. *Shipwreck Anthropology*. Albuquerque: University of New Mexico.

Haneca, K. and Daly, A. Tree rings, timbers and trees: a dendrochronological survey on the cog *Doel 1*. *IJNA* 43. (in press)

Hasslöf, O. 1958. Carvel construction technique, nature and origin. *Folkliv* 21-22: 49-60.

Hasslöf, O. 1972. Main principles in the technology of ship-building. In O. Hasslöf, H. Henningsen and A.e. Christensen (eds) *Ships and Shipyards, Sailors and Fishermen: Introduction to Maritime Ethnology*: 27-72. Copenhagen.

Hocker, F. 2004. Bottom-based shipbuilding in northwestern Europe. In F.M. Hocker and C. Ward (eds) *The Philosophy of Shipbuilding: Conceptual Approaches to the study of Wooden Ships*: 65-94. College Station: Texas A & M University Press.

Hocker, F. and A. Daly 2006. Early cogs, Jutland boatbuilders and the connection between east and West before AD 1250. In L. Blue, F. Hocker and A. Englert (eds) *Connected by the Se: Proceedings of*

the Tenth International Symposium on Boat and Ship Archaeology Roskilde 2003*: 187-194. Oxford: Oxbow Books.

Hocker, F. and K. Vlierman 1997. *A Small Cog Wrecked on the Zuiderzee in the Early Fifteenth Century*. NISA Excavation Report 19, Flevobericht 408. Lelystad.

Jézégou, M.-P. 1985. Eléments de construction sur couples observes sur une épave du Haut Moyen-Age découverte à Fos-sur-Mer (Bouches-du-Rhône). In *VI Congreso Internacional de Arqueologia Submarina*: 351-356. Madrid.

Kahanov, Y., J. Royal and J. Hall. 2004. The Tantura wrecks and ancient Mediterranean shipbuilding. In F.M. Hocker and C. Ward (eds) *The Philosophy of Shipbuilding: Conceptual Approaches to the study of Wooden Ships*: 113-128. College Station: Texas A & M University Press.

Lemeé, C. 2006. *The Renaissance Shipwrecks from Christianshavn: An Archaeological and Architectural Study of Large Carvel Vessels in Danish Water, 1580-1640* (Ships and Boats of the North 6). Roskilde: Viking Ship Museum.

Loewen, B. 2007. The Basque shipbuilding trades: Design, forestry and carpentry. In R. Grenier, M.-A. Bernier and W. Stevens (eds) *The Underwater Archaeology of Red Bay: Basque Shipbuilding and Whaling in the 16th century III*: 253-298. Ottawa: Parks Canada.

Loewen, B. and M. Delhaye 2006. Oak growing, hull design and framing style. The Cavalaire-sur-Mer wreck, c. 1479. In L. Blue, F. Hocker and A. Englert (eds) *Connected by the Sea: Proceedings of the Tenth International Symposium on Boat and Ship Archaeology Roskilde 2003*: 99-104. Oxford: Oxbow Books.

Maarleveld, T. 1994. Double-Dutch solutions in flush-planked shipbuilding. Continuity and adaptations at the start of modern history. In C. Westerdahl (ed.) *Crossroads in Ancient Shipbuilding: Proceedings of ISBSA 6*: 153-164. Oxbow Monograph 40. Oxford: Oxbow Books.

Marsden, P. 2009. Understanding the *Mary Rose*. In P. Marsden (ed.), *Mary Rose Your Noblest Shippe: Anatomy of a Tudor Warship*: 20-33. Archaeology of the *Mary Rose* 2. Portsmouth: Mary Rose Trust.

Nielsen, S. 2006. Experimental archaeology at the Viking Ship Museum in Roskilde. In L. Blue, F. Hocker and A. Englert (eds) *Connected by the Se: Proceedings of the Tenth International Symposium on Boat and Ship Archaeology Roskilde 2003*: 16-20. Oxford: Oxbow Books.

Ollard, R. 1991. *Pepys, a Biography*. London: Sinclair Stevenson.

Pomey, P. 1988. Principes et méthodes de construction

en architecture navale antique. In *Navires et commerce Méditerranée antique. Homage à Jean Rougé.* Cahiers d'Histoire 33.3-4: 397-412.

Pomey, P. 1994. Shell conception and skeleton process in ancient Mediterranean shipbuilding. In C. Westerdahl (ed.) *Crossroads in Ancient Shipbuilding: Proceedings of ISBSA 6*: 125-130. Oxbow Monograph 40. Oxford: Oxbow Books.

Pomey, P. 2004. Principles and methods of construction in ancient naval architecture. In F.M. Hocker and C. Ward (eds) *The Philosophy of Shipbuilding: Conceptual Approaches to the study of Wooden Ships*: 25-36. College Station: Texas A & M University Press.

Pomey, P., Y. Kahanov and E. Rieth 2012. Transition from shell to skeleton in ancient Mediterranean ship-construction: analysis, problems and future research. *International Journal of Nautical Archaeology* 41.2: 235-314.

Rieth, E. 1981. La construction navale à fond plat en Europe de l'ouest. *Ethnologie française* 11.1: 47-62.

Rieth, E. 1984. Principe de construction 'charpente première' et procédés de construction 'bordé premièr' au XVII siècle. *Neptunia* 153: 21-31.

Rieth, E. 2008. *Concevoir et construire les navires.* Ramonville Saint-Agne.

Rival, M. 1991. *La charpenterie navale romaine.* Paris : Presses du CNRS

Schama, S. 1987. *The Embarrassment of Riches: An Interpretation of Dutch Culture in the Golden Age.* New York: Harper Collins.

Steffy, J.R. 1985. The Kyrenia ship. An interim report on its hull construction. *American Journal of Archaeology* 89: 71-101.

Steffy, J.R. 1994. *Wooden Ship Building and the Interpretation of Shipwrecks.* College Station: Texas A & M University Press.

Varenius, B. 1992. *Det nordiska skeppet. Teknologi och samhällsstrategi i vikingatid och medeltid.* Stockholm Studies in Archaeology 10. Stockholm: Stockholm University.

7

Experiencing Shipwrecks and the Primacy of Vision

Jon Adams

The lure of water

Shipwrecks, particularly those discovered under water, have always had an allure for the general public and if the truth be told for many archaeologists too. Not for all it has to be said and there has been some criticism of what was seen as maritime archaeology's undue focus on shipwrecks as well as the ways in which they have been investigated (e.g. Lenihan 1983; Gould 2000; Ransley 2005). Yet this book explores some of the reasons why they remain a fertile area of enquiry. Personally I feel no guilt in admitting that I find shipwrecks fascinating, primarily as archaeological sites but also as places to be. If someone who is not an archaeologist visits a wreck site (either in person or remotely), their sense of wonder will be rather different to mine. But although I am there with particular questions and will probably notice different things about the site than them, I still experience what Philip Barker (1977:259) referred to as the 'frisson of discovery'. For all of us perhaps, some of that sense of wonder engendered by wrecks relates to their existence in that 'other' medium. It is dangerous to define any human behaviour let alone feelings and emotions as 'evolved universals' (Steele 1995:81), those behavioural characteristics apparently common to us all, but archaeological evidence suggests that water has held a deep-seated fascination for human kind for thousands of years. Much has been written about the nature of water as a mysterious element, magnetic to human activity and as a place of intentional deposition for many culturally significant objects (e.g. Bradley 1990). Water was that Quixotic and enigmatic element of allure and danger into which humans could, however briefly, go to glimpse that other state of existence.

Today, with the benefits of various technologies we can enter and remain in the water for extended periods. However, doing so to carry out archaeological work raises questions about how we experience, get to know, understand and interpret what we find, and this in turn is related to the nature of our discipline.

In Poseidon's domain

A great deal has been written about the difficulties of working under water and the ingenious ways maritime archaeologists have developed to mitigate them. Along with the perceived obsession with shipwrecks, this focus on method has also been the source of a certain amount of self-criticism within the field (Ransley 2005) as well as from outside it. However, there are valid reasons why a concern with methodology was inevitable in a developing field, and much of the critique of shipwreck research is now out of date (Staniforth 1997; Flatman 2003; Adams 2006). In any case, depending on the conditions, it is not always more difficult (or more expensive) to work under water even though that is the tacit assumption by almost everybody including some within the discipline. It certainly can be but not for example, on a wreck site in nine metres of warm, clear Bermuda water such as the *Sea Venture* (Adams 2013: ch 6) or the *Warwick* (Bojakowski & Custer Bojakowski 2011) (Fig. 7.1). Given the choice between these or a land excavation in central Europe in July with temperatures of over 50 degrees centigrade in the trench, I know which I prefer.

Indeed it was Keith Muckelroy who, in writing about archaeological work under water, was the first to identify those things that are *easier* to do as well

Figure 7.1. Work on the 'Warwick' (1619) during 2011. In less than 10m of warm, clear water, working conditions are ideal (Photo J. Adams).

as those that are harder (Muckelroy 1978:49). From his perspective it was a matter of recognising that when working under water we simply exchange one set of constraints for another and from this follows a more proactive approach to meeting the challenges of wreck sites in particular. Inevitably perhaps almost all discussion in the literature about mitigating environmental and physiological conditions is related to methodology. But what is just as important is how these constraints influence our interpretation throughout the practice of archaeology: from before we go under water, when we're immersed in it and afterwards as we ponder the meanings of our data.

This raises the question of whether it is necessary to go underwater at all? Are there not ways of investigating sites remotely? There are indeed and the advances made in their capabilities in the last 20 years mean we can carry out entire wreck investigations with various robotic and remotely operated systems (e.g. Ballard et al. 2000; McCann & Oleson 2004). However, just as we still resort to excavation on land when we cannot answer our research questions by other means, so we do under water (Adams 2002). Certainly a greater proportion of our data is now captured using systems that were unavailable until recently but to answer the question another way, if a site offers conditions benign enough

to allow safe diving, I doubt that any archaeological team would choose to restrict their enquiry to remote techniques. This is because being on the site confers distinct advantages to archaeological enquiry subject to various provisos discussed below.

Is seeing believing?

While we may successfully mitigate disadvantages and exploit advantages in developing elegant methods of excavating and recording our sites, there are some differences in being under water that are inescapable and one of these concerns perception. All our senses are affected to some extent by being in another medium and so alter our perceptions of what we are trying to understand. This is especially pertinent in the context of discussions about the senses in general, particularly those concerned with cultural aspects of what and how we see as opposed to bio-physical processes.

If asked what the most important sense is, many people would quickly say 'vision' because it seems to be dominant in many ways. It is certainly the sense that most people state they'd be most reluctant to lose. Someone with no sight might beg to differ and on reflection even those who are sighted often suggest that touch is equally important or perhaps more so. But in post-Enlightenment Europe and throughout Western art, it is the primacy of vision and the presumed correlations between 'seeing' and 'knowing' that have been the subject of considerable analysis and debate (see for example Merleau-Ponty 1962; Jenks 1995; Jay 1993). My aim here is not to engage directly in this debate but I can nevertheless pose the question: can we investigate a wreck site without being able to see it? If touch is the most important sense then technically yes and in fact people do (for example see Tilburg 1998) but there are certain provisos. I am reminded of a civil engineering project that I worked on in the 1980s, moonlighting between archaeology seasons on the *Mary Rose*. It wasn't directly relevant to archaeology except that I was one of three Mary Rose Project divers on the team and most importantly, I learnt something about perception that made me aware of some of the issues involved in understanding complex structures under water, something I have continued trying to do ever since.

'Seeing' in the dark

The project involved the repair of a marine outfall, configured as a double pipe, each 2m in diameter and running a mile out to sea. It was built in 20m long concrete sections, each one looking like the barrel of some gigantic shotgun. The units were fitted with watertight bulkheads so that they could be floated into position and lowered into a trench dredged several metres into the seabed. They were then fastened on the outside by divers and from the inside by tunnel workers who removed the bulkheads. The installation process worked well but unfortunately the sub-sea geology proved less stable than anticipated. Some of the concrete sections continued to settle, fracturing the bolts and flooding the 'tunnel' (luckily when no one was inside). As each section weighed over a hundred tons this movement was irreversible. The only solution was a complex repair to seal the dislocated joints with GRP panels individually fabricated to cover the unique configuration of each break. Installing these inside the flooded 'tunnel' is another story but outside we had to drill the concrete and install large stainless steel mountings and tie-bolts to prevent the concrete sections from moving any further. This would have been reasonably straightforward except that the tunnel had subsided so deep into the Solent mud that the joints were now inaccessible. A coffer dam c. 8 x 6m had to be installed within which large airlifts were used to dig the mud away and reveal the joints. This was all done in absolutely zero visibility and yet it was remarkable how easily one entered the water and switched into an unsighted mentality and how familiar one became with

every feature in an invisible word. This comes as no surprise to the unsighted or indeed fire service personnel who train in smoke-filled rooms. The point of the story concerns a young engineer who was sent to inspect our work. In preparation for his dive he was carefully briefed on where he would find the all-important bolts. The conversation ran something like this:

'*The down-line will take you to the south-west corner of the coffer dam. On the upper brace you'll find the ladder. Go down that and once you've made bottom, make your way along the south side of the coffer dam to the tunnel. You'll see the tie-bars and the bolts which stick out about 150mm – you can't miss them.*'

The engineer was clamped into his helmet, helped over to the ladder and into the water. He made his cautious way down to the coffer dam. There then followed a pregnant pause – we heard slow, deliberate breathing over the comms but no apparent activity or comment. The supervisor asked:

'Surface to diver, are you well?'

'Yes, er, I mean, "Roger".' came the reply.

Time passed, still nothing. Then the obviously embarrassed engineer said:

'Diver to surface'.

'Come in diver' said the supervisor.

'Er, which way should I go?

The supervisor raised his eyes to heaven and said:

'Face the ladder then make your way left along the bracing and when you get to the tunnel you'll see the bolts.'

Erratic breathing followed as the engineer groped his way around. Then forgetting protocol he burst out:

'But I can't see anything!'

Visibly annoyed the supervisor was just about to tell him he was an idiot when we realised we were using the word 'see' in a different way. We were 'seeing' in our minds eye those things we had come to know intimately through touch. The engineer not unreasonably, when told he would 'see' the bolts was nonplussed when he found himself in pitch blackness. Thirty years later I can still visualise those light grey GRP panels, their rubber sealing, the bright stainless steel bolts and the rough concrete they were fastened to, and yet I never 'saw' any of these things.

As far as I know the 'Browndown tunnel' is still disgorging treated sewage into the Solent but what about archaeology? Could we have excavated the *Mary Rose* without ever seeing it? Perhaps, but with considerably more difficulty and almost certainly a far greater loss of information. The fact is that while we can investigate an underwater site without taste, smell, hearing or even touch, to do so without sight, though perhaps not impossible, is challenging to say the least and certainly much slower.

Distortions of reality

Under water then, vision *is* the primary sense. Even so, all senses are fallible and those experienced in recording underwater will not assume that 'seeing is knowing' especially at first glance. For even when one can see, one does so in a medium that affects the way light behaves. Water attenuates the spectrum of light visible to the human eye and refracts what is left, so we do not see the site as we would in air. Neither can we see as far through water so we rarely see the whole site at one time. Add to that the physiological constraints of working at depth, particularly the narcotic effect of nitrogen, then it can be seen that the practice of recording requires us to understand how we are affected and take appropriate measures, especially as the tools we use are continually developing.

But irrespective of the level of technology utilised, there are certain processes of coming to understand a site that do not change so much. At the site level, systems such as swath bathymetry can, in an hour or so, bypass weeks of conventional topographic survey and this is just one of an increasingly powerful range of systems employed for imaging underwater sites (Singh et al. 2000; Bates et al. 2011). But at the intra-site level there is less correlation between the sophistication of the technology used and how well or how quickly one comes to understand it or develop a strategy for recording. Here we are concerned with the construction and the sorts of analyses of space, contents, organisation, status, role, symbolism, etc., discussed by Eriksson in this volume. Much of this cannot be perceived acoustically or even photographically. I have often been frustrated by apparently crisp video taken in clear water or by sharp photographs from which I was unable to identify let alone interpret what was shown. What I have found to be much more effective are sketches. If the reader is shocked by such an admission in this scientific age of digital electronics let me explain. Firstly I am no luddite, being only too happy to use the aforementioned hi-tech systems such as the 3D Chirp sub-bottom profiler developed at Southampton and used so successfully to visualise the buried hull of Henry V's *Grace Dieu* (Plets et al 2009) (Fig. 7.2). But where wreck structure is visible to any degree I argue that sketches can fulfil an important role in the cognitive process of coming to know and understand. A sketch can show far more than is ever visible on the site at one time as well as clarifying structural relationships that are often so difficult to see in a photograph. Perhaps most importantly, I find that if I can draw it I understand it, at least spatially. Then there's memory. Mine is horribly fallible after a dive of simply looking, however hard I have concentrated. By contrast drawing embeds the subject far more effectively

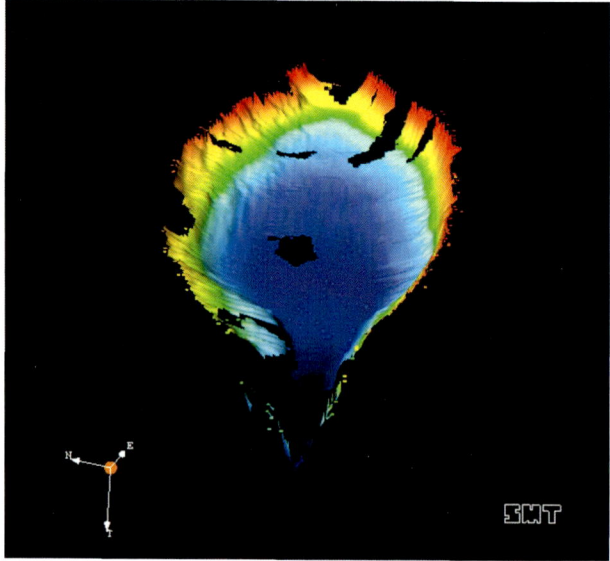

Figure 7.2. An acoustic model of the lower hull of Henry V's Grace Dieu buried in the Hamble riverbed, Hampshire, England. This was obtained with a revolutionary 3D chirp sub-bottom profiling system designed and built at the National Oceanography Centre, Southampton. (after Plets et al. 2009).

and for the long term. I find it easy to recall structural relationships of timbers that I drew thirty years ago. Without drawing them, 30 minutes would be more like it.

'But I can't draw' or 'I'm not artistic' people say when it is suggested they have a go at this. You don't have to be for we are concerned with spatial relationships as a basis for building understanding and interpretation. In our first dive on a 16th-century wreck on the Nämdofjärd kravel in 1991 (Adams & Rönnby 1996), I concentrated on sketching structural aspects that were specific to the ship's time period, while Johan Rönnby made a sketch of the whole site in a dive of 20 minutes at 35m depth, breathing air. I do not think he would mind if I said that it was not exactly a work of art! but it remained in the files for years as a reliable reference for briefing other members of the team on the geography of the site.

Art and archaeology

Having said that, some drawings explicitly do incorporate the intention to illustrate and this leads us to other interesting considerations on how and why we do what we do. Illustration in various forms has been an integral component of archaeological practice since its emergence as a distinct discipline around the end of the 19th century. Quite early we see the development of two distinct traditions. One is associated with formal recording and the production of images for publication, while the other allows the artist freer rein in reconstructing the past. At first sight the production of publication images using measurement seems objective and scientific, while reconstructions are 'freehand' and imaginative, albeit informed by archaeological discovery. The former, typically stippled and cross-hatched finds drawings, site plans, sections and crisp photographs of clean trenches provide apparently objective representation of artefacts, features, structures, etc., but with reconstructions, it is more difficult to assess their veracity. Moser (1998) for example has examined the ways that the past has been represented and shown how it is inexorably bound up with constructed ideas of our own histories and identities. All too often, images of 'how it was' in the past propagate an almost indelible lexicon of visual motifs even in the face of new discoveries that show them to be erroneous. For these reasons, while finds drawings have been regarded as obligatory in an archaeological report, the reconstruction drawing was an optional extra.

Today the traditional media of archaeological illustration and of reconstruction have been augmented by various scanning technologies and computer modelling but they are still primarily used in the same roles: recording, in which production of plans and illustrations is governed by various Cartesian conventions of scale, orthographic projection and representation (e.g. Adkins & Adkins 1989) and for interpretative images of increasing sophistication, where their veracity and hence their usefulness rests on demonstrable links between the source data and the final reconstruction (see for example, Earl et al. 2002; Earl 2013). Yet there is more, and I think this is bound up with the fundamental nature of the discipline: our source material is everything that was created or affected by past human action: from the most ephemeral residues and the smallest things made, to buildings, settlements and the landscape itself. Small wonder then that the production of images and the whole process of visualisation are fundamental to the ways we research, practise, teach and publish. So while it is not uncommon in many of the humanities and social sciences to see seminars given without the aid of a single image or diagram, it is very unusual in archaeology. Inevitably then images comprise more than the plan, the finds drawing and the virtual reality model, exciting and vital though they are. Many recent research projects explicitly incorporate art in various forms (Tilley et al. 2000) and there are also organisations devoted to exploring the relationship between art and archaeology and the theory of so doing is being increasingly explored (Tilley 1991; Renfrew 2006; Smiles & Moser 2005; Pollard 2004).

A Baltic tradition

Where shipwrecks are concerned, producing drawn or painted images of them both to illustrate and as an aid to archaeological recording is something of a Baltic tradition stretching back half a century, notably manifested in the drawings of Finnish wrecks by Henry Forsell (Fig. 7.3) and of Baltic wrecks in general by Harry Alopeaus (Fig. 7.4a and b). Niklass Eriksson

Figure 7.3. Perspective drawing alongside a plan of the galliot St. Michel *in the Finnish archipelago by Henry Forsell (Cederlund 1983:31).*

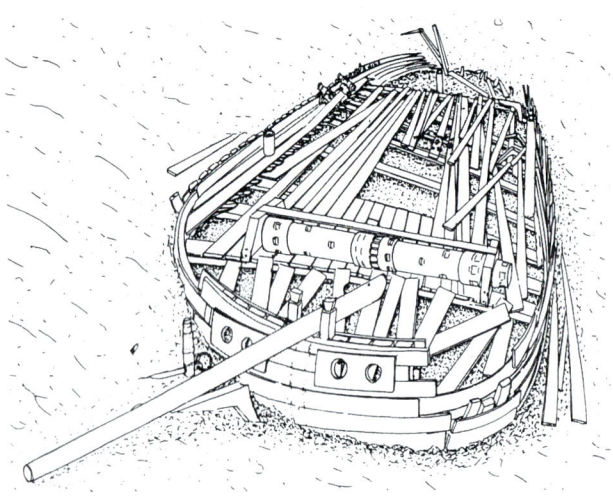

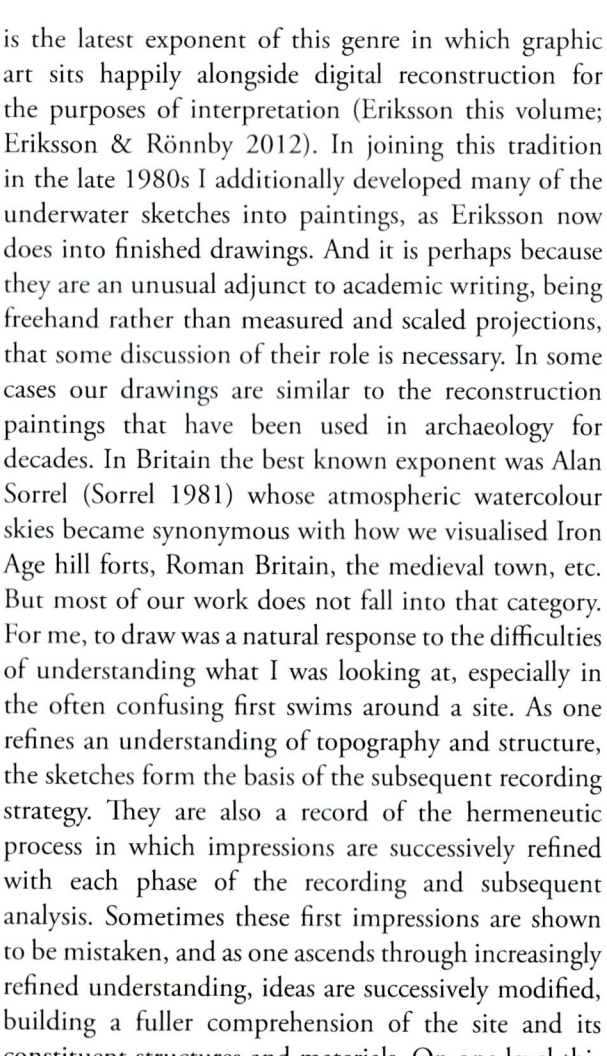

Figure 7.4a. Above: Perspective drawing of the 19th century Jussarö wreck in the Finnish archipelago by Harry Alopaeus.
Figure 7.4b. Right: Model of the 19th century Jussarö wreck in the Finnish archipelago by Harry Alopaeus. Even in a digital age his models continue to be commissioned by museums, research institutes and sponsoring companies.

is the latest exponent of this genre in which graphic art sits happily alongside digital reconstruction for the purposes of interpretation (Eriksson this volume; Eriksson & Rönnby 2012). In joining this tradition in the late 1980s I additionally developed many of the underwater sketches into paintings, as Eriksson now does into finished drawings. And it is perhaps because they are an unusual adjunct to academic writing, being freehand rather than measured and scaled projections, that some discussion of their role is necessary. In some cases our drawings are similar to the reconstruction paintings that have been used in archaeology for decades. In Britain the best known exponent was Alan Sorrel (Sorrel 1981) whose atmospheric watercolour skies became synonymous with how we visualised Iron Age hill forts, Roman Britain, the medieval town, etc. But most of our work does not fall into that category. For me, to draw was a natural response to the difficulties of understanding what I was looking at, especially in the often confusing first swims around a site. As one refines an understanding of topography and structure, the sketches form the basis of the subsequent recording strategy. They are also a record of the hermeneutic process in which impressions are successively refined with each phase of the recording and subsequent analysis. Sometimes these first impressions are shown to be mistaken, and as one ascends through increasingly refined understanding, ideas are successively modified, building a fuller comprehension of the site and its constituent structures and materials. On one level this

may lead to little more than an appreciation of dating evidence, constructional aspects and the vessel as a functional object, etc. But as Rönnby has discussed in this volume, other questions are ever-present, some are inevitably generated as the work progresses, to be integrated with those that may have prompted research in the first place. As the process continues one's capacity to tackle these increases. Questions - observation - answers - new questions, and so on in hermeneutic oscillation, that progressively allow one to address broader, contextual questions in which the site-specific data are related to a wider whole. Of course this is a cognitive process that an archaeologist investigating a land site will also go through, as in fact we all do in any learning situation. However, for the land archaeologist who may be on site all day every day, this process is continuous and often subconscious. Underwater it is more episodic because it can only happen during or as a result of a dive. The process is therefore iterative rather than continuous and arguably therefore a more conscious one.

In a way the archive of sketches made during fieldwork track this process (Figs 7.5 & 7.6). And, as most people will never see these sites, the paintings and drawings worked up from the underwater sketches convey an impression of how these wrecked ships look in what is now their natural setting (Fig. 7.5b & 7.7). Images then fulfil an important role of communication as well as being part of research process.

But what about accuracy? Can they be valid

Figure 7.5a. Underwater sketch of the wreck of the Swedish brig Margareta (1898). (J. Adams).

Figure 7.5b. Painting of the wreck based on the underwater drawing 7.5a. Since this was painted in 1992 the bowsprit has collapsed and the stern half of the hull has opened about 50mm. (J. Adams).

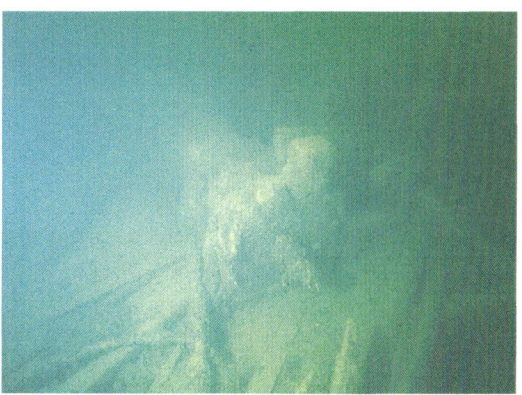

Figure 7.6. Photograph of Margareta taken from the same vantage point (though closer) as from which the drawing was made (J. Adams).

archaeologically if they are freehand? In fact many are produced with the aid of measurements, but these are used more to assist in achieving realistic proportions rather than accuracy of projection. In producing an image to convey an impression of the site as well as technical information some are worked up straight from the underwater drawing with no attempt to adjust the distortion resulting from being under water and looking through the relatively crude optics of a diving mask. Having said that we attempt to depict the structure as it is, not with any pretensions of photo-realism but with the aim of evoking the 'feel' of the site as much as anything. There is an element of artistic licence but this is restricted to giving the impression of rather better visibility than there ever really is, and to sharpen edges and seams between structural components and different surfaces. The artist's brush is used to clean away a little of the weed and other marine growth, rather as a photograph might be retouched, though in this case we are not removing blemishes, quite the opposite. Most importantly, nothing is (intentionally) exaggerated in the sense that no timbers are replaced; no existing structure is heightened, reconstructed or otherwise extrapolated in order to make it look more impressive. Every timber represented in every image was on the site at the time it was drawn as is the case for Eriksson's recent drawings of the Dalarö wreck and the 'Ghost wreck' (Eriksson this volume). From this point of view, certain aspects that would be accepted in a reconstruction, and art in general, are intentionally suppressed. They are therefore closer to conventional archaeological illustration than it might appear, for this also involves selective representation of certain qualities of the object being drawn. The illustrator makes judgements about what to emphasise and what to omit. Even though this is done using accepted conventions it is often possible to distinguish the style of individual 'artists'. Indeed many finds drawings have undeniably aesthetic qualities so are they craft or art?

The science of Art

This is a question one might also ask of the illustrations in this volume although that leads us straight to the oft-debated question: what is art? For William Hazlitt writing in the early 1800s the answer had been provided by Lord Bacon for whom art was:

> '*the proper disposal of the things of nature by human thought and experience, so as to answer the several purposes of mankind; in which sense art stands opposed to **nature***' (Hazlitt 1838:1). (my emphasis)

Interestingly, in the context of the following discussion

Hazlitt continued:

> '*Art is principally used for a system of rules serving to facilitate the performance of certain actions ; in which case it stands opposed to **science**, or a system of speculative principles*' (*ibid.*). (my emphasis)

Of course definitions of art have ranged broadly since then and to each of them we can find another that is diametrically opposed. Marcel Duchamp famously proclaimed that something was 'art' if he said it was, but where underwater sketches used as the basis for painted illustration were concerned my initial instinct was to do the opposite and suppress any claims of artistic status for these images lest they be seen as unscientific and hence suspect. I would also have denied they were scientific in the sense of measurement and procedure so they existed in a sort of limbo. Hazlitt would have agreed notwithstanding the differences in what was meant by science at that time. In fact today, recognition of the role these images have, and particularly the process of making them described above, suggests they can be both an active and legitimate component of archaeological practice. Scientific status does not depend on a skeleton of Cartesian coordinates and so perhaps, like archaeology at large, is a subject which integrates the arts and sciences more explicitly than any other (see for example Jones 2002), they are a product of both modes of enquiry and expression. In this way they are maritime equivalents of the archaeological paintings of Wessex by Heywood Sumner an artist and archaeologist whose obituary ironically mourned his loss to scientific archaeology. The author and artist Mervyn Peake said that without craft, art cannot exist (Peake 1946:1). Not a view with which Duchamp or many of today's conceptual artists would agree but one with which archaeological art sits rather well. It implies that art needs to be born of craft which in turn implies that both are related facets of how we make things in general: tools, paintings, ships, cars, toys or houses. This challenges the rather arrogant distinctions made between what in Western thought is understood to be 'fine art' as opposed to merely 'craft'. In reality they are part of the same continuum. For irrespective of the quality of the underlying intellectual process in creating a 'work of art', if the artist is not competent to handle the medium of expression it is rather like trying to write a poem in a language one cannot speak. Whether one takes Duchamp's line, Peake's, or somewhere in between, a Baltic tradition of creating images of wrecks through graphic art (and craft) will continue to play a role in the ways in which we come to understand and interpret them, not in denial of new technologies but as complementary means of visualising these fascinating monuments.

Figure 7.7. Painting of the Jutholmen wreck, a 17th century fluit ship (J. Adams). In reality what you would see at this distance from the wreck is a dark shape looming up in the water. The painting combines this with the detail that you see as you swim nearer (Rönnby & Adams 1994).

Inset: photograph taken from a similar viewpoint – considerably less detail is visible (Photo: K. Keighley)

CAVEs of experience

A final thought is related to the fact that we do archaeology not just for ourselves but everyone. In that context images also have the important function of bridging what is often a divide between academic and popular publications. In the context of the Baltic there has already been an EU-funded research project (MoSS) in which the visualisation of shipwrecks was a key component (Cederlund 2004; Leino et al. 2004). The efficacy of images in transmitting research results can be seen in a variety of media including TV documentaries but especially in museums. Watching visitors to museums who are not specialists, one might expect to see them spending most time in front of the objects on display but often it is the graphic representations, reconstructions and dioramas that claim an equal amount of their attention. In the case of children it can be even more so. What begins for us under water as a means of coming to understand, here becomes the means to communicate that understanding. Perhaps it is here that the two formerly distinct branches of formal vs reconstructive archaeological illustration are already coming together. Digital media have recently been used to construct what are referred to as *cave automatic virtual environments* (CAVE). These are rooms or spaces created by clusters of adjacent projection screens and audio speakers in which the viewer gains an immersive, three-dimensional experience of places, structures and things. The images can be photographic or computed reconstructions, or indeed a combination of both. Archaeologically, the virtual reconstruction can be overlaid or integrated with the recorded remains or alternatively, plans, sections and reconstructions can be explored in three dimensions as though one was moving downwards through the site and back in time (DeFanti et al. 2009; Levy et al. 2012) (Fig. 7.8). The CAVE therefore utilises human perception not just as the medium for visualising and auralising the

results of research but in opening up new pathways for engaging with and understanding the source material. This form of multidimensional communication has particular potential for visualising, exploring and coming to understand shipwreck sites. Muckelroy, invoking Binford, once described the shipwreck as the static seabed remains of a formerly dynamic, organised machine (Muckelroy 1978:157). We (as he was) are of course interested in a lot more than the technology but it is part of what the ship was in terms of maritime materiality. Shipbuilding and seafaring were social practice and so what a ship was as a thing cannot be separated from the people who conceived, designed, built, used and either lost or disposed of it. Yet even to experienced eyes the relationship of many wrecks to the complete entity they once were is often far from clear. But in the CAVE the viewer can experience the wreck site as it is now and through sequential reconstructions pass back in time. In this way wrecks that will never be salvaged or even fully excavated can populate the galleries of museums and the pages of electronic media and, as Rönnby has stressed in this volume, fire the imagination.

Figure 7.8. A CAVE environment. To the viewer the edges of the screens are not apparent and an almost hyper-real sense of being there is created by a synthesis of stereoscopic sounds and images. Viewing can be passive as shown here or interactive where movement through time and space can be controlled by a console held by the viewer. (After DeFanti UCSD; Levy UCSD)

References

Adams, J. 2002. Excavation methods under water. In: C. Orser (ed.) *Encyclopaedia of Historical Archaeology*: 192-196. London: Routledge.

Adams, J. 2006. From the water margins to the centre ground. *Journal of Maritime Archaeology* 1.1: 1-8.

Adams, J. 2013. *A Maritime Archaeology of Ships. Innovation and Social Change in Medieval Europe.* Oxford: Oxbow Books.

Adams, J. & Rönnby, J. 1996. *Furstens Fartyg.* Stockholm: National Maritime Museum.

Adkins, L. & Adkins, R.A. 1989. *Archaeological Illustration.* Cambridge: Cambridge University Press.

Ballard, R.D., McCann, A., Yoerger, D., Whitcomb, L., Mindell, D., Oleson, J., Singh, H., Foley, B., Adams, J., Piechota, D., Giangrande, C. 2000. The discoveries of ancient history in the deep sea using advanced deep submergence technology. *Deep-Sea Research* Part 1: 1591-1620.

Barker, P. 1977. *Techniques of Archaeological Excavation.* London: Batsford.

Bates, R., Lawrence, M., Dean, M. & Robertson, P. 2011. Geophysical Methods for Wreck-Site Monitoring: the Rapid Archaeological Site Surveying and Evaluation (RASSE) programme. *International Journal of Nautical Archaeology* 40.2: 404-216.

Bojakowski, P. and Custer Bojakowski, K. 2011. The Warwick: survey results of the early 17th-century Virginia Company ship. *Post-Medieval Archaeology* 45.1: 41-53.

Bradley, R. 1990. *The Passage of Arms.* Cambridge: Cambridge University Press.

Cederlund, C.O. 1983. *Old Wrecks of the Baltic Sea.* BAR International Series no. 186. Oxford: British Archaeological Reports.

Cederlund, C.O. 2004. What is Visualisation? *MoSS Project Newsletter* 1. Helsinki: National Board of Antiquities.

DeFanti, T., Dawe, G., Sandin, D., Schulze, J., Otto, P., Girado, J., Kuester, F., Smarr, L. & Ramesh, R. 2009. The StarCAVE, a third-generation CAVE and virtual reality OptlPortal. *Future Generation Computer Systems* 25. 2: 169-178.

Earl, G. 2013. Modeling in archaeology: computer graphic and other digital pasts. *Perspectives on Science* 21.2: 226-244.

Earl, G. & Wheatley, D. 2002. Virtual reconstruction and the interpretative process: a case-study from Avebury. In, D. Wheatley, G. Earl, & Poppy, S. (eds) *Contemporary Themes in Archaeological Computing*: 5-15. Oxford: Oxbow Books.

Eriksson, N. & Rönnby, J. 2012. The Ghost Ship'. An Intact Fluyt from c.1650 in the Middle of the Baltic Sea. *International Journal of Nautical Archaeology* 41.2: 350-361.

Flatman, J. 2003. Cultural biographies, cognitive landscapes and dirty old bits of boat: 'theory' in maritime archaeology. *International Journal of Nautical Archaeology* 32.2: 143-157.

Gould, R.A. 2000. *Archaeology and the Social History of Ships.* Cambridge: Cambridge University Press.

Hazlett, W. 1838 The Fine Arts. In: B.R. Haydon & Hazlitt, W. *Painting and the Fine Arts.* Edinburgh: Charles black.

Jay, M. 1993. *Downcast eyes. The denigration of vision in twentieth century French thought.* Berkeley: University of California Press.

Jenks, C. (ed.) 1995. *Visual Culture.* London: Routledge.

Jones, A. 2002. *Archaeological Theory and Scientific Practice.* Cambridge: Cambridge University press.

Leino, M., Jöns, H., Wessman, S & Cederlund, C.O. 2004. Visualizing Underwater Cultural Heritage in the MoSS-project. In C.O. Cederlund (ed.) *MoSS Project Final Report.* Helsinki: National Board of Antiquities.

Lenihan, D. 1983. Rethinking Shipwreck Archaeology: A History of Ideas and Considerations for New Directions. In R. Gould (ed.) *Shipwreck Anthropology*: 37-64. Albuquerque: University of New Mexico.

Levy, T., Smith, N.G., Najjar, M., DeFanti, T., Yu-Min Lin, A., & Kuester, F. 2012. *Cyber-Archaeology in the Holy Land. The Future of the Past.* California Institute for Telecommunications and Information \technology (Calit2), UC San Diego. Biblical Archaeology Society.

McCann A.M. & Oleson J. P. (eds) 2004. Deep-water Shipwrecks off Skerki Bank: the 1997 Survey. *Journal of Roman Archaeology*, Suppl. Series.

Merleau-Ponty, M. 1962. *Phenomenology of Perception* (trans. by Colin Smith), London: Routledge & Kegan Paul.

Moser, S. 1998. *Ancestral Images: The Iconography of Human Origins.* London: Routledge.

Muckelroy, K. 1978. *Maritime Archaeology.* Cambridge: Cambridge University Press.

Peake, M. 1946. *The Craft of the Lead Pencil.* London: Alan Wingate.

Plets, R., Dix, J., Adams, J., Bull, J., Henstock, T., Gutowski, M. & Best, A. 2009. The use of a high-resolution 3D Chirp sub-bottom profiler for the reconstruction of the shallow water archaeological site of the Grace Dieu (1439), River Hamble, UK. *Journal of Archaeological Science* 36.2: 408-418

Pollard, C.J. 2004. The art of decay and the transformation of substance. In C. Renfrew, E. DeMarrais & C. Gosden (eds) *Substance, Memory,*

Display. Archaeology and Art. McDonald Institute Monographs: 47-62. Cambridge: McDonald Institute.

Ransley, J. 2005. Boats are for boys: queering maritime archaeology. *World Archaeology* 37.4: 621-629.

Renfrew, C. 2006. *Figuring it out: What are we? Where do we come from?* London: Thames & Hudson.

Rönnby, J. & Adams. J. 1994. *Östersjöns Sjunkna Skepp: En marinarkeolisk tidresa.* Stockholm: Tiden.

Singh, H., Adams, J., Mindell, D. & Foley, B. 2000. Imaging Underwater for Archaeology. *Journal of Field Archaeology* 27.3: 319-32.

Smiles, S. & Moser, S. (eds) 2005. *Envisioning the past: archaeology and the image.* New Interventions in Art. Oxford: Blackwell.

Sorrel, M. (ed.) 1981. *Alan Sorrel. Reconstructing the past.* London: Book Club Associates.

Staniforth, M. 1997. The Archaeology of the Event - The Annales School and Maritime Archaeology, In: Lakey, (ed.) *Underwater Archaeology*: 17-21. Society for Historical Archaeology.

Steele, J. 1995. Talking to each other: why hominids bothered. In: I. Hodder et al (ed.) *Interpreting Archaeology*: 81-86. London: Routledge.

Tilburg, H van 1998. Zero Visibility Diving. In L. Babits & H van Tiburg (eds) *Maritime Archaeology. A Reader of Substantive and Theoretical Contributions.* New York: Plenum.

Tilley, C. 1991. *Material Culture and Text: the Art of Ambiguity.* London: Routledge.

Tilley, C., Hamilton, S. & Bender, B. 2000. Art and the Re-Presentation of the Past. *Journal of the Royal Anthropological Institute* 6.1: 35-62.

8

Sailing, Sleeping and Eating on board 17th century ships: Tapping the Potential of Baltic Sea Shipwrecks with regard to the Archaeology of Space

Niklas Eriksson

Introduction

Conditions for the preservation of organic material are remarkably good in the Baltic Sea due to the absence of the shipworm *Teredo navalis*. Hulls of old ships can remain virtually intact for hundreds of years, with decks, masts, cargo and crew's belongings in place, providing unique archaeological opportunities. But the underwater location, as well as the fact that the hull structures are so unbreachable, prevents detailed recording of building techniques.

The reconstruction and analysis of construction sequences is a common point of departure in the archaeology of ships, and a natural continuation of the recording process of wrecks. But such an approach is not that simple when discussing Baltic wrecks as these well-preserved ships do not release such information easily. Questions regarding shell- or skeleton first construction tend to bounce against the coherent hull-side. As it is neither possible nor desirable to raise, dismantle and minutely record all the Baltic shipwrecks of possible archaeological interest, we need to devise a strategy for recording them while under water. But for this to be meaningful, we must be aware of what we are looking for before donning wetsuits, casting ourselves into the water and diving down to the empirical data. Once there, perhaps 30 meters below the surface, it is too late for decisions about where to place a measuring *tape* or where to direct a camera shot. Regarding this great pile of more or less structured timbers, the choice of which aspects should be recorded, collected and brought to the surface, must derive from an idea of how this material could be used as a point of departure for a more thorough understanding of human kind.

With this in mind, the concept of standardizing methods for underwater documentation of wrecks seems otiose. Methods must be open to selection, based on a balance of the information preserved at the site, the research questions in focus, and – this is fundamental – the practical possibilities of collecting relevant information.

Treasure chests and tautology

These well-preserved Baltic wrecks have not been used to any great extent within research on ship construction sequences, on account of the compactness of the hull structures and the difficulties of carrying out detailed recording under water (but see Adams 2003, for an exception). Thus the construction sequence analysis of wrecks has evolved to a large extent without regard to Baltic material. Well-recorded wrecks found on land or raised intact provide a more suitable point of departure (cf. Hocker & Vlierman 1996; Lemée 2006).

Baltic wrecks have served other uses in marine archaeology, such as treasure chests from which to salvage objects for museum exhibitions, or as illustrations of great legends. Consequently, many of the objects that formed the initial exhibition of the Swedish Maritime Museum when it opened in 1938, had their provenance on the floor of the Baltic Sea. The interest of the Swedish naval officers in shipwrecks derived primarily from their focus on their own history (see Cederlund 1983a, 1997). The artefacts raised by the Navy in the early 20th century also provided images substantiating the imposing History of the Swedish Navy published in 1942 (Lübeck 1942). This custom was common in the Baltic area. At the Centralne Muzeum Morskie in

Gdansk, Poland, one of the explicit aims of maritime archaeology was the salvaging of artefacts in order to redress the losses sustained during the Second World War, when most historic districts in Poland's coastal towns and cities were reduced to ruins (Ossowski 2008:35; Smolarek 1985:421-35).

In the 1980s, when Swedish maritime archaeology was formalized into academia, the well-preserved remains of large carvel-built ships from the early modern period became a special concern. In his dissertation from 1983, Carl Olof Cederlund made an important contribution by outlining the research history of these ships; one important research topic being a methodology for recording and collecting clues leading to the identity of a wreck (Cederlund 1983a:69, 1997:126). The Finnish historian Christian Ahlström might be considered to have continued the task defined by Cederlund, with his Doctoral thesis concerning the identification of wrecks from written sources (Ahlström 1995, translated into English in 1997).

The underwater recording of shipwrecks to supplement written sources as a means of identifying them became a sort of paradigm in Baltic Sea ship archaeology from the mid 1980s. Several wrecks were examined on these grounds and some regained their original identities (Rönnby 2003:123-30; Rönnby & Adams 1994). But in a number of cases the archival search gave no results and the identities of those wrecks remain unknown. Over the years, quite a few such attempts have proved fruitless, despite serious efforts.

Unidentified shipwrecks create an interesting problem. They cannot be worthless just because they are unidentified. This circumstance calls for a discussion of the relationship between written sources and material remains (for an overview, see Andrén 1998). Is there an inherent archaeological potential in well-preserved shipwrecks or is such potential mere tautology? Is a shipwreck primarily a point of departure for archival research, as an illustration of history already retold by other means? Are written accounts indispensible to the appreciation of shipwrecks? What other possibilities exist? (cf. Adams 2003:42; Muckelroy 1978:6).

Architecture

As already mentioned, perhaps the most unique aspects of the well-preserved Baltic shipwrecks are their coherence and totality. They resemble complete ships and should be understood as such. If we view the Baltic wrecks from this vantage point, it becomes possible to regard them as the achieved goal of a sequence of construction. The preserved hulls should be viewed as buildings, as architecture; and they should be recorded, but most important, be interpreted, as such.

To regard ships as architectural creations is nothing new. Maritime treatises written in the 17th and 18th centuries were often given titles with architectural themes. Examples include Witsen's *Architectura Navalis*, first published in 1671 (1979), Deane's *Doctrine for Naval Architecture* from 1670 (Lavery 1981), or Sutherland's *The Ship-builders Assistant*, subtitled *Or Some Essays Towards Completing the Art of Marine Architecture* (1711). The most well-known is perhaps Chapman's *Architectura Navalis Mercatoria* (Chapman 1768).

The considerations of the ship's architects when creating their designs have also been used as inspiration by archaeologists when interpreting the material remains of old ships. Consequently, the term 'naval architecture' commonly appears in the archaeological literature as well as inventive terms such as 'reverse naval architecture' (see for instance Lemée 2006:97ff; Pomey 2004). However, the theory of naval architecture tends to circulate around aspects of hydrodynamics and carrying capacity on the one hand and methods of constructing hulls on the other. A comparison could be made with general architectonical theory, which involves a wide variety of approaches towards the relationship between humans and the built environment, besides the engineering of erecting buildings. Might some be applicable to shipwrecks? Can we learn anything about human interaction and the mindset of the people on board these ships from an analysis of ship architecture? Approaches such as these may gain meaning if applied to unidentified shipwrecks where written accounts are non-existent.

Space

It was once stated that one of the prime aims of architecture was to arrange space (cf Markus 1992:8). Clearly spatial arrangement has a crucial impact on the social interactions possible in a building, so why not on board a ship? The preserved 17th century naval architectonical treatises reveal some information in this context regarding naval ships. However, when it comes to merchant ships the information is scarce, or rather, non-existent. Distribution of space can be described in terms of volume, priority and value. Spatial volume and value can in some cases be argued as going hand in hand; for example a ship intended for heavy loads was equipped with greater space for this purpose. Such a functional approach sees space as a container wherein actions take place (see for instance Bollnow 1994; Eriksdotter 2005:237ff; Tilley 1994:9).

Onboard ships a variety of functions were conducted within a limited space. This makes them perfect architectonical metaphors. The functionalist architect, Le Corbusier, conceived the Atlantic steamer as the perfect arrangement for a concentrated population where all activities had their given place (Rådberg 1998:142-153). The Swedish nobleman, Axel Oxenstierna, the architect of Swedish public administration, also used the ship as a metaphor to describe his ideas of the state (Adams 2003:33; Rönnby & Adams 1994:68). The relationships between different spaces reflect the relationships between the persons that inhabit them. The way rooms are arranged may be understood as a form of grammar (Glassie 1983; Johnson 1996). If one extends this linguist analogy, then a ship's hull forms a sentence whose meaning can be gleaned from the totality of its arranged words (special units).

Archaeologists sometimes avail themselves of space syntax (see for instance Hillier & Hanson 1989; Hanson et al. 2003), which is a theory to describe the arrangement of rooms. Access patterns are revealed through converting the arrangement of rooms into interlinked boxes and are commonly applied in two dimensions. The applicability is obvious when interpreting site-plans and similar archaeological data but space syntax has attracted some criticism lately precisely because of being two-dimensional, which is important with regard to the three-dimensionality of ships, where functions, fittings and people are squeezed into every available space. Aspects other than 'depth into a building' and 'privacy' may be relevant when defining, for instance, status, power, or social interaction. How rooms and other elements are disposed, given dimension and most notably, how they are to be perceived, may be a more relevant analytical point of departure.

In this context, the physical experience of space has been pointed out as a supplementary element. The concept of the coin of vantage determines the impression and the experience of architecture. Archaeologists, art-historians, architects and others, variously discussing how we perceive our surrounding world, sometimes invoke the notion of the 'isovist' (viewshed). An isovist is the area in a spatial environment directly visible from a particular location in space (Turner et al. 2001). The appearances of things shift as one moves and a structure that appears simple may have complexity inherent in its design. As expressed by Giles 'the use of this technique may, in part, reflect the fact that the relatively simple formation (ground-plan) of these buildings does not lend itself so readily to space syntax' (Giles 2007:108).

The perception of a structure held by a person influences the way they experience it, but the reverse is also true. As a consequence, architectural historians and others have applied an empathic approach to the study of architecture, by trying to understand how people felt and behaved while moving through buildings

(Nagbøl 1983; Eriksdotter 2005). Architecture may be regarded as a stage set for performers whose progress is governed by class and gender. People make buildings but buildings also make people (cf. Johnson 2002:11-12). The actions performed within architecture define not only the architecture but also its inhabitants, on a ceremonial as well as a daily basis.

In such discussions the term 'everyday life' is sometimes used. The concept is intricate as it involves the variety of seemingly trivial activities carried out each day (for a discussion of the term, see Goodwin 2002:188-190). But what is important in the present context is the debate related to standard architecture. Henri Lefebvre thought of architecture as 'everyday space'. The study of architecture, in this sense, is the study of the material setting for human life (Upton 2002). If architecture has a role in everyday life then the architecture of our well-preserved wrecks could unveil aspects of the behavioural patterns of the people on board, irrespective of whether the ships can be identified in written sources or not. Perhaps we can supply a different form of identity by 'populating' these wrecks?

Two 17th century wrecks

I wish to briefly mention two recently surveyed Baltic wreck sites, namely the 'Edesö' wreck, dated by style and associated artefacts to the second half of the 17th century, and the so-called Jutholmen wreck, which foundered around 1700 or shortly thereafter. Consequently, their respective periods of activity would have coincided, at least briefly. Both lie along the same sailing route beyond Edesö in the Stockholm archipelago, resting a mere five kilometres apart. The points I wish to make in relation to the potential for studying spatial configuration on board wrecks, could have been done using almost any well-preserved and fairly well-recorded shipwreck. I have chosen the Edesö and Jutholmen wrecks for the simple reason that I am familiar with them. Let us start with sorting out the spatial configuration on board the Edesö ship.

The Edesö wreck was found in 2003 and was surveyed in 2007 and 2008 (Fig. 8.1). The survey, which was carried out by the National Maritime Museum in cooperation with Södertörn University and the University of Southampton, involved the recording of the visible hull structure and all visible artefacts and their contexts (Eriksson 2012a, forthcoming). The hull measures a mere 20 metres between posts and is at the most 5.8 metes wide amidships. It rests 30 metres below the surface and has a 17-degree list to starboard (Fig. 8.2). The bow is rather sharp for a 17th century ship in contrast to the Dutch constructions that were common

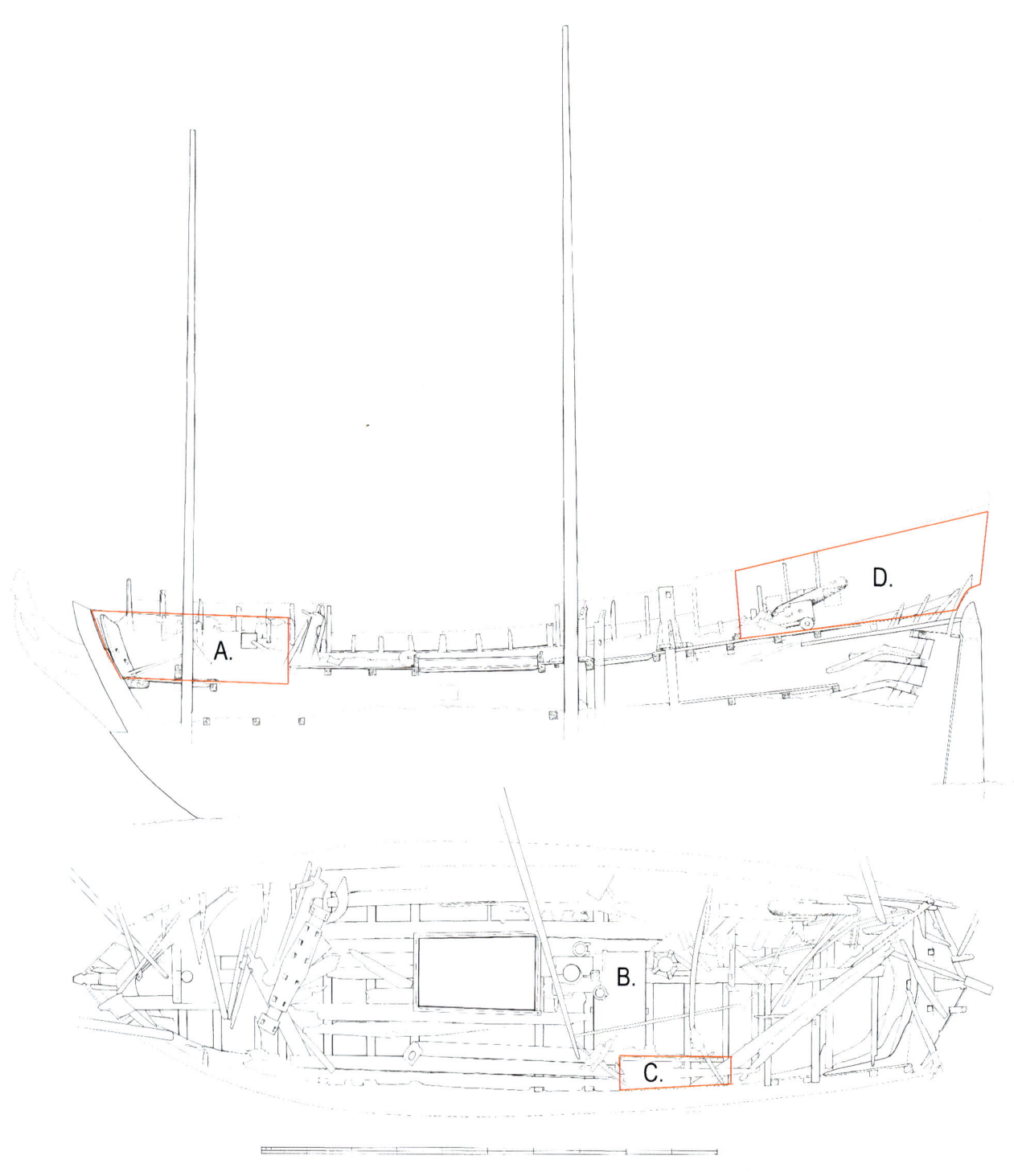

Figure 8.1. Longitudinal section and plan of the Edesö wreck. The letters indicate; A = the forecastle in which the galley was located together with two guns, B = the smaller hatchway abaft of the mainmast, C = small cubbyhole in which tools have been observed, D = stern cabin (Jon Adams/Niklas Eriksson).

Figure 8.2. The starboard bulwark and the deck. Note the grinding stone and the loose rigging elements that have slid over to starboard (photo: Jens Lindström/SMM).

during the same century. The stern is round-tucked, the lower planking ending at a rabbet in the sternpost, the upper planks terminating at the wing transom. This kind of stern construction became common during the 18th century (Landström 1980:105; Laughton 2001:105ff). However, when the Edesö ship was built this procedure was commonly found on English-built ships or those built by masters trained in that tradition. Dendrochronological analysis of one timber indicates that it may derive from northeast England. As the results of this analysis rely on a single match and therefore may not be fully convincing, such a provenance does not conflict with the stylistic features of the ship itself (Eriksson in press).

The ship originally had three masts. The lower masts of the fore and mainmasts are still standing, while the mizzenmast is missing. Most likely it is the lower mizzenmast that is lying towards the starboard side in the stern. Bits of rigging lie scattered all over the site and it would appear that the wreck has been more or less untouched since capsizing. The fine state of preservation and the large number of visible objects throughout the wreck enable a rather full reconstruction of the spatial

configuration of the ship, the organization of zones and their various functions (Fig. 8.1). Starting in the bow, the beakhead has fallen down. All the component parts, including the lion figurehead, are found beneath their original positions, on the seabed ahead of the bow, enabling full reconstruction.

The ship originally had a forecastle, inside which the main deck was stepped down (Fig. 8.1-A). The deck that covered this space has collapsed, but the knees that supported the beams covering this space are preserved in their original position, revealing that the height inside here was a mere 1.4m. Artefacts deriving from several different activities have been recorded inside the forecastle. Ropes appear all over the wreck in differing states of fragmentation, but some of these may have been stored inside the forecastle. The location and height of the hawse-holes on either side of the stem, and the windlass abaft the forecastle, show that the anchor cable or at least the messenger cable passed through here. The forecastle also had one gun port on either side. The portside cannon has fallen down below deck, while its starboard counterpart is most likely buried under the sediments and loose boards on that side of the hull.

Loading equipment, such as rams and powder scoops, have also been found here. The presence of scuppers reveals that water occasionally found its way into this section.

Fragments of bricks and a copper cauldron remain from the ship's stove, indicating that the forecastle also served as the galley. The stove was placed in the aftermost end of the space, directly before the windlass. Perhaps the loose grating found in the bow area was originally located above the stove. A similar grating and stove arrangement in the forecastle of an English pink is shown by Rålamb (1943:22-24, plate F), in his treatise on shipbuilding, first published in 1691. Eating utensils consisting of wooden plates have also been spotted in this area. The forecastle is all but voluminous. It ends some four meters from the stem. Besides housing guns and associated equipment as well as the lower end of the foremast and the galley, the forecastle also served as lodgings for some of the men on board, a condition we will return to below.

The main hatch out on deck has an opening that measures 260cm, which is large by comparison with the fluyts of the period (see for instance Eriksson 2012b:21; Eriksson & Rönnby 2012:355). Another, smaller hatch is located directly abaft the mainmast providing access to the lower level underneath the main deck in the stern (Fig. 8.1-B). The line of the main deck follows the sheer of the hull. Towards portside and in front of the bulkhead enclosing the helmsman's stand, there once stood a small cubbyhole (Fig. 8.1-C) in which different woodworking tools were found together with a shoe. Did the carpenter keep his personal belongings alongside his tools?

The deck is more horizontal abaft the bulkhead originally demarcating the helmsman's stand. It is not certain if the helmsman's stand and the main cabin were also divided by a bulkhead (Fig. 8.3). If so, which is possible, the latter would have been located between the two gun ports. This, to judge by the length of the tiller, is also where the mizzenmast would have been placed. (The tiller was originally fitted with an iron head, which would have made it slightly longer than drawn here in figure 8.1).

A gun, still in its carriage, stands *in situ* on deck in the stern with its muzzle pointing aft. Two pistols, one flintlock and one wheel-lock, as well as a musket, were found nearby (Fig. 8.4). Besides these guns, good quality pottery and about fifteen Bartman jugs have been recorded in connection with the cabin area in the stern, along with a number of glass bottles.

There is a short portion of an orlop deck below the main deck in the stern, abaft the main mast, and in the bow before the windlass. In the stern at least one bulkhead has been noted. A system of beams and carlings is all that remains of the orlop deck planking. Bottles and ammunition have been found down in the hold, below the orlop. These objects may derive from upper deck levels or may lie in or close to their intended location, stowed away. In English and Dutch shipbuilding treatises from this period, naval vessels had their bread stores located in the stern (cf. Witsen 1979:56ff, plate XLII; Sutherland 1717:33).

As with the facade of a house, the architecture of a ship gives the surrounding world an impression of its owner. As the profile of the Edesö ship appeared on the horizon, with its beakhead and artillery, at least three gun ports per side distributed along the hull, there would have been no mistaking that this was a naval ship. In this sense, the exterior as well as the interior speaks an articulated architectonical language. Thus the architecture of the ship made the people on board perform in certain ways, creating their specific roles.

The Jutholmen wreck

The so-called Jutholmen wreck is one of many discoveries made in the 1960s as a consequence of the increasing popularity of recreational diving. But not only is the Jutholmen wreck an example of a pioneer discovery, it has also been the subject of a pioneer underwater archaeological excavation. The investigation was made between 1970 and 1974 and involved the excavation of a major part of the hull. The prime aim of these investigations was the development of methods of recording, and several innovative measuring techniques were tested, with varying results. The recovered artefacts have been conserved and are stored at the National Maritime Museum (see Cederlund 1983b; 1982; Kaijser 1983; Ingelman-Sundberg 1976; Eriksson 2010).

In 2008 a renewed investigation of the site was undertaken with the main objective of producing material in advance of heritage site management and to collect information regarding the hull structure. This had been partly recorded in the 1970s but complementary information was desired (see Eriksson 2010). The structure of the hull was now recorded using the Direct Survey Method (see Adams & Rule 1991; Marsden 2003:48) and produced a plan and a section drawing of the hull that revealed the supporting structures of the deck (Fig. 8.5). Four more drawings of cross-sections of the hull defined its shape. By combining the information gathered in the 1970s with the results from the survey in 2008; and also the original sketches made by Sven Olof Johansson, the diver who found the wreck in the 1960s; it has been possible to get a detailed picture of the internal arrangement of the ship.

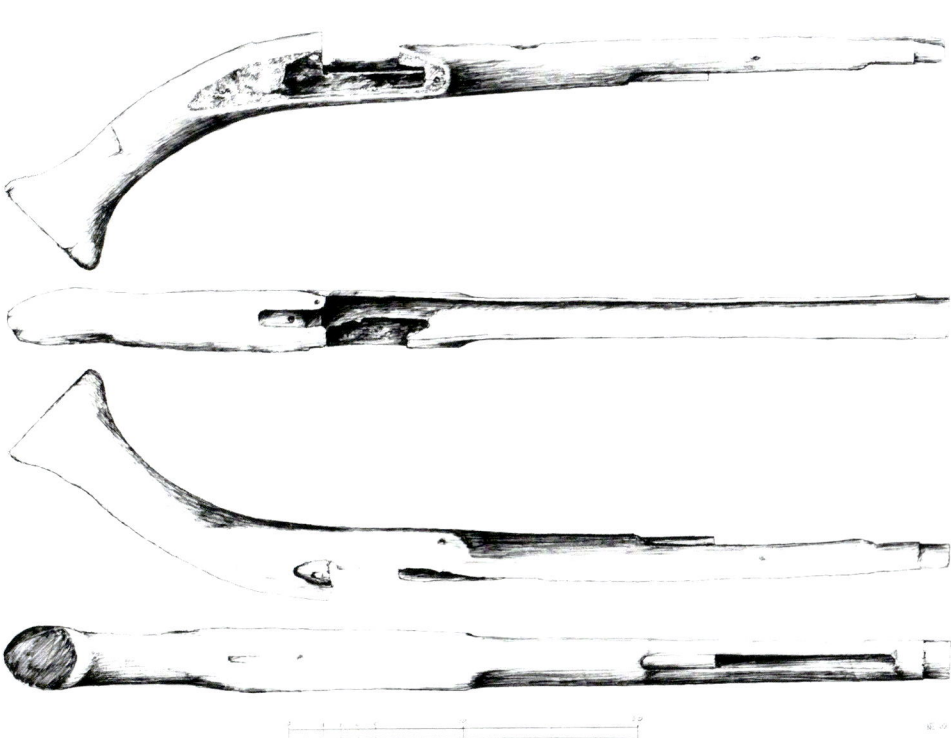

Figure 8.3. The capstan on the Edesö wreck, abaft of which there was originally a bulkhead enclosing the sterncastle (photo: Jens Lindström/SMM).

Figure 8.4. Two pistols and a musket have been observed in the stern of the Edesö wreck. This pistol, originally equipped with a flintlock, was lifted during the survey. After recording it was placed back in situ (Niklas Eriksson).

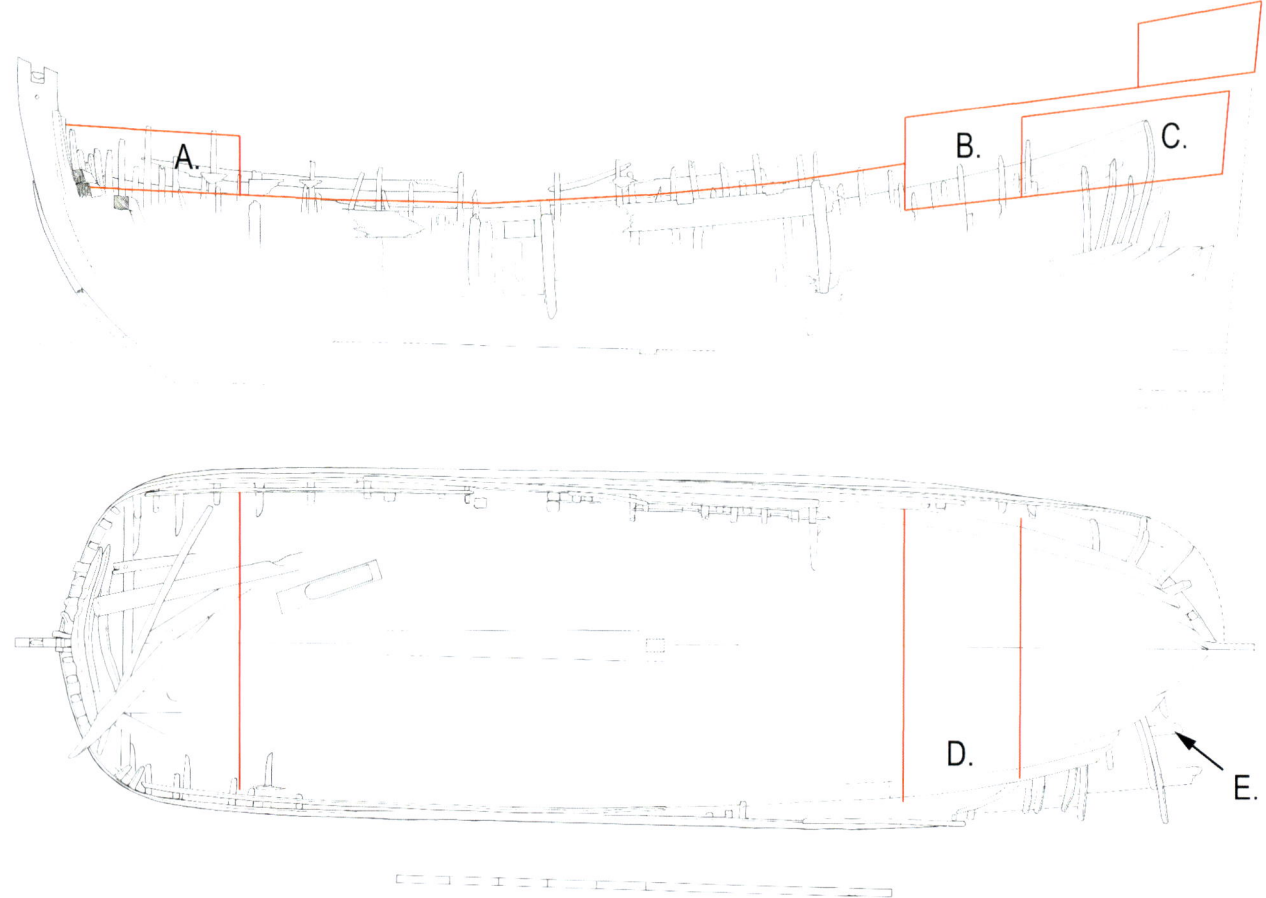

Figure 8.5. Longitudinal section and plan of the Jutholmen wreck. Letters indicate; A = forecastle, B = galley, C = cabin, D = hearth, E = discharge hole for the privy. The cargo room stretches from bow to stern underneath the living quarters (Niklas Eriksson).

Based on the artefacts recovered, the estimated time of sinking has been set to around 1700 (the youngest coin found dates to this year (Kaijser 1983:8, 45; Cederlund 1983b:25; Ingelman-Sundberg 1976). There is, however, reason to question this date for the sinking, as Swedish minting in the early 18th century was disrupted by ongoing wars. The clay-pipes recovered from the wreck suggest a later date for the sinking (Åkerhagen 2009; see also Kaijser 1983:39-44). The remains of the cargo proved to consist of iron ore and tar, typical Swedish export products, suggesting that the ship was on her way from Sweden when she sank (Cederlund 1983b; Kaijser 1983). The reason why this happened outside Jutholmen is not known. Historian Christian Ahlström has made extensive efforts to identify the ship by name, but without result.

However, neither cargo nor ship were totally lost, whatever the reasons for not reaching its destination. Traces of various salvage operations are clearly visible all over the site. In his 1734 treatise entitled *Konsten at lefwa under Watn* (The Art of Existing under Water),

Triewald discusses the practice of salvaging goods from sunken ships, and describes the different machinery used. He explains how decks were removed using saws and various devices powered by capstans on barques in order to get access to the goods stored in the holds. Truncated deckbeams and saw marks on their supporting knee timbers correspond to the methods described by Triewald. However, while the deck itself has perished, some of the structural supports are still in place. As we shall see, enough information survives to reconstruct the configuration of spaces on board the ship.

The interior starboard side is the best preserved section of the hull of the Jutholmen wreck (Fig. 8.5). Along the edge we find a shelf clamp, a thick timber attached to the wall of the hull to support the deck beams. The position of these beams is revealed by notches in the shelf clamp and by hanging knees. The Jutholmen ship had a low forecastle in the bow. The deck that covered this space has disintegrated together with most of the sides of the hull and its height is only indicated by the surviving top-timbers. The character of this space (Fig. 8.5-A) suggests storage rather than a living area, unlike the arrangement on the Edesö wreck.

The situation is less clear when it comes to the quarterdeck, where no structural elements are preserved *in situ*. Some general comments may however, be made regarding the height and location of this deck. The length of the sternpost indicates that the tiller enters the hull immediately above its upper end. The quarterdeck is commonly located immediately above the tiller for technical reasons, as the whipstaff bearing would have been integrated into the quarterdeck construction (see for instance Harland 2011; Pipping 2003:329-333), with the helmsman standing on the quarterdeck.

In 1965, when the wreck was first discovered, the floors of the sections below the quarterdeck were still intact. Diver Johansson made a sketch of the ship in this state of preservation (reproduced in Eriksson 2010:5). In the foremost part of the deck towards the portside, there is a pile of bricks, originating from the ship's stove (Fig. 8.5-D). Although scattered, they are still visible on the site of the wreck. Besides the stove, this room contained another feature of shared interest to the crew, namely armament. A bench or chest containing cannon balls and bar-shot was also found (Kaijser 1983:10, 45). It was common on fluyts of the period to locate the guns in the foremost space under the quarterdeck, this section being sometimes referred to as the gunroom (see for instance Hoving 1995:49). It is likely that they were retrieved during early salvage operations. In the same sketch a laterally running bulkhead is located abaft the stove, dividing the space below the quarterdeck. As the portside tilted outwards the floor of these rooms disintegrated and fell down into the hull.

A shelf clamp found out of place is the only supporting structure deriving from this floor, (cf. Cederlund 1983b:99), indicating that the floor was of a lighter construction than the main deck. But although no shelf clamps or knees have been preserved *in situ*, other traces reveal the location of beams and the level of the floor. When inserting a beam into the hold its end had to be fitted between the frames. If the space was too tight, the frames would be notched to accommodate the beam. Two such cut-outs have been noted on the starboard side and their position recorded, revealing the level of the floor of the sections under the quarterdeck.

Underneath this floor and all the way to the bow, was the hold where the cargo of iron and tar was stowed. This contrasts with the Edesö wreck where various stores were located in the aftermost part of the hold. Access to the hold was provided by the main hatch in the deck situated before the mainmast, along with a small loading hatch in the side of the hull amidships.

There was also a loading port in the stern intended for long objects such as planks, timbers and the like.

In conclusion, we have two ships of somewhat equal size and from approximately the same period. Both are three-masted with square sails and consequently would have required an equal number of hands for sailing. Yet they reveal obvious differences regarding the distribution of space, fittings and crew. Let us now try to understand what kind of impact these differences would have had on those on board. What roles did these hull structures assign to their inhabitants?

Eating and sleeping

The repeated unconscious rituals performed and mediated between the individual and the architecture on a daily basis, shape not only the architecture but also the individual and his/her place in the social community (Giles 2007:105-121; Upton 2002:707-723; Johnson 2002:10ff). The boatswain becomes a boatswain by carrying out boatswain activities and by dressing as a boatswain; similarly the area for the boatswains' quarters becomes defined as such by the presence there of the boatswains (cf. Hacking 1999:161-171).

One act that is done on a repeated basis and is most certainly a part of 'everyday life', is eating. A commonly used term when analysing the eating of food is foodways, which includes 'the whole interrelated system of food conceptualization, procurement, distribution, preservation, preparation and consumption shared by all members of a particular group' (see for instance Deetz 1977:50; Fahlander 2010; Landon 2002:220-221). Repeatedly carried out, foodways enable an understanding of the impact a ship's architecture may have had on the individuals on board and how the process was conducted. From a performative as well as a spatial point of view, foodways on a ship should be recognized as the way the food moves from the storage room via the galley to the plate, in order to be consumed by the crewmember. For this reason let us stay on board the Jutholmen wreck for a while and examine its foodways.

The stove on board the Jutholmen wreck was located in the foremost section under the quarterdeck (Fig. 8.5-B). Access to this space was through a door in the bulkhead, at the breach in the quarterdeck. Stepping through this door and having adjusted your eyes to the darkness, you would make out the stove towards portside. During excavation of the wreck, cooking utensils such as copper cauldrons were found associated with the pile of bricks that once belonged to the galley. Three-legged pots and other utensils deriving from this space for cooking activities had fallen towards the bow.

After passing the guns and the carefully stacked pile of firewood, you would enter the main cabin (Fig. 8.5-C). Light entered this room through two windows in the stern (one window frame was found at the site) (Kaijser 1983:26, 48, 80-81). This is where the food would have been consumed. The majority of the eating utensils, such as plates, were found astern of their original location at the dividing bulkhead. Seven pewter spoons were found, the majority in the stern area although some seem to have fallen towards the bow (cf. Kaijser 1983:15). This number may well correspond to the likely size of the crew on board the Jutholmen when she sailed.

The Jutholmen wreck shares many similarities with the so-called Baltic Ghost Ship (Spökskeppet) and many other fluyt-like vessels from the 17th and early 18th centuries. It may not be that farfetched to imagine that the Jutholmen ship was originally fitted out similarly to the Ghost ship, with two bench chests flanking a table. On the Ghost ship this furniture would have provided seating for the entire crew around the same table (Eriksson & Rönnby 2012). In any case, preparation and consumption is not separated by more than the bulkhead, and nothing indicates that any specific group of people ate separated from any others. Eating and sleeping was carried out in the same space, the main cabin, which seems to be the standard arrangement on fluyts (cf. *ibid.*, also Eriksson 2012b).

If we leave the Jutholmen now and examine the situation on board the Edesö wreck we find several points of difference. The Edesö ship shows a spatial distinction between the area where the food was prepared and where it was consumed. The stove was located in the forecastle (Fig. 8.1-A). We can recognize this spatial solution in written descriptions of warships. In Sutherland's *Britain's Glory: or Ship-Building Unvail'd* published in 1717, we find accounts of the interiors of naval vessels of various sizes. Despite the difference in time, some 20-40 years or so, between that publication and the Edesö ship sinking, and despite the fact that Sutherland is describing much larger ships; his accounts show too much agreement with the Edesö ship to be neglected. According to him on a 'sixth rate' ship (as well as on larger ships) on the 'Fore Castle…are Cabins for the Cooks' (*ibid.*:33). In the bow there are 'Apartments for the Carpenters and Boatswains…Stores as also their Lodgings' (*ibid.*). The eating utensils, plates and pottery found in the forecastle of the Edesö wreck suggest that people ate or at least kept their dishes there.

The artefacts spotted in the bow however, are not the only ones associated with eating on board the Edesö wreck. In the main cabin in the stern, an agglomeration of Bellarmine jugs and a couple of wine bottles have been recorded. Bellarmine jugs were also spotted in the cargo room, but the jugs in the cabin should be seen as the separate wine store of the inhabitants of the cabin. From a purely functional point of view, it seems impractical to locate the stove in the bow if you intend to eat in the stern. The transportation of food from the forecastle out onto the open deck and into the stern would not only cool the dish but be rather risky on a rolling deck. A disastrous solution from a strictly functional point of view, but seen as a staged performance, the transportation of the dish would have been a great success. The path the food travels every day would be visible to the whole crew and would be a reminder to all on board, at repeated instances, of the distinction between those who serve and those who receive. The foodways of the common seamen and the officers on board the Edesö wreck seem to create destinations at separate ends of the ship. The ship's architecture in this sense acts on behalf of a concept of a hierarchal social structure. By controlling peoples' movements one controls their identities (cf. Upton 2002:719).

The separated destinations of the foodways on board the Edesö wreck should be seen as an expression of great professionalization and social range. The spatial relationship between preparation and consumption of food has been discussed by Matthew Johnson with regard to 16th century England. He notes how a more segregated and privatized architecture reflects a more individualized society in the transition from feudalism to capitalism (Johnson 1996:174-178). The conditions on board the Jutholmen wreck (as well as other fluyts, see Eriksson 2012b) reveal the opposite situation. Here the individual seems to have been erased; the shared space for eating and sleeping creates an impression almost of familiarity. Sharing food brings about a subconscious sense of intimacy. Eating together conveys a sense of belonging and tightens the bond between members of a household. In this sense eating is a way to build relations and express confidence. The common meal constitutes an arena where hierarchies, social structures and gender are renegotiated (cf. Fahlander 2010:37ff).

The vital seat

There is however more to daily life on board a ship than sailing, eating and sleeping. Ships, as with buildings in general, also need sanitary accommodation. The disposal of human waste on board ships has been of major concern throughout history (for an overview see Simmons 1997). Most well known are perhaps the 'seats of ease' in the ship's beakhead, a location that led to a ship's privy being called 'the head'. As a general rule, when there is a beakhead there is a seat of ease inside it. The beakhead of the Edesö wreck has collapsed and there is no clear evidence that this extremity contained such a facility (cf. Simmons 1997; Munday 1978:125-140). If such a seat existed in the beakhead, which I find very likely, it would hardly have served all on board. Those who ate in the cabin would have found a closer place to answer the call of nature. Sanitary accommodation would have been placed close to their quarters in the stern, in a manner similar to that on larger ships.

What about ships without beakheads? Although about five metres longer from stem to stern, the Jutholmen wreck never had a beakhead. Fluyts were rarely equipped with such a feature. Sanitary accommodation was of course available. In the stern of the Jutholmen wreck, towards the portside, there is a small square hole in the bottom planking. This hole was depicted by diver Johansson in his sketch of the wreck mentioned earlier, but did not attract attention during excavation (Cederlund 1983b; Kaijser 1983). When surveying the so-called Lion shipwreck, a 17th-century fluyt of smaller size than the Jutholmen ship, in 2010 a similar opening was noted (see Eriksson 2012b). After more careful examination this proved to be a discharge hole for a privy. The interesting aspect of this solution is its location inside the cabin. The square hole noted on the Jutholmen wreck no doubt served the same purpose.

According to Unger seven men and a boy could handle a fluyt of 150 tons in the Norwegian trade and the size of the crew did not rise proportionally to tonnage (Unger 1994:122). This number could have fitted inside the cabin on the Jutholmen wreck. The spatial configuration suggests that the crew shared the cabin in the stern. This is where they would have eaten and slept, and this is also the place where they kept their personal belongings. One should regard this as a shared domestic space, a condition that would form a shared coin of vantage with regard to the rest of the ship. We know from the toll registers of the Danish Sound that the majority of the men involved in the Dutch merchant service on board ships like the Jutholmen wreck came from approximately the same area in northern Holland. Dutch shipmasters recruited their crews from their immediate geographical and even social environment (van Royen 1992:154ff). The standardized distribution of space apparent on board ships built in a Dutch manner reflects these relations, while the naval architects formed a wooden world of far less private character. Perhaps the need to distance the ship's officers from the crew was not so pressing when the captain was a neighbour or a relative?

The architecture of the Edesö wreck presents quite a different picture. Not only does the ship contain the armament of a warship, but its naval character is further revealed in its spatial and social organization which is that of a warship. In spite of its puny size, the Edesö ship articulates hierarchy and power. It divided up the people on board. Their movement through the hull required performing different roles and in this sense the ship controlled their identities. The social range on board spanned from the lowly seaman in the forecastle to the exalted nobleman in the stern. In this context one may recall the words already referred to of the Swedish nobleman Axel Oxenstierna, when he described society as a ship at sail, steered by the firm hand of the king. Society was seen as a pyramidal hierarchy with the king and the aristocracy at the top. A warship was organized along similar lines, with a nobleman as admiral placed high above the officers and the lower ranks ranged below (Adams 2003:33; Rönnby & Adams 1994:68).

How to define identification?

I will end here even though this analysis of performance and daily life on board these two ships is far from exhausted. One could further discuss the distribution of space and explore the private areas of both the officers and the crew more deeply. The point I wish to make in this article is that shipwrecks, in particular the well-preserved and coherent ones of the Baltic, have great analytical potential even when their names remain unknown. A ship's 'identity' can embrace more than the written sources have to offer.

References

Adams, J. 2003. *Ships, Innovation and Social Change – Aspects of Carvel Shipbuilding in Northern Europe 1450-1850*, Stockholm Studies in Archaeology 24.Stockholm: Stockholm University.

Adams, J. & Rule, N. 1991. A comparison of the application of a three-dimensional survey system on three underwater archaeological sites. In: R. Reinders, & R. Oosting, (eds) *Scheepsarcheologie: prioriteiten en lopend onderzoek, flevobericht* 322: 145-154. Lelystad: Ministerie van Verkeer en Waterstaat.

Ahlström, C. 1995. *Spår av hav, yxa och penna – historiska sjöolyckor i Östersjön avspeglade i marinarkeologiskt källmaterial*. Doctoral dissertation, Stockholm University. Helsinki: The Finnish Society of Sciences and Letters.

Ahlström, C. 1997. *Looking for Leads – shipwrecks of the past revealed by contemporary documents and archaeological record*. Helsinki: The Finnish Society of Sciences and Letters.

Åkerhagen, A. 2009. *Kritpipor funna i Sverige och på Åland*, unpublished report (CD).

Andrén, A. 1998. *Between Artifacts and Texts: Historical Archaeology in Global Perspective* (trans. Alan Crozier). New York: Plenum Publishing.

Bollnow, O. F. 1994. Vara-i-rum och ha-rum. Swedish translation by William Fovet and Björn Sandmark, chapter 1, part V, in Mench und Raum. *Nordisk Arkitekturforskning*, 1/94.

Cederlund, C.O. 1983a. *The Old Wrecks of the Baltic Sea*. BAR International Series 186. Oxford: BAR.

Cederlund, C.O. 1983b. *Vraket vid Jutholmen – fartygets byggnad*, Statens Sjöhistoriska museum rapport 19. Stockholm: National Maritime Museum.

Cederlund, C.O. 1997. *Nationalism eller vetenskap: svensk marinarkeologi i ideologisk belysning*. Stockholm: Carlssons.

Chapman, F. H. 1768. *Architectura Navalis Mercatoria*. Stockholm. (Reprint 1971. London: Adlard Coles)

Deetz, J. 1977. *In Small Things Forgotten – the Archaeology of early American life*. New York.

Eriksdotter, G. 2005. *Bakom fasaderna: Byggnadsarkeologiska sätt att fånga tid, rum och bruk*, Lund studies in Medieval Archaeology 36, Lund: Almqvist & Wiksell International.

Eriksson, N. 2010. *Jutholmsvraket – ett handelsfartyg från sent 1600-tal*. Sjöhistoriska museet, Arkeologisk rapport 2010:1. Stockholm: National Maritime Museum.

Eriksson, N. 2012a. Recording a large three-dimensional ship-structure – thoughts rendered from the Dalarö-wreck project, In: J.C. Henderson (ed.) *Beyond Boundaries*. The 3rd International Congress on Underwater Archaeology, IKUWA 3, London 2008. Römisch-Germanische Kommission.

Eriksson, N. 2012b. The Lion Wreck: a survey of a 17th-century Dutch merchant ship—an interim report. *International Journal of Nautical Archaeology* 41.1: 17-25.

Eriksson, N. The Edesö Wreck: the hull of a small, armed ship wrecked in the Stockholm archipelago in the latter half of the 17th century, *The International Journal of Nautical Archaeology* (in press).

Eriksson, N. & Rönnby, J. 2012. 'The Ghost Ship'. An Intact *Fluyt* from *c.*1650 in the Middle of the Baltic Sea. *International Journal of Nautical Archaeology* 41.2: 350–361.

Fahlander, F. 2010. The Nose, the Eye, the Mouth and the Gut: Social Dimensions of Food-Cravings and Commensality. In: F. Fahlander, & A. Kjellström (eds) *Making Sense of Things: Archaeologies of Sensory Perception*. Stockholm Studies in Archaeology 53: 35-50. Stockholm: Stockholm University.

Glassie, H. 1983. *Folkhousing in middle Virginia – a structural analysis of historic artifacts*. Tennesse: Univ. of Tennessee Press.

Giles, K. 2007. Seeing and Believing: Visuality and Space in Pre-Modern England. *World Archaeology* (*Viewing Space*) 39.1: 105-121.

Goodwin, L. 2002. Everyday Life, In: C. Orser (ed.) *Encyclopedia of Historical Archaeology*: 188-190. London & New York: Routledge.

Hacking, I. 1999. Making up people, In: M. Biagioli, (ed.) *The Science Studies reader*. London and New York: Routledge.

Hanson, J. (ed.) 2003. *Decoding homes and houses*. Cambridge: Cambridge University Press.

Harland, J. 2011. The Whipstaff. *The Mariner's Mirror*, Vol. 97.1: 97-102.

Hillier, B. & Hanson, J. 1989. *The Social Logic of Space*. Cambridge: Cambridge University Press.

Hocker, F. & Vlierman, K. 1996. *A small cog wrecked on the Zuiderzee in the early fifteenth century*. Excavation Report 19. Flevobericht 408. NISA, Lelystad.

Hoving, A. 1995. Seagoing Ships of the Netherlands, In: R. Gardiner & P. Bosscher (eds) *The Heyday of Sail – The Merchant Sailing Ship 1650-1850*. (Conway's History of the Ship). London: Conway Maritime Press.

Ingelman-Sundberg, C. 1976. Preliminary report on finds from the Jutholmen wreck, *International Journal of Nautical Archaeology and Underwater Exploration* 5: 57-71.

Johnson, M. 1996. *An Archaeology of Capitalism*. Oxford: Blackwell.

Johnson, M. 2002. *Behind the castle gate: from Medieval to Renaissance*. London & New York: Routledge.

Kaijser, I. 1983. *Vraket vid Jutholmen, dokumentation*

last och utrustning. Stockholm: National Maritime Museum.

Landon, D. 2002. Food and foodways, In: C. Orser ed. *Encyclopedia of Historical Archaeology:* 220-221. London & New York: Routledge.

Landström, B. 1980. *Regalskeppet Vasan – från början till slutet.* Stockholm: Interpublishing.

Lavery, B. 1981. *Deane's Doctrine of Naval Architecture, 1670.* London: Conway Maritime Press.

Lübeck, O. (ed.) 1942. *Svenska flottans historia 1.* Stockholm.

Laughton, C. L. 2001 (1925). *Old Ship Figure-heads and Sterns.* Mineola.

Lemée, C. 2006. *The Renaissance shipwrecks from Christianshavn: an archaeological and architectural study of large carvel vessels in Danish waters, 1580-1640.* Ships and boats of the North, 6. Roskilde: The Viking Ship Museum.

Markus, T. 1992. On re-discovering space – a critical editorial summary. *Nordic journal of architectural research* 2: 7-10.

Marsden, P. 2003. *Sealed by Time. The loss and Recovery of the Mary Rose.* The Archaeology of the Mary Rose Vol 1. Trowbridge: Mary Rose Trust.

Muckelroy, K. 1978. *Maritime Archaeology:* Cambridge: Cambridge University press.

Munday, J. 1978. Heads and tails: The necessary seating, In: P. Annis (ed.) *Ingrid and other studies.* National Maritime Museum Monographs and Reports 36: 125-140. Greenwich: National Maritime Museum.

Nagbøl, S. 1983. Makt och arkitektur – försök till en upplevelseanalytisk arkitekturtolkning, *Magasin Tessin: Tidskrift för arkitektur, estetik och miljökritik* 2.

Ossowski, W. 2008. Archaeological underwater excavation of wreck W-32, In: W. Ossowski et al. (eds) *The General Carleton Shipwreck, 1785.* Gdansk: Centralne Muzeum Morskie.

Pipping, O. 2003. Whipstaff and Helmsman. An Account of the Steering-gear of the Vasa, In: C. Beltrame (ed.) *Boats, Ships and Shipyards.* Proceedings of the Ninth International Symposium on Boat and Ship Archaeology, Venice. Oxford: Oxbow Books.

Pomey, P. 2004. Principles and Methods of Construction in Ancient Naval Architecture, In: F. Hocker & C. Ward (eds) *The Philosophy of Shipbuilding: Conceptional approaches to the study of wooden ships.* College Station: Texas A&M University Press.

van Royen, P.C. 1992. Seamen and the Merchant Service, 1650-1830, In: R. Gardiner (ed.) *The Heyday of Sail. The Merchant Sailing Ship 1650-1830.* (Conway's History of the Ship). London: Conway Maritime Press.

Rådberg, J. 1998. Atlantångaren och den moderna staden – maskinmetaforen som ledbild i stadsbyggandet, In: R. Pettersson & S. Sörlin (eds) *Miljön och det förflutna – landskap, minnen, värden*: 142-153. Umeå.

Rålamb, Å.C. 1691. *Skeps byggerij Eller Adelig Öfnings Tionde Tom, Medh behörige Kopparstycken.* Stockholm. (reprinted 1943).

Rönnby, J. 2003. En flygande holländare i Oxelösund. *Kulturell mångfald i Södermanland,* 2: 123-130.

Rönnby, J. & Adams, J. 1994. *Östersjöns sjunkna skepp. En marinarkeologisk tidsresa,* Stockholm: Tiden.

Simmons, J. 1997. *Those Vulgar Tubes, External Sanitary Accommodations aboard European Ships of the Fifteenth through Seventeenth Centuries (Studies in Nautical Archaeology).* Texas A&M University Press. College Station TX.

Smolarek, P. 1985. The development of the archaeology of boats and ships in Poland, In: C.O. Cederlund (ed.) *Postmedieval Boat and Ship Archaeology, Papers based on those presented to an International Symposium on Boat and Ship Archaeology.* Report 20. Stockholm: Swedish National Maritime Museum.

Sutherland, W. 1711. *The Ship-builders Assistant; or, some Essays Towards Compleating the ART of Marine Architecture.* London.

Sutherland, W. 1717 (2011). *Britain's Glory; or, Ship-building unvail'd, being A General Director, for Building and Compleating the said Machines.* London.

Tilley, C. 1994. *A Phenomenology of landscape, Places, Paths and Monuments.* Oxford: Berg.

Trievald, M. 1734. *Konsten at Lefwa under Watn.* Stockholm (Facsmile edition: Anders Engwall).

Turner, A., Doxa, M., O'Sullivan, D. & Penn, A. 2001. From isovists to visibility graphs: a methodology for the analysis of architectural space. *Environment and Planning B: Planning and Design* 28: 103-21.

Unger, R.W. 1994. The Fluit: Specialist Cargo Vessels 1500 to 1650, In: R. Gardiner (ed.) *Cogs, Caravels and Galleons. The sailing ship 1000-1650.* (Conway's History of the Ship). London: Conway Maritime Press.

Upton, D. 2002. Architecture in Everyday Life. *New Literary History* 33.4: 707-723.

Witsen, N. 1671 (1979). *Aeoloude En Hedendaegshe Scheeps-Bouw en Bestier.* Amsterdam.

9

The Sovereign's Cabin: Material Culture and Symbolic expression. A case study of the wooden sculptures and wall panelling in the great cabin and stern gallery of the warship *Vasa* of 1628

Shaun Wallace

The great cabin of the warship *Vasa* was adorned as a palace-like room rather than a ship's cabin, containing over seventy wooden sculptures. The herm pilasters and console heads certainly held symbolic meaning, as did the exterior sculptures of the ship. Why was so much money spent on the cabin? Who was its intended audience? How was the great cabin decorated and why? A study of the archaeological remains within their wider maritime and decorative historical context, can give the reasons for the designing and building of this highly decorative and expensive cabin. The "Sovereign's Cabin" is a demonstration of the complex role of material culture as symbolic expression onboard a ship.

Research scope

In order to establish the original placements of the oak wood carvings found on or near the floor of the great cabin and stern gallery of the warship *Vasa* during its recovery, it was necessary to study the archaeological remains in combination with the photographs and database records held at the Vasa Museum, as well as information connected to the excavation of the ships interior (Cederlund & Hocker 2006). The woodcarvings consist of herm pilasters, console heads, lintels and herm pilaster doorposts or tall pilasters, and hypotheses exist as to how the cabin would have looked (Soop 1992; Landström 1988). The *Vasa* Museum's current life-size cabin reconstruction is based on photographic evidence from a 1978 reconstruction. The latter made use of the most well preserved pilasters and console heads, although no attempt was made to determine their original positions.

The great cabin and stern gallery were where most

of the interior wooden sculptures were found. In order to determine the function of the carvings and whether or not the imagery used had symbolic meaning or was merely used according to contemporary workmanship or trends, it was necessary to look further than to other ships of the time. Due to a lack of contemporary maritime archaeological material, one must instead look to the style of decoration found in contemporary castle and palace state rooms and northern European churches, these being places where a wood panelling and sculpture style similar to that established within the *Vasa* can be found.

The study also investigated what the woodcarvings can tell us about power, status and division of space, and whether or not the decoration of the great cabin and stern gallery may have been unique in a contemporary European warship context.

Ship cabin decoration of the 17th century

Little is known about 17th century cabin decoration. In order to attempt to understand the symbolism that may have been attached to it during the late Renaissance/early Baroque period in Sweden, it is necessary to consider the influence of the previous two centuries. During this time, European symbolic religious art, which had taken the form of paintings, etchings, carvings, sculptures and other expressive images based on human ideology, in attempting to influence the ways people thought, became increasingly secular, plausibly linked to the reformation of the church.

Ecclesiastical art as a whole was designed to tell stories to the largely illiterate population in comprehensible and visually striking terms (Day 2003:

9). Interior wall paintings, as well as the skilfully carved expressions on the gargoyles adorning the outside of the buildings, would have added to this atmosphere (Figs 9.1 & 9.2). By the time of the late Renaissance/early Baroque the influence of the Reformation would have led to a general decline in religious art being used even on the European ships of the period. One exception was in Catholic countries where religious artwork was still being widely used.

The few archaeological remains from timber framed warships of the period include the odd railing decorations, figureheads, single stern ornaments and coats-of-arms. This is probably due to the working

life cycle of a warship often being not only brief, but sometimes even violent, due to bad weather, being caught on the rocks while navigating through uncharted waters, or being set on fire or sunk. The wood of which it was made was considerably less durable than stone, brick, porcelain or metal.

In order to aid reconstruction of the great cabin of *Vasa*, the archaeological remains were looked at in combination with other representational evidence of the period including ship models, etchings, paintings and drawings, although there is a lack of relevant maritime pictorial evidence regarding the interior decoration of ships.

Figure 9.1.
A warning to blasphemers in the 15th century. Wall painting in Corby Glen Church, Lincolnshire, England (photo: author).

Figure 9.2. Gargoyle from the north wing, St. Andrews Church, Heckington, Lincolnshire, England (photo: author).

Cabin design and placement

With a lack of comparative material to the 17th century *Vasa* cabin, the only existing great cabin reconstruction with which any slight comparisons can be drawn is the Swedish *Kronan*. One of the largest warships of the century, *Kronan* was built by an Englishman, Francis Sheldon the elder, the ship differing from the dominating Dutch style of the *Vasa*, its hull being more V-shaped and with a less lofty stern (Einarsson 2001:18). *Kronan* was launched in 1668, forty years after the *Vasa*, and therefore the interior can already be identified as being later Baroque (Einarsson 2001:28) with more gilding than is presumed would have been in the *Vasa* interior. As can be seen in figure 9.3, there is a use of wall panelling with column pilasters and sculptures, and the light blue colour used on the walls is not necessarily accurate. From what is already known about its exterior, the interior sculptures of the *Vasa* would have instead been painted in bright, natural colours.

The great cabin of the *Vasa* was approximately 14m long. It had originally been completely panelled, using herm pilasters, console heads, decorated panel rails and built-in benches with fold-down berths along all the walls. Towards the port side of the wall to the fore was a door leading into the helmsman's cabin. A light transverse bulkhead with a doorway towards the starboard side of the aft wall provided access to the stern gallery behind. The stern gallery was about 2.3m long and overhung the transom and the head of the rudder.

It provided access to the quarter galleries via doors on either side and to the upper cabin by a staircase on the port side (Fig. 9.4), and had built-in lockers on both sides (Cederlund & Hocker 2006:311).

Swedish Stately Mansions, Castles and Churches

Pilasters and herm pilasters are visible in a number of kinds of interior, the space between the pilasters often housed by panelling. Some rooms in Swedish stately mansions have wall panelling and framing of a simple design and others incorporate more elaborate sculptures into the pilasters.

The Gentleman's Room (often mistakenly called Gustav Vasa's study room) in the tower accommodation at Rydboholm was designed for Per Brahe the elder, nephew to Gustav Vasa, in 1548, and is one of Sweden's oldest existing Renaissance interiors. The painted illustration in the wall panelling was meant to depict true ancestors, a practice continuing until the end of the 17th century (Bedoire 2004:57). There is more brick wall in evidence here than wood panelling, and in later interiors more panelling and imagery can be found.

An example of this development can be seen at Gripsholm Castle. Duke Karl's bedroom from around the 1570s, has benches, panelling and painted flower and fruit decoration around the walls. Unlike the gentleman's room at Rydboholm, there is no depiction of ancestors, instead rather a variation on a theme. The use of pilasters on the outside of each frame can be seen, as well as smaller pilasters with top and bottom wooden decorations inside the frame panelling. By the end of the 16th century, additional wooden pilasters were being used.

More examples of panelling and pilasters with varying degrees of decoration can be seen in two rooms from Kalmar Castle. Rutsalen was designed some time shortly after 1553, and Erik XIV's chamber was created in 1562. Rutsalen, with veneered panelling, was Queen Katarina Jagellonica's living room, and possibly designed by the chief builder at the castle, Domenicus Pahrs. Erik XIV's chamber is considered one of Northern Europes finest Renaissance veneered rooms and includes panelling by the German architect Hans Blum (Bedoire 2004:54). Similar pilaster sculptures can be seen on fireplaces at Skokloster Castle and Skara Cathedral, and are similar to those found on the *Vasa*.

Following the Thirty Years War, and on the return of the Swedish nobility, interiors continued to develop in lavishness. The diary author, Lorenzo Magalotti from Florence, Italy, wrote that he was amazed at the affluence and ostentation surrounding the Swedish stately mansions (Kylsberg 2006:6-7).

Figure 9.3. A full scale reconstruction of the admiral's cabin on the upper deck of 'Kronan' (Einarsson 2001:45).

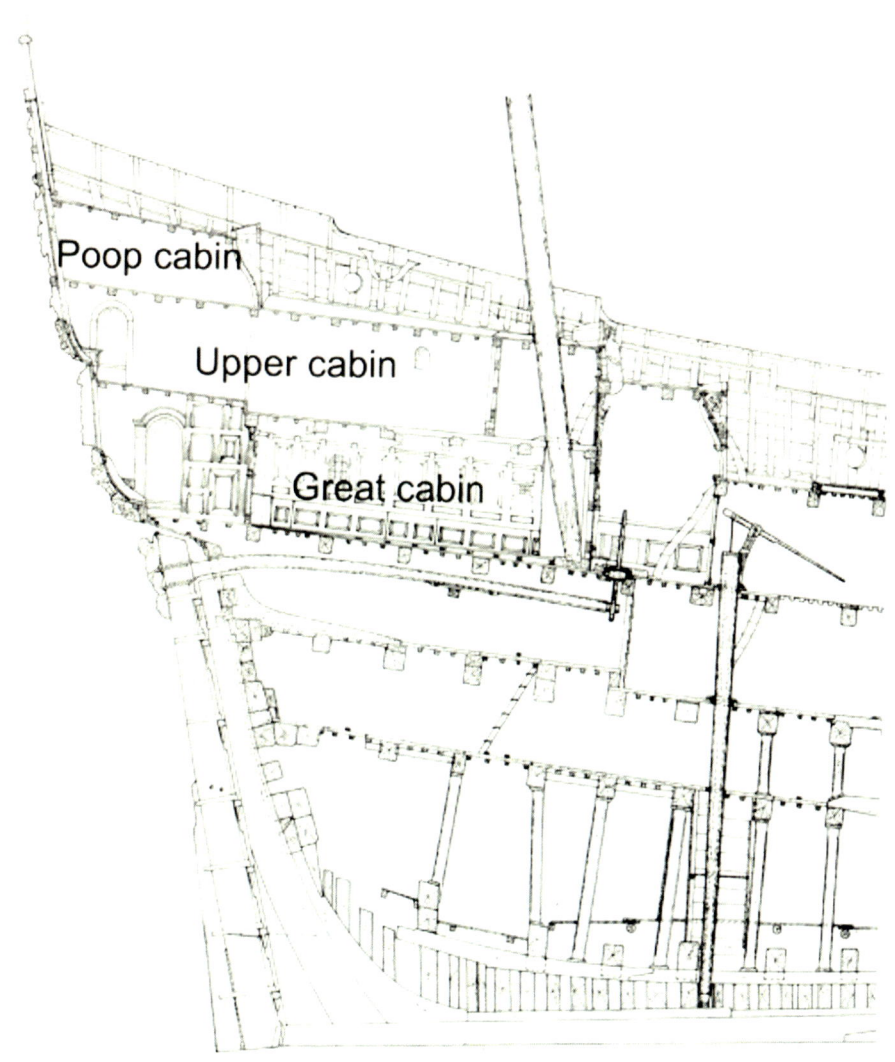

Figure 9.4. Longitudinal section of Vasa's sterncastle, showing the three principal cabins (based on Cederlund & Hocker 2006:166).

Cabinets, chests and church pilasters

Examples of herm pilasters and panelling can be seen in a number of Northern European churches from around the same time as the building of the *Vasa*. An example of some of the best remaining herm pilasters similar to those found in the great cabin of the Vasa can be seen at Gårdstånga Church, Stockholm, also known as the German Church.

In the German Church, we find what is possibly the closest reference material to show what the walls may have looked like in *Vasa*'s great cabin (Fig. 9.5). Although created 1659–1665, the particular structure or use of the framing is similar to that on the warship, a console head being separated by herm pilasters, and with wood decoration between each framed biblical picture. The carved foliage and fruit motifs are also similar. Many of the herm pilasters run in a male-female-male-female pattern, although on the opposite side of this balcony there are herm pilasters that show a different pattern, for example with a male-male or female-female combination. Also within this balustrade, above the pilasters, are console heads that are smaller than those found in the great cabin, and the herm pilasters in this example are gilded, along with the framing and console heads. One of the herm pilasters in the German Church has what looks like the face of a demon on it, and this is very similar to one of the herm pilasters from the *Vasa* great cabin.

The archaeological remains

The herm pilasters, console heads, tall pilasters and lintels believed to be originally placed in the great cabin, stern cabin and entrance to the great cabin (from the helmsman's cabin) were studied in the Vasa Museum magazine rooms. A number of measurements were taken and plans of the finds' locations made following the salvage were studied. Photographs were taken and corresponding descriptions made.

The herm pilasters – pairs and singles

All the *Vasa* herm pilasters are made of oak, are approximately one metre in length, and were located in, or just outside, the great cabin. Some of them are very badly worn, although it is still possible to make out some of the markings that can help identify the kind of decoration or meaning they may have had. The thirty-one herm pilasters (which excludes one herm pilaster apparently misplaced after the recovery of the ship) can be divided into thirteen pairs of similar decoration plus five singles. The singles were either meant to be single or they have been unable to be identified as matched with another. Clues as to the original placement of the pilasters include the 'drop location' recorded during the recovery of the ship, identification of the original holes via which they were attached to the wall panelling, and the angle at which the base of the pilaster was made. For example, if the base of a herm pilaster slants up to the right, it may indicate a placement on the port side of the cabin, following the angle of the deck. An example of a herm pilaster pair can be seen in figure 9.6.

Conclusions

This research examined the archaeological remains from the great cabin and stern gallery of the warship *Vasa* (including the entrance to the great cabin from the helmsman's cabin) in order to identify how they would have originally been arranged and what meanings would have been portrayed. This was approached against a historical backdrop lacking in comparative contemporary maritime archaeological material. However, some model, print and painting

Figure 9.5. German Church, Stockholm (photo: author)

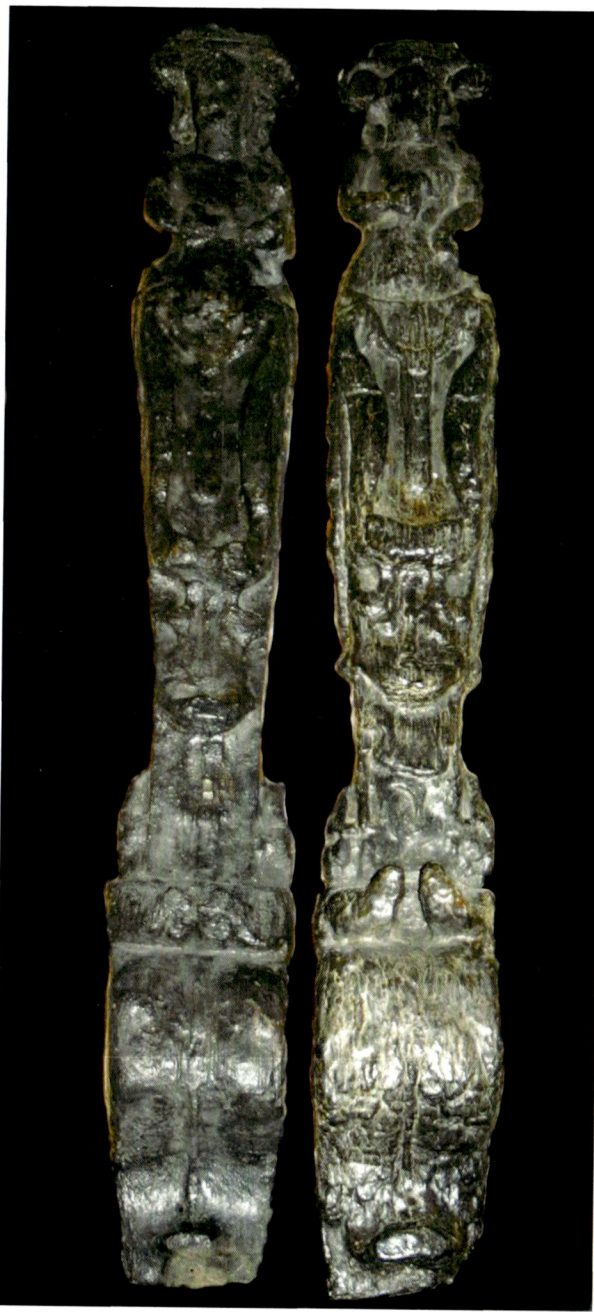

Figure 9.6. Herm pilasters (photo: author).

about the archaeological remains of the *Vasa*.

We know that the exterior of the *Vasa* was painted in bright, natural colours and that the exterior sculptures drew on several influences from classical Greek and Roman mythology as well as heraldic sources, giving us clues about the imagery used in the great cabin and stern gallery. Another source of information has been provided through actual or pictorial visits to a number of contemporary castles, stately homes, palace state rooms and northern European churches, in order to examine the wood panelling decoration style that has proved to be similar to that established on the *Vasa*. Even though some of the most similar herm pilasters and console heads are found in the German Church, Stockholm, their woodcarving differences lead to the suggestion that a contemporary master craftsman's book or catalogue of sculptures could have been in existence. That sculptural thematic ideas were chosen by a designer from such a book is not unthinkable. It is also interesting that some of the sculptures on the organ originally built for the German Church and now housed in Övertorneå Church were crafted by Mårten Redtmer, identified as Mester Mårten on the payroll of the *Vasa* as one of its woodcarvers.

The design of the benches at Gripsholm Castle is not dissimilar to that of the benches in the great cabin of the *Vasa*, and the development of wall panelling and decoration from less to more in the second half of the 16th century was certainly reflected in the use of more sculptures by the time the *Vasa* was built, state room adornment very probably having an impact on the decoration of ships' great cabins. Another source of comparative information was provided by the only existing great cabin reconstruction of a ship from the 17th century, *Kronan*, although *Kronan* was launched some forty years after the *Vasa*, and it has been identified as having a later Baroque interior, presumably more gilded than the *Vasa* great cabin would have been. The evidence found in Swedish stately mansions, castles and churches leads to the conclusion that design fashion from both the Netherlands and Germany had an influence on the interior design of the *Vasa*. As the wall panelling between herm pilasters was often painted with coats of arms, flowers or other scenes, any evidence that may be found through possible future paint analysis on the interior archaeological remains of the *Vasa* will be of great interest.

The great cabin represented the boundary between the classes on board ship, and it also follows that the decoration would have been designed with upper ranks and upper social class visitors in mind. Based on what is known about the great cabin and the similarities between the Swedish navy and the class system in the British navy, the senior officers of the *Vasa* were also

evidence from the 16th and 17th centuries helped to show a progression from painted adornment in the early 16th century to more sculptural decoration in the 17th century, representing an explanation as to why warships of the period became more embellished amidst possible rivalry between master shipwrights. It also appears that the most lavishly decorated part of the ship in this period was the stern, due to this being the accommodation and main working area of the officers. However, so far no artwork has been found that documents the decoration inside a ships cabin, in order to be able to compare this with what is known

to the giving of ideas, as well as the projection of values and opinions, not unlike the function of a modern billboard or television advertisement. The use of such symbolic decorative function within the *Vasa* points us in the direction of another function – that the great cabin was intended as a mobile royal court for the King when on board, a place where it was possible to hold council and entertain the upper classes or show off the wealth of the country to foreign nobility and diplomats. It was meant to be a home from home in times of war, giving the sovereign power, status and the ability to relax in relative comfort. That it was decorated as a stateroom rather than a cabin would have made it different from other warships of the period.

Acknowledgements

I would like to thank Dr. Fred Hocker, Director of Vasa Research, for his guidance and for allowing my research to take place at the Vasa Museum, and my supervisor at Södertörns Högskola, Professor Johan Rönnby.

Thanks also to the following people: Hans Soop, Stockholm, for his insight into the *Vasa* sculptures and cabin design; Diederick Wildeman, Curator of Navigation and Library Collections, VOC, Amsterdam; Anton Oortwijn, Scheepvaartmuseum, Amsterdam; Marcel Kroon, Maritiem Museum, Rotterdam; Pia Melin, Statens Historiska Museum, Stockholm; Bengt Kylsberg, Museum Curator, Skoklosters Castle, for his guided tour; Lars W. Andersson, Museum Curator, Kalmar Castle, for his museum images; Tina Björkbacka, The Royal Palace, Stockholm, for room design information; Lars Einarsson, *Kronan*, Kalmar, for project information; Lena Palmqvist, Nordiska Museet, Stockholm, and Ab Hoving, Dr. Frits Scholten and Paul van Duin from the Rijksmuseum, Amsterdam, for their help regarding contemporary interior decoration.

References

Bedoire, F. 2004. *Svenska slott och herrgårdar; en historisk reseguide.* Stockholm: Bonnier.

Cederlund, O.C. & Hocker, F. 2006. *Vasa I; the archaeology of a Swedish warship of 1628.* Stockholm: National Maritime Museums of Sweden.

Day, E. 2003. Revealed: the medieval church fresco depicting Judgement-Day in Coventry. *The Sunday Telegraph*, 21st December.

Einarsson, L. 2001. *Kronan.* Kalmar: Sund Tryck AB.

Kylsberg, B. 2001. *Sekelringar: klosterkyrkan på Sko.* Värnamo: Fälth & Hässler.

Landström, B. 1988. *The royal warship Vasa.* Stockholm: Interpublishing.

Soop, H. 1992. *The power and the glory: the sculptures of the warship Wasa.* Uddevalla: Bohusläningens Boktryckeri AB.

10

Things on Board. The Interpretation of Three 18th Century Shipwrecks from the Gulf of Finland

Riikka Alvik

In this article I will present three shipwrecks dating from the Age of Enlightenment, and will discuss possible research perspectives from which to view them and their sites. The wrecks were once merchant ships destined for St. Petersburg in Russia. This was the town founded by Tzar Peter the Great in 1703 as a new strategic seaport, and a 'bridge' to Europe, and was a fast developing, lively city. By combining written sources and archaeological studies, it is possible to offer a more complete story of the three ships: *St. Michel, Vrouw Maria* and *De Catherina,* even more so when considering them together as part of a historical and cultural continuum. In conclusion, I will suggest various approaches to the artefacts on board, and the cargoes carried by these ships; material which represented more than economic value, revealing also a new ideology and way of thinking. Ships and seafaring were important means of spreading trends and innovations from Western Europe to Russia.

Historical background

During the early 17th century seafaring had developed into a global activity. Ships from countries such as England and the Netherlands transported goods from India, China and South America, and traded them further on to Europe. New cities and ports grew rapidly around the world and one of the most important was St. Petersburg. This city was a destination for colonial and European merchandise and the ships transported back the raw materials and food supplies needed in Western Europe such as rye and wheat.

In this 'Age of Enlightenment', science, philosophy and the arts were highly appreciated among the upper classes of European society and education was a desired accomplishment. The founding of St. Petersburg by Tzar Peter had military and strategic reasons, but it also sprang from his ambition to change and reform Russian society. He desired to develop the country in a European manner and elevate its levels of culture and education. Foreign merchants soon established themselves in the city which included German, English and Dutch settlements (North and Snapper 1990:263-266). St. Petersburg, and also the old port of Archangel in the North, became important places for trade to other parts of Russia such as Moscow (Gelderblom 2003:96-97).

To get to St Petersburg required sailing through the Gulf of Finland, a dangerous route due to a lack of proper marine charts and the rudimentary navigation equipment carried aboard most ships (Ahlström 2000a:11-19). Many merchantmen went astray and sank in what are today Finnish territorial waters. The shipwreck register of Finland lists 57 wrecks that date roughly to the 18th century. It is three of these wrecks that are the focus for this case study: the *St. Michel,* the *Vrouw Maria* and the *De Catherina;* which all sank between 1747 and 1782. Towards the end of the 18th century some sectors of the once strong Dutch tradition of shipbuilding were beginning to stagnate. However, all three merchant ships in this study represent the Dutch trade at this period in the Baltic, which although less significant than that of the British by this time, Gelderblom (2003:98) suggests that Dutch ships still accounted for the majority of carriage in some routes.

Presentation of the wrecks

St. Michel

The merchant ship, *St. Michel,* was on her way from Amsterdam to St. Petersburg in the autumn of 1747 when she sank near the island of Borstö in the archipelago of Finland. In the 1950s local fishermen complained that their nets were catching at a depth of 30-40 meters. In 1956 marine divers located an extremely well preserved wreck which was named 'Borstö I' from her location. She was lying on her keel on the seabed with all three masts still standing. The find was officially announced to the National Board of Antiquities in 1958 and it soon became known as a sensational wreck on account of its well-preserved cargo and the excellent state of its hull. It was even compared to the Swedish warship *Vasa* and raising it was discussed (Åbo Underrättelser 6.10.1957 and 6.8.1961, HS 30.5.1965, Suomen sosiaalidemokraatti 5.9.1961). The notion was also conceived that the jewellery recovered from the wreck was intended for Catherine the Great (Uusi Suomi 27.4.1971).

The artefacts contained in the wreck date to the mid 18th century. The ship type and form (probably a galliot) indicate that it was Dutch. The divers found a great many items including ceramics (Fig. 10.1) and other luxury items such as snuff boxes, watches, dishes, and personal belongings of the crew. Human bones

were also discovered. In the early 1960s an exceptional find consisting of parts of a two-wheeled horse-drawn carriage, were salvaged by divers from the cargo hold (Hbl 8.9.1961, Uusi Suomi 16.2.1964). The ship's cargo originated in different parts of Europe and included colonial goods such as dyes and tobacco. This was a very typical combination for Russian transport (cf. e.g. Jonker & Sluyterman 2000:39).

Despite the vast number of artefacts found, tracing the ship's identity was not an easy task. Archival research carried out by Christian Ahlström has indicated how important it is to find exact dates and origins for the artefacts on board. Ahlström followed several leads in his research, such as the French origin for both the lead seals on the cloth, and the mysterious horse-drawn carriages. One clue was found in Åbo where Ahlström unearthed an auction protocol from 1748 regarding a salvaged sea-chest. The list of contents included religious literature in German and French. Clearly a foreign ship had been in difficulties in the archipelago in 1747. Despite this, no records of any sunken ship could be traced (Ahlström 2005:88-92).

A stronger indication of the identity of the wreck was a letter concerning a horse-drawn carriage bought for the Russian Empress Elizabeth I. The letter was found in the Sound Toll Register archives. The Russian ambassador to Denmark was requesting a free passage or a return of the toll payment for a carriage transported

Figure 10.1. Meissen porcelain vessels from wreck of St. Michel. (Photo: National Board of Antiquities)

by ship under the direction of shipmaster Carl P. Amiel. A response to the letter from the King of Denmark, instructed the toll officers to repay the fee because the horse-drawn carriage was intended for the personal use of the Russian empress. At that time it was customary that royal courts were exempt from custom charges. The name of the ship was not mentioned, but the name of its captain led to a ship called *St. Michel*. This evidence was found in Amsterdam, among records of ships required to pay a certain fee called '*galjootsgeld*' (galliot money) when entering Amsterdam (Ahlström 2005: 92-97).

The question of the home harbour of the *St. Michel* proved to be interesting. In the Amsterdam records captain Amiel's home city is given as Amsterdam, but in the Sound Customs register the *St. Michel* is mentioned as a Russian ship (Ahlström 2005:93,97). The ship possibly sailed under a Russian flag or had some connection with Russia; maybe her owners lived in St. Petersburg.

Oddly, no written evidence of the capsizing of the *St. Michel* has been found; the ship and its cargo just seem to have disappeared. If this ship is *St Michel*, most likely no one survived. However the ship's boat is missing, so an attempt may have been made to escape from the sinking vessel. Some human bones were found on the wreck, along with the skull of a small dog which makes this ship a grave site as well (Bojner 1965; Telkkä 1962; Ericsson 1970).

Unfortunately for archaeological analysis, the first lifting of artefacts from the wreck was more a matter of salvage than retrieval for research and valuable information has probably been lost. When the horse-drawn carriage was put on exhibition in the Maritime Museum of Finland in 2008, it was discovered that not all the pieces fitted together and that there were probably two carriages, a model and one intended for use (Mäntynen pers. comm.). Most parts of the carriage were salvaged at the beginning of the 1960s. They were found in the cargo hold and kitchen area, but we only have written descriptions of these locations (Bojner 1965). Today the *St. Michel* is a protected site and only scientific diving is permitted. Though much cargo was salvaged there are still a large number of artefacts, and perhaps even human remains, inside the ship's hull and on the seabed alongside.

These questions emphasise that, even if this is the *St Michel*, the story is not yet complete. Not only is there more work required on the recovered material but further research could be carried out on the wreck. Neither have the Russian written sources been studied yet and these, together with other information still being located in the Sound toll records may clarify the intriguing anomalies referred to above.

Vrouw Maria

The master of the Dutch merchant ship *Vrouw Maria* was Reynoud Lourens. He was experienced and highly esteemed despite his young age (24 or 25 when the *Vrouw Maria* sank). His name appears in several documents concerning the *Vrouw Maria* and another ship, the *Johanna en Pieter*. According to these documents he sailed to St.Petersburg annually in the late 1760s and carried the goods of 34 merchants on the final voyage of the *Vrouw Maria* in 1771 (Gelderblom 2003: 100-101).

Her cargo on this fateful trip consisted of zinc, mercury, dyestuffs, sugar, coffee beans and cloth, as well as provisions such as cheese, butter and fish. From other sources it is known that the ship carried valuable items of art belonging to the Russian Empress Catherine the Great and the Russian Prince Gallitzin (Gelderblom 2003: 101). These were paintings bought at an art auction held earlier in Amsterdam. They had belonged to the then deceased Dutch merchant and art collector Gerrit Braamcamp. (Ahlström 2000a:26; Gelderblom 2003:101-104).

When the *Vrouw Maria* reached the Gulf of Finland it strayed off route and struck rocks in the Finnish archipelago. The ship lost her rudder and began letting in water. Master Lourens and nine crew members tried to save the ship and her cargo for several days, staying overnight on a tiny island nearby. Local men representing the Northern Diving and Salvage Company helped in this task. While silver, ship's equipment and luxury items including paintings were salvaged, most of the cargo was lost. The coffee beans filled the pumps and the hold soon filled with water. On the fifth day the ship sank. The captain and crew, with salvaged cargo and some equipment belonging to the ship, were transported to Turku (Åbo). The value of the salvaged goods was assessed and the ship's equipment and the shipmaster's cargo were sold at auction in Turku. The rest of the salvaged cargo was transported to St. Petersburg after negotiations between the Swedish authorities and representatives of the cargo's owners in Russia.

The Russian nobility was very anxious to retrieve their lost paintings and initiated correspondence with the Swedish authorities immediately on receiving news of the accident (Gelderblom 2003: 114). According to the records, at least 11 paintings went down with the ship. In 1772 a number of failed attempts were made to locate her and salvage her submerged cargo. But the ship remained lost for more than 200 years. In the early 1970s archival documents were discovered by Ahlström and the wreck was located by him in 1999, in co-operation with a group of divers who searched the area with a side-scan sonar. The two-masted, snow-rigged ship lies almost intact on her keel at a depth of 41 m on the seabed (Fig. 10.2). The upper deck and stern were damaged when it went down, and also during the salvage operations carried out while the ship was still afloat. Only a few artefacts have been retrieved, to help towards its correct identification.

A number of written sources exist concerning the *Vrouw Maria,* from the date she was sold to her last owner until the day she sank off the Finnish coast. These include the sea protest and ship's log of the days surrounding the accident, written by shipmaster Lourens, and the list of salvaged cargo and the auction protocol of the salvaged items sold in Turku. The diplomatic correspondence about the lost art is housed in archives in Stockholm (Ahlström 2000b:8-12).

In the case of the sinking of the *Vrouw Maria* the process after the accident is fairly well known from the written sources, offering an interesting glimpse of jurisdiction in practice with regard to a shipwreck in Swedish waters. According to Swedish law it was the duty of the salvage companies to assist in cases of shipwreck. Off the Finnish coast this would fall on the Northern Diving and Salvage Company. Locals participated in these operations and were led by the

local authorities, a diving commissioner. Companies were entitled to a 25% commission on salvaged cargo, making a successful salvage operation a profitable venture.

By comparing different written sources it is clear that the sugar, zinc, most of the dyestuffs and the Tzarina's paintings are missing and are most likely still in the cargo hold of the sunken ship. Several goods mentioned in the list of salvaged items are not mentioned in the toll registers. These include tobacco, coffee, tea and books. Indeed, during research conducted in 2010-2012, coffee beans, indigo, grapes, pumice, madder and several other items were found. Some of these correlate with the Sound Toll Records or the list of salvaged items such as the salvaged coffee which was sold in St. Petersburg in 1772. Other items are not mentioned in the written sources at all, for example the tobacco pipes (Fig. 10.3) and glass lenses, which are still visible in the cargo hold (Ahlström 2000:7-11; Gelderblom 2003:104-105, 109-111; Leino 2004:8).

The National Board of Antiquities has surveyed and monitored the site since 2000. There have been discussions in the media about lifting the wreck in order to carry out an archaeological excavation inside her hull. Although an enormous undertaking this would naturally be very interesting should sufficient resources be made available.

De Catherina

The Dutch merchant ship, *De Catherina,* sank off Ekenäs in 1782. Her cargo consisted of roof tiles and mixed goods. According to the ship's protocol, the owner of the ship was Thomas Gotthard Sabeck who lived in St. Petersburg. Most of the cargo was owned by the traders Michael Falejeff and Henrik Bt.von Lilaer from St. Petersburg (Ahlström 1997:163-167). The cargo also included silver that belonged to the merchant Lodewijck Hovy. This same person owned the silver carried on the *Vrouw Maria.* This time the silver cargo was salvaged and auctioned in Ekenäs. Mr. Hovy asked his representative to lodge a complaint against the auction and the 25% salvage reward to the Salvage Company but his complaint did not lead to a satisfactory result.

A wreck was found in the early 1970s and presumed to be *De Catherine.* Some divers had looted the wreck before the official announcement of the discovery and survey by the National Board of Antiquities. The wreck is badly damaged and broken into several pieces. Two large 16-19m sections of the sides of the ship and a brick stove surrounded by loose finds and roof tiles still remain. The wreck lies in quite shallow water and is probably partly buried in the sediment.

Figure 10.2. Wreck of Vrouw Maria from the starboard side. (Illustration by Tiina Miettinen, National Board of Antiquities.)

Figure 10.3. Dutch clay pipes from the wreck of Vrouw Maria. (Photo Ulla Klemelä, National Board of Antiquities)

The divers in the 1975 survey salvaged some roof tiles, glass bottles, china and clay pipes as reported by Harry Alopaeus in the Annual Report of the Bureau of Maritime History in 1975 (Wreck no. 1447, Archive of underwater finds, National Board of Antiquities, The Maritime Archaeology Unit). The wreck is also known as the Rysskär wreck from her location. The survey of the site and archival research is not yet completed and excavation is required to obtain all the available archaeological data.

Combining different source material

As shown above the source material for this study includes not only the ships themselves and the archaeological remains on board, but also various archival records concerning these sites. Important additional information to the archaeological data has been provided by several written sources from archives in the Netherlands, Sweden, Finland, Denmark and Russia.

Establishing the identity of a ship in some ways makes its story more complete (Ahlström 1995:152-168, 2005:86-100; see however, Eriksson in this volume). The wrecks in this article have been identified from archaeological data combined with written sources gathered from several countries. In the case of

the *St. Michel* archival research was carried out in five European countries (Nurmio-Lahdenmäki 2005:85).

In the 18th century the handling of lost material possessions through accidents at sea was quite well organized (Gelderblom 2003:96, 102, 106-108, 112-114). Attempts to make trading safer for the owners of ships and cargo included insuring and spreading the risk among several owners (Unger 1978:44). Thus the legal paperwork connected to the loss of a ship is an important source of detailed information. The relative status of a ship can probably also be evaluated by the amount of archive material that accumulated after its loss. The cargo of the *Vrouw Maria* was for example considered of such high value that a considerable amount of diplomatic correspondence was amassed after it sank.

One important additional source for many wrecks in the Baltic is the Sound Toll Register, which provide information about ships and their cargoes that enter and leave the Baltic. The marine archaeological investigations of identified shipwrecks sometimes show however, that these registers and other documents do not contain full information about the entire content of the cargo, nor about other artefacts on board. There are sometimes other difficulties in combining and interpreting the written records together with archaeological data. A case in point is the *Vrouw*

Maria, the life of which can be followed starting with a document of her sale at auction in Amsterdam in 1766 (GAA, Notarial Archives 12043/483).

If this is the same ship that sank in 1771 in Finnish territorial waters and was found in 1999, there is a contradiction in the measurements of the shipwreck and those reported in the auction inventory. The *Vrouw Maria* sold at auction was a koffship almost three metres shorter than the wreck. Furthermore, the ship's equipment salvaged off the wreck in Nagu belonged to a snow-rigged ship, as also does its rigging, which better fits a snow ship than a koffship (Laitinen 2000:2-4). One possible solution is a mistake in interpreting the measurements and ship classification of the inventory, or perhaps the same owners had several ships with the same name.

Future research

The potential of a shipwreck to provide reliable information must be critically evaluated. What significance do shipwreck sites hold and how should they be interpreted? What kind of questions do they address? What kind of stories do they relate? One obviously important aspect is the structure of the ship itself. All ships in this article are most likely of Dutch origin. Rotterdam and Zaanstreek were important ship building docks in 18th century Holland and employed hundreds of people. A merchant ship was built to fulfil the need for transporting goods between people and between centres of commerce. The ships contained technical innovations but were also part of a long building tradition. At this time there was a tendency towards the standardization of ship designs, whereby the adaptability of the ship was important (Unger 1978:41-44). Once the hull was built, it was up to the buyer to choose whatever modern and effective rigging he liked.

Another possible perspective is to study the ship as a work-place and temporary home for a limited group of people. In the case of the *Vrouw Maria,* a nine-man crew shared a very limited space. A shipwreck can offer information about life on board, daily routines and even such things as attitudes to safety. In the legal testimony and ship's log written by Reynoud Lourens, the shipmaster of the *Vrouw Maria,* he reports that the ship hit an unseen rock while two members of the crew were on duty and the rest were at prayer with the shipmaster (Ahlström 2000b:7). This small notice in the log of the final voyage of the *Vrouw Maria* provides evidence of the role of religion in the activities of the seafarer. Today it may seem rather odd to occupy a crew with prayer while the ship is manoeuvring through dangerous waters in darkness and high wind, but religion was no

doubt an important element of life then, especially at sea. A merchant ship was hardly a safe workplace and religion possibly gave some form of comfort.

Another principal aspect of life onboard concerns the division of space. This can raise interesting questions when researching shipwrecks of the historical period when the internal division of space on ships becomes progressively more complex and influenced by social factors as well as role and function. In many cases there were cabins for those uppermost in the ship's hierarchy, but tracing the crew's space, interspersed as it was with functional areas, is not always an easy task (see Eriksson's analysis related to different types of ship in this volume). However, the ship's galley and different types of tableware can be studied in all three ships in this case study, revealing the nature of life at sea, interesting not least for comparisons with life ashore.

In contrasting life at sea and ashore, another question concerns gender. Men seem to have been the dominant sex in seafaring, although as Adams (2003: 31) has pointed out, women were often aboard in various roles and in many circumstances that did not necessarily appear in the official records. In fact there is a case here of exactly that. In the written sources on the three ships in this study there is no evidence for the presence of women or of passengers, but the archaeological data tells us otherwise. Judging from finds of women's clothing and female human bones, *St. Michel* had a young woman on board, possibly a passenger (Telkkä 1962). In other ways too, although the world of trade in the 18th century was very male dominated in some aspects, stories surrounding the *St. Michel* and *Vrouw Maria* show there were also outstanding women who held political power and owned much property. This too was not unusual particularly in the sphere of merchant shipping, for when the men went to sea it was often the women who ran the business (Doe 2009).

The Russian connection

A Russian connection is very clear in all of these ships. The owners of the *De Catherina* lived in St. Petersburg; the *St. Michel* possibly sailed under the Russian flag; but the shipmaster of the *De Catherina*, Jochem Andreas, was Dutch (Ahlström 1995:139-140). Whether the ships themselves were Russian is an interesting question, because late 18th century merchant ships were able to sail under the Russian flag if half of the crew was Russian (Ahlström 1995:134). This was an ingenious way of avoiding custom fees. Whether this was possible before the maritime law declared by Catherine II in 1781 is uncertain. The ownership of the *St. Michel* is still unresolved.

The *Vrouw Maria* was Dutch according to archival sources. Her owner, Coenraad Vissering, and her co-owner and book keeper Tamme Ysbrantsz Beth, both lived in Amsterdam; the successful history of Tamme Beth is well known (Gelderblom 2003:99-100). Important merchants like Lodewijck Hovy also left their mark in history. His ownership of the silver cargo of the *Vrouw Maria* and *De Catherina* has left traces in archives and at least part of his life can be reconstructed. He was the son of a surgeon of the Russian fleet who moved from Moscow to Amsterdam (Gelderblom 2003:97). Perhaps this ancestry was one reason for his participation in Russian trade.

Unique to all three ships is that the Russian Empresses Elizabeth I and Catherine II and other members of the Russian court had close connections with them, linking them directly with the important objectives of the leading powers. This is where the explanatory power of these ships is seen as a group, in addition to the stories they tell us individually.

Things in action

The theoretical perspective of seeing meaningful constructs in material culture is relatively well established in archaeology today. Objects are not just the result of functionalism or accidental processes, but are both created and used for specific reasons. They are 'symbols in action', expressing someone's will to change, or in some cases to preserve. Their meaning is also regarded as strongly connected to the context within which they existed (see Hodder 2003, 2009).

The cargoes from the *St. Michel*, *Vrouw Maria* and *De Catherina* have been shown to consist of a remarkable assemblage of different products and artefacts. Items such as zinc, mercury, dyestuffs, sugar and coffee beans reflect the new contemporary trade and colonial economy. The import of luxury items such as horse-drawn carriages and exclusive paintings as well as simple objects such as ice skates, snuff-boxes and watches bear witness to a process whereby old Russia was seeking to become more European.

Today, these artefacts belong to old shipwrecks lying off some rocky islands in the Finnish archipelago. The challenge for future research is to examine them in the light of their various past historical contexts. How were they used, seen and valued in the places where they originated? For example, the paintings from the *Vrouw Maria* are at present under investigation by Eero Ehanti, curator at the National Board of Antiquities, Finland. The material preservation of artwork in underwater conditions is uncertain. But because information exists in several written sources, the titles of the paintings, their artists, art collectors and art dealers can be traced. What was the intended use at the end destination for the items carried by the wrecked ships? Who dressed in the new fashions in St Petersburg? Who skated for fun on the Neva in the winters? Where were the paintings to hang? Who was meant to see and be impressed by all these exotic imports from Holland? Such perspectives allow maritime archaeology not only to study lost ships in their present locations, but also to understand the contribution of material culture to the process of social change.

References

Adams, J. 2003. *Ship, Innovation and Social Change.* Stockholm Archaeological Monographs 24. Stockholm: Stockholm University.

Ahlström, C. 1995. *Spår av Hav, Yxa och Penna: Historiska Sjöolyckor i Östersjön Avspeglade i Marinarkeologiskt Källmaterial.* Helsinki: Societas Scientiarum Fennica.

Ahlström, C. 1997. *Looking for Leads.* Saarijärvi. Helsinki: Finish Academy of Science and letters.

Ahlström, C. 2000a. *Syvyyksien sylistä.* Karisto: Hämeenlinna.

Ahlström, C. 2000b. Venäjän keisarinna ja hollantilainen koffi-laiva Vrouw Maria. *Nautica Fennica 2000*: 4-16.

Ahlström C. 2005. Johtolankoja maalta ja mereltä - arkistotiedot ja hylkylöydöt auttoivat tunnistamaan

St. Mikaelin. In: A. Nurmio-Lahdenmäki (ed.) *S:t Mikael*: 84-110. Jyväskylä.

Doe, H. 2009. *Enterprising Women and Shipping in the Nineteenth Century.* Woodbridge: The Boydell Press.

Gelderblom, Oscar 2003. Coping with the Perils of the Sea: The Last Voyage of *Vrouw Maria* in 1771. *International Journal of Maritime History*, Vol. XV. 2: 95-115.

Hodder, I. 2003 (1986). *Reading the Past: Current Approaches to Interpretation in Archaeology.* Cambridge: Cambridge University Press.

Hodder, I. 2009 (1982). *Symbols in Action: Ethnoarchaeological Studies of Material Culture.* Cambridge: Cambridge University Press.

Laitinen, M. 2000. Vrouw Maria – hylky ja 1700-luvun hollantilaiset purjealustyypit kirjallisissa lähteissä. www.nba.fi/fi/purjealustyypit Published also in

SKAS 4/2000 (Sällskapet för medeltidsarkeologi i Finland)

Leino, M. 2004. Nauvo, Trunsjö *Vrouw Maria – hylky.* In: M. Laitinen (ed.) 2001. *Raportti hylyn kenttätutkimuksista.* (Field studies report on the wreck). Suomen merimuseo.

North, M., & Snapper, F. 1990. The Baltic Trade and the Decline of the Dutch Economy in the 18th Century. In: J. Ph. S. Lemmink, & J.S.A.M van Koningsbrugge (eds) *Baltic Affairs. Relations between the Netherlands and North – Eastern Europe 1500-1800*: 263- 286. Nijmegen: Instituut voor Noord-en Oosteuropese Studies.

Nurmio-Lahdenmäki A. (ed.) 2005. *S:t Mikael 1747.* Jyväskylä: Fingrid Oy.

Unger, R. W. 1978. *Dutch Shipbuilding before 1800. Ships and Guilds.* Amsterdam: Van Gorcum.

Vilkuna, Kustaa H.J. 2005. *Viha. Perikato, katkeruus ja kertomus isosta vihasta.* Jyväskylä: Suomalaisen Kirjallisuuden Seura.

Archives

Gemeentearchief, Amsterdam, Notariele Archieven (NA) 12043/483: Inventaris Tamme Beth Ysbrandzs, Makelaar. A inventory protocol of the koffship *Vrouw Maria* sold at auction September 1766. In this source there is also mention of the captain of *Vrouw Maria*, the repairs made in 1761 and the equipment belonging to the ship. Copy in the archive of the National Board of Antiquities, Finland.

Newspapers

Åbo Underrättelser 6.10.1957: Skeppet vid Börstö kan vara en världssensation.

Åbo Underrättelser 6.8.1961: Vraket vid Börstö kan vara ett unikum i hela världen.

Helsingin Sanomat 30.5.1965:

Hufvudstadsbladet 8.9.1961: Engelskt guldur, 200-årigt vin vrakfynd i Nagu.

Suomen sosiaalidemokraatti 5.9.1961: Hämmästyttävän nykyaikaista muotoilua 1700-luvulta 40 metrin syvyydessä.

Uusi Suomi 16.2.1964: Kellolasti 200 vuotta Suomenlahden pohjassa.

Uusi Suomi 27.4.1971: Katariina Suuren koruja sukelletaan Borstössä.

Unpublished sources

Bojner, G. 1965. "Börstö I". Tremastad galliot förlist omkring 1750 söder Borstö på ett djup av ca 40 m. Unpublished report.

Telkkä, A. 19.1.1962: Analyses of the lower part of the chine, found from wreck *St. Michael.*

Ericsson, C. 1970. A note on the skull of a dog found in the cabin of *St. Michael.* Archives of the National Board of Antiquities.

Personal communication

Jenni Mäntynen, Conservator.

11

RECYCLING SHIPWRECKS - EXAMPLES FROM THE 18TH CENTURY FORTRESS ISLAND OF SUOMENLINNA

Minna Leino

Suomenlinna Sea Fortress is a unique monument of military architecture located just off the coast of Helsinki, the capital city of Finland. This group of islands is a UNESCO World Heritage Site, receiving 700,000 visitors annually. It is one of the most important cultural heritage sites in Finland. Recently Suomenlinna has provided rare opportunities to research, develop and promote the field of maritime archaeology. This article presents a re-evaluation of wrecks recorded already in 1981. The re-evaluation was made possible thanks to an intensive archaeological survey of the underwater parts of Suomenlinna. As a result, for the first time these previously unknown wrecks were identified as the scuttled part of the original 18th century Army Fleet.

In maritime archaeological studies in Finland, wrecks are most commonly seen as unique time capsules, and these en-route wrecks have been documented. This article proposes another way of viewing wrecks. The ships discussed here are instead seen as part of an active society's ambitions and strategies after they are no longer seaworthy. They are rescued and transformed into constructions under the sea. The recycling of a ship is naturally a more complex process than just the convenient reuse of an old vessel. The process of recycling ships is discussed in connection with recycling practices in Suomenlinna and Karlskrona in southern Sweden. Karlskrona and Suomenlinna served as naval bases and dockyards for the Swedish crown in the 18th century. Naturally, both areas contained several ships in various states of repair and inevitably a considerable number of the military vessels found their last resting places in their home waters as recycled objects.

This research forms part of a larger cultural project, which has already concluded with an exhibition at Suomenlinna Museum. The exhibition *Bubbling Under, the Underwater Cultural Heritage at Suomenlinna* displayed the history of the waters surrounding Suomenlinna. In addition, this case study is also a part of the author's PhD study: *Recycling Ships, Maritime archaeological aspects of Suomenlinna, UNESCO World Heritage Site.*

Karlskrona

The city of Karlskrona was founded in 1680 when the Royal Swedish Navy was relocated there. The new city had, at the time, a strategic position with short sailing distances to important areas in the Baltic Sea (Ericson 1993:9). Recycling ships' hulls was common in the 18th century Swedish Navy (Wachtmeister 1912: 56). In Karlskrona, at least 60 vessels were deliberately scuttled and the sites of most of these recycled shipwrecks were even marked on maps (Ekberg 2008; Cederlund 1983; Wachtmeister 1912). These wrecks were incorporated into various new structures, such as bridges, piers, and breakwaters. Ships were also used as landfill material. Naturally, most of the reused wrecks in Karlskrona had a military origin, as they were former navy ships (Wachtmeister 1912: 5).

In Karlskrona, the recycled ships were not necessarily old. In fact, some were fairly new, but so badly damaged in battle that they were judged to be beyond repair at reasonable cost. It seems that scuttled ships usually lay useless in the dockyard for quite some time before that decision was reached (Wachtmeister 1912:5). The hulls were filled with stones before they were sunk, which seems to have been the normal procedure in Sweden in the late 17th and early 18th centuries.

Suomenlinna

During the 17th century, Swedish military action concentrated on the southern part of the Baltic Sea. The situation changed after Russia gained a connection to the Baltic. One of the biggest influences on the strategic focus on the Baltic Sea was the founding of the city of St. Petersburg by Peter the Great in 1703 (Fig. 11.1). During the 18th century, military activity increased in the surrounding countries. New fleets were established, enabling battles at sea. At this time Finland was part of Sweden and under constant threat of Russian occupation. For this reason, the Swedish crown decided to build a major fortress in 1747. This fortress was called Sveaborg, the fort of Sweden (in 1918 the name was changed to Suomenlinna, the fort of Finland), and it was located off the coast of Helsinki. The location was carefully chosen in the middle of the Finnish coastline in a favourable spot for a big fortress, offering a sheltered water area for the fleet.

The main architect of the fortress was Augustin Ehrensvärd, a lieutenant colonel in the artillery at the time (Gardberg & Palsila 1998:2; af Hällström 1986:11). Within ten years of its establishment, Suomenlinna became a naval base and a dockyard for a new Swedish fleet. It was an important addition to Sweden's naval stratagem, complementing Karlskrona. The location of Karlskrona on the eastern shore of Sweden was too distant to protect Finland against Russia. After several wars, Finland eventually became part of Russia (1809-1917) and Suomenlinna became the home of Russian troops, leaving an interesting record in the underwater landscape. However, this study focuses on the Swedish period, that is, 18th century Suomenlinna, which was the equivalant of Karlskrona.

Underwater Suomenlinna

In the underwater cultural landscape around Suomenlinna, over 50 different kinds of sites including pole structures, log barriers, embankments, and wooden and iron wrecks have been recorded (Leino 2008:101). The surrounding waters, covering 80 hectares, have been subject to considerable interest over the past ten years due to dredging and other activities changing the underwater landscape. The underwater cultural heritage at Suomenlinna is nevertheless still very rich in character. The Finnish National Board of Antiquities conducted a maritime archaeological survey from 2007 to 2010. This survey made the cultural seascape more accessible with the use of side-scan and multibeam sonars. The multibeam data was especially useful when combined with Lidar material, producing a comprehensive 3D model of the whole landscape.

The wooden wrecks are preserved only up to the lowest parts of the hull. These are the so-called skeleton wrecks. It seems that everything valuable had been removed leaving only the wooden shell. The impression is that nature has cleaned the shorelines, slowly absorbing the abandoned ships into the underwater

Figure 11.1. Map showing the location of the places mentioned in the article (Minna Leino).

landscape. If we take a closer look at the geographical location of the wrecks, other interpretations become possible. In the larger straits, ships were scuttled to function as obstacles to sailing, as described already by maritime archaeologist Harry Alopaeus (1984a:27-53). A block ship is scuttled as a wartime defensive measure designed to block passage into a waterway. This is one of the oldest naval tactics on record (Richards 2008:29). An especially interesting location is Lilla Varvet (see below), where the most extensive marine archaeological documentation of the fortress area to date took place in 1981.

Case Study, the Little Wharf

The Little Wharf is located on the eastern coast of the island of Iso Mustasaari (Stora Öster Svartö) and is today one of the largest small shipping harbours in Suomenlinna (Fig. 11.2). It houses mostly motorboats belonging to a local yachting club (Fig. 11.3). The Swedish name Lilla Varvet means the Little Wharf or a minor dockyard, and it originated in the late 18th century. The main dockyard for the fleet was the drydock in Susisaari (Vargön), the construction of which started soon after the establishment of the whole fortress. In addition, this Little Wharf was established because there was a need to build boathouses to shelter new, smaller gunboats. The Little Wharf was placed in a good geographical location for mooring ships; the island creates a shelter from prevailing winds from the southwest. The challenge to be solved was instead its openness to waves caused by north-eastern winds.

The Little Wharf was not in active use in the 1970s and hence the decision was made to change it into a modern harbour. For that reason, the last heavy construction work there, making it a viable harbour, took place in 1982. The old breakwater was rebuilt as a pier by adding boulders of bedrock to the structure. At the same time, the Maritime Museum of Finland had the opportunity to make a quick record of the site which contained four wrecks and a timber caisson structure (Fig. 11.4). These were partly dredged away (Fig. 11.5) and partly left *in situ* beneath the new pier after completion of the archaeological documentation, which also included lifting up the most important structural parts of the wrecks.

Recording the site, 1981-1982

Archaeological documentation of the site by the staff of the Maritime Museum took place in December 1981. Additional volunteer work was also conducted during that winter. Due to poor visibility, wintry conditions and the impending construction work, it was decided

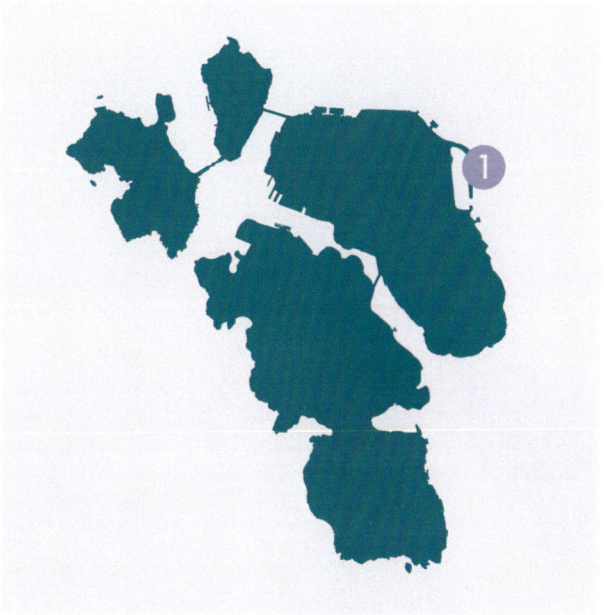

Figure 11.2. Location of the Little Wharf in Suomenlinna. (Tiina Miettinen, National Board of Antiquities, Finland).

to raise the most important structural parts for documentation on land (Fig. 11.6). Also the log-frame construction of the breakwater was photographed and measured, but none of its components were removed from the site. Before lifting, the wreck parts were also measured and photographed *in situ* by Harry Alopaeus. He also photographed the wreck elements separately in their new location in the Maritime Museum of Finland. The elements were included in the museum collections, but stored outside in the maintenance area unconserved. All in all, wooden parts were removed from the four different wrecks, which were named 1A, 1B, 2 and 3 (see Table 11.1). Some of the wreck elements were even relocated underwater into a safe place in front of the Coast Guard Station in Suomenlinna.

Already in 1982, a brief summary of the archaeological fieldwork had been published in the Annual Report of the Maritime Museum of Finland. At that time, the wrecks were interpreted as having operated in the Crimean War (1853-1856) or earlier. The dating was influenced by the discoveries of two shot (92 mm and 142 mm) from wreck 1A and one shot (200 mm) from wreck 1B. The shot in wreck 1B had gone through the keelson (Maritime Museum of Finland 1982:53). One shot included a fuse, which clearly dates to the Crimean war or later (Alopaeus 2009: pers. comm., see also Alopaeus 1984b). At that time, the origin of these wrecks remained unsolved. Over the years, these wooden pieces of different wrecks were forgotten and their historical value remained unrecognized.

These wreck elements were re-evaluated with

Figure 11.3. The Little Wharf as a modern small shipping harbour (photo: Markus Kivelä).

the latest maritime archaeological survey of the Suomenlinna water area in 2007-2010. Re-evaluation became relevant, because these pieces of wood were going to be destroyed in a cleaning operation of the maintenance area at the Maritime Museum of Finland. At the same time, the survey around Suomenlinna was active and the surveyors were consulted about the future of these pieces originating from the Little Wharf. As a result, the original documentation pictures and maps were recovered from the Maritime Museum archives, archiving was completed and information was combined with the preserved wreck elements. As a result new information was found and the mystery of these wrecks could be solved. Eventually they did not end up being destroyed; instead they were put on exhibit in a museum.

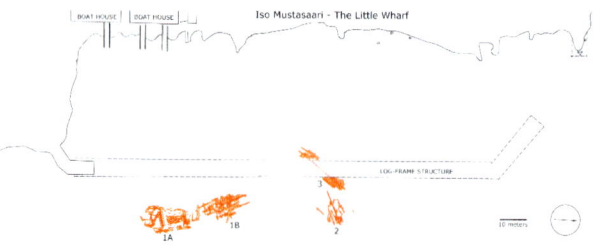

Figure 11.4. Site map of the Little Wharf by Harry Alopaeus, 1982, redrawing Ville Leino 2013. (National Board of Antiquities, Finland.)

New information - a new interpretation

It is challenging to attempt to uncover a historical context for a group of skeleton wrecks thirty years after their salvage, especially in a place like Suomenlinna, where the archives are spread across three different countries and the wealth of information is vast. For an archaeologist, it was easiest to start with examining the geographical location through old maps. In this way, a new piece of information about the Little Wharf came to light. This discovery was made in a series of nautical maps of the Finnish coast stored in the National War Archives (Krigsarkiv) in Stockholm (Laitinen 1999; Harju & Tiilikainen 2009). This new information is marked on a map dating to 1794. Against the waterfront

Figure 11.5. Dredging of the wrecks after the archaeological recording in 1982 (National Board of Antiquities, Finland).

	Wreck 1A	**Wreck 1B**	**Wreck 2**	**Wreck 3**
Building Material	Oak	Oak	Softwood/ Pine?	Oak
Hull Structure	Clinker built	Clinker built	Clinker built	Clinker built
Estimated Length	25-26 m	22-23 m	18.5-20 m	25-27 m
Estimated Width	7.4 m	7 m	5.4-6.5 m	5.5-8 m
Location	Partly under the wreck 1B	Partly above the wreck 1A	-	Under breakwater construction
Estimated amount of Rocks inside the wreck	18 tons	60 tons	-	-

Table 11.1. The Little Wharf, results from the 1981 recording (National Board of Antiquities).

Figure 11.6. The new breakwater construction was built in 1982 during the archaeological fieldworks in wintry conditions. Wreck elements on top of the ice (Harry Alopaeus, The National Board of Antiquities in Finland).

of Lilla Varvet was written: '*2ne nedsänkte Gallioter på hvilka* är *6 fot djupt*' (two submerged galliots at a depth of 6 feet) and beside this, '*vrak*' (wreck) (Fig. 11.7).

The identification of a ship type, galliot, was the important piece of information. It was easy to combine with historian Oscar Nikula´s (1933) list of the Swedish archipelago fleet, where five galliots are mentioned (Matikka 2009). They were named *König v. Preussen, Prinz Heinrich, Prinz Wilhelm, Prinz v. Preussen* and *Alte Treu*. According to Nikula (1933:366-367), all of them had been captured from the Prussians in 1758-1759 during the Pomeranian war. They were added into the Swedish fleet, and later on, these five galliots became part of a 33-vessel fleet forming the core of the Suomenlinna squadron. This new Army Fleet was created during the Pomeranian war under the command of Augustin Ehrensvärd. The famous ship designer F. H. Chapman was also involved with the fleet. Co-operation between Ehrensvärd and Chapman started in Stralsund and led to the building of new ship types. At the end of the war, the new fleet, including old and modified vessels and some genuinely new ships, settled in Suomenlinna (Nikula 1933:126; Matikka 2008:30).

However, after a brief period in Suomenlinna, the galliots were removed from the ship list of the naval fleet in 1766 and 1767 (Nikula 1933:366). In their minutes for 11 June 1766, the Helsinki Auction Rooms record the sale of the equipment of four galliots, namely the *Prinz Wilhelm, Prinz von Preussen* and *Alte Treu*, which were mentioned in Nikula's list, and a fourth galliot named *Ancklam*. (Malinen 1997:37; HKA Ga:7). Their condition is described in an inventory made two years earlier in 1764 to estimate the cost of the rigging. The auction minutes from 1766 also describe how the value of the items had decreased because the rigging had suffered during stripping ('*slopningen*') and sinking ('*försänkningen*'). These actions clearly indicate that the ships had been deliberately submerged rather than having sunk in a battle. This information was discovered by maritime historian Ismo Malinen, who had been studying a famous merchant, Johan Sederholm from Helsinki. Sederholm had made successful discoveries from public auctions of shipwrecked vessels. For example, he had bought all four tackles of the galliots for the price of 20,000 copper daler (= Finnish taaleri), including also some of the sails, which were partly

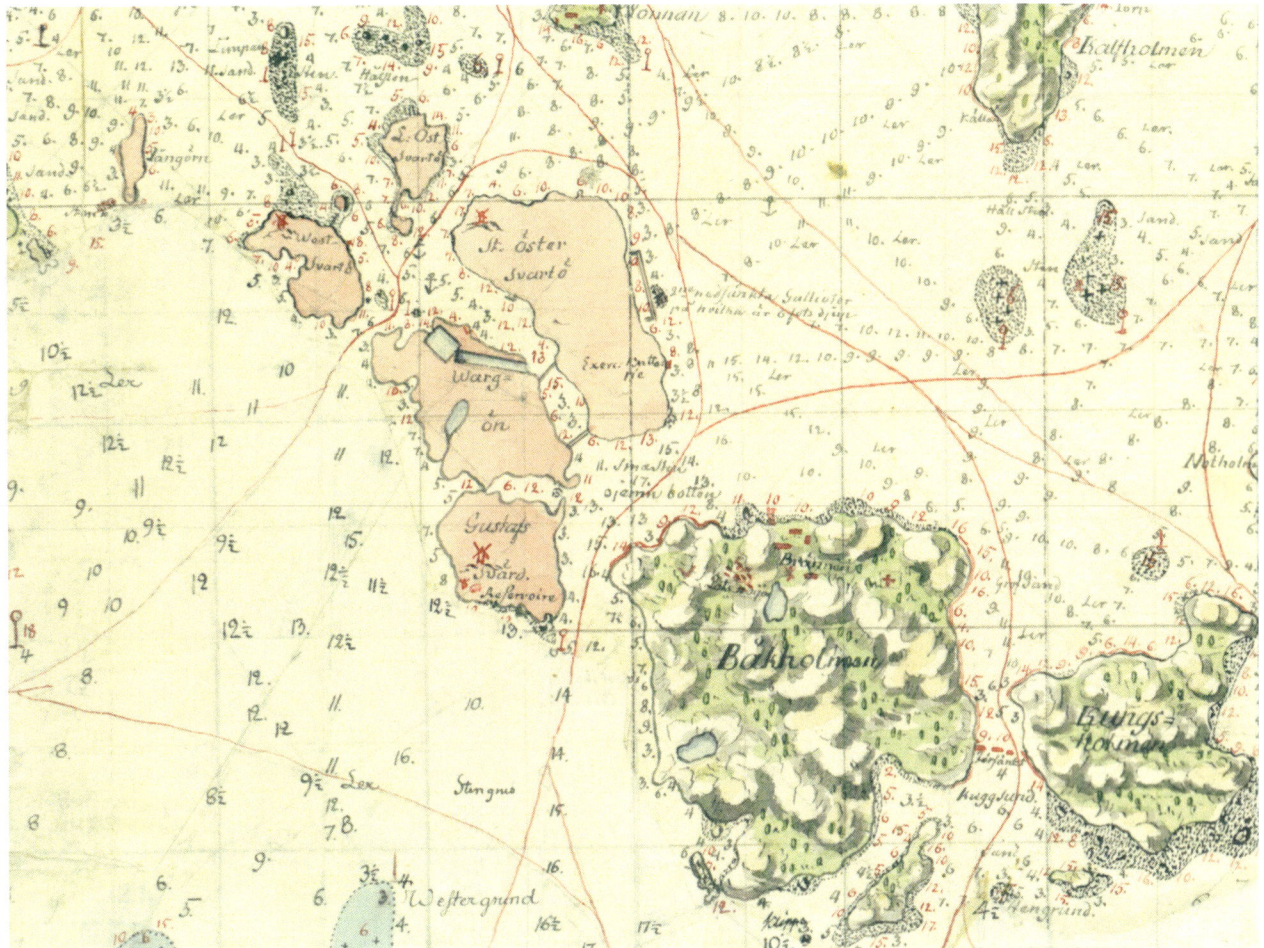

Figure 11.7. Map of Suomenlinna and the Little Wharf by Gustav Fred, af Klerck 1794 (Harju & Tiilikainen 2009).

worn out. At the time, the value of one galliot was approximately 50,000 copper daler (Malinen 2009: pers. comm.).

In 1767, the last two galliots, *König von Preussen* and *Prinz Heinrich,* were recorded as sold at the Helsinki Auction Rooms (HKA Ga:8), implying that also the ships' hulls were sold at the auction. They were also described as being in poor condition. *König von Preussen* was rebuilt as a hospital ship (Nikula 1933:126). *Prinz Heinrich* was rebuilt as a transport vessel, and later on it served as a merchant vessel in private ownership (Hornborg 1950: 336). The vessel also took part in a famous operation where troops were transported from Finland to Stockholm during the revolution of Gustav III in 1772. Altogether 992 men from Finland were transported in different vessels (Nikula 1933:85).

According to historian Petterson, who has studied the history of the drydock (1952:3), four merchant vessels were scuttled in the harbour area. Combining this information with the description of the two galliots in the old map led to a new conclusion. According to this new interpretation, these merchant vessels are most likely some of the galliots from the Army Fleet, the

tackles of which had been sold in the auction, namely the *Ancklam, Prinz Wilhelm, Prinz von Preussen* and *Alte Treu.* The ships' hulls were scuttled to create a breakwater before the inventory in 1764, the minutes of which were preserved in the Helsinki Auction Rooms, as described earlier. Combined with archaeological evidence from 1981, they could be wrecks 1A, 1B and 3. The fourth wreck, built from pine, cannot be interpreted as the fourth galliot. In the 1980s, it was thought to represent a different building tradition and is described as "a peasant vessel" (*Nautica Fennica* 1982:16). All in all there was a correlation between the number of vessels in the Helsinki Auction Rooms and in Petterson's writing, but one galliot was still missing in the archaeological documentation. This new hypothesis needed archaeological proof, and for that reason the wreck elements remaining from the recording in 1981 were re-evaluated.

Re-evaluation of the wreck parts

The pile of wreck parts lifted in 1981 and stored outside in the maintenance area of the Maritime Museum of

Finland was re-evaluated in the context of the recent survey from 2007 to 2010. New evaluation was carried out in three different phases. It was a challenge to start with, since without any conservation, the long period outside had affected the condition of the wood, and over the years the pile had grown with additional wreck elements from different sites. Sorting and comparing was carried out first in 2009 by opening up the pile and trying to find the original pieces. The physical remains were compared to photographs and drawings from the 1981 documentation (Vakkari 2009). In addition, military archives in Sweden were visited to collect supplementary information, revealing a list of inventories of the galliots *Anclam*, *Alte Treu* and *Prinz Wilhelm*, which were described as being of clinker construction and built of oak.

The second phase was taking samples for tree-ring studies in order to reinforce the new interpretation. The dendrochronological datings were carried out at the Laboratory of Dendrochronology at the University of Eastern Finland. The sampling was successful (Table 11.2) with two of the wrecks, 1A and 3. All four samples from wreck 1A were oak (*Quercus robur L*), and the growing region indicated was the Pomerania district of northern Germany. The last growth-rings were the years 1666, 1698, 1707 and 1721, dating the ship after the year 1721. From wreck 3, five samples of oak (*Quercus robur L*) were analysed, and they matched districts in northern Germany and Poland. The last year-rings were 1674, 1695, 1705, 1708 and 1726, meaning that the ship dates after the year 1726. Wreck 2 yielded only one sample of pine (*Pinus sylvestris L*) and one of alder (*Alnus glutinosa/incana L*). The dating was 1641, but no interpretations can be made based on these samples, since they are not representative. As described earlier, information from literature suggests that the Prussian galliots were old merchant ships, which were taken for military purposes in the Pomeranian war (1756-1762). This matches perfectly with the dendrochronological dating results.

The third step of the re-evaluation was done in 2011, when wreck elements from Hylkysaari were photographed and drawn by students from the University of Helsinki attending a practical course in maritime archaeology. Several pieces were re-evaluated and compared with information of the inventory lists from Swedish military archives. Combining information from ship inventories with preserved wreck elements in order to identify wrecks turned out to be a challenging task. At least the galliot *Prinz Wilhelm* was, according to the inventory list, clinker-built out of oak. Wrecks 1A, 1B, and 3 had the same features, being built out of oak with the clinker technique. Although only three of the wrecks have features that correlate

with information from the galliots, there was originally also a fifth wreck, which had already been dredged away in 1978 without any recording of the remains. With all this new information, it can be concluded that the galliots *Ancklam*, *Prinz Wilhelm*, *Prinz von Preussen* and *Alte Treu* were scuttled in front of the Little Wharf.

One interesting feature can be seen in these wrecks compared with scuttled vessels in Karlskrona. At least two of the four wrecks (1A and 1B) at the Little Wharf contained a large amount of stone, based on a document from 1981. Loading stones inside a vessel in order to keep it in place makes sense if it is to serve as the foundation for a jetty. Wreck 3 lies under the 18th century wooden breakwater, and hence it cannot be ascertained whether or not it contained stones. The wooden log-framed breakwater construction has not yet been dated, but it was most likely constructed during the active building period in the 1790s (Petterson 1952:3). As a matter of fact, Harry Alopaeus had taken samples from the structure in 1981, but they were never analyzed at the time. They were now discovered after 30 years. Unfortunately, without proper storage, they were unsuitable for dating. The log-frame construction is still visible under the modern jetty, and it could be dendrochronologically dated to validate this interpretation.

Historical context of the galliots

With this new interpretation, it is relevant to take a closer look at the kind of information that is preserved concerning these very galliots in different sources. It is known that after the Pomeranian war, monetary problems were severe in Sweden. The parliament was even called in to discuss the bankruptcy of the whole nation (Nikula 2011:367). The whole political climate in Sweden changed and building activities at Suomenlinna were scaled back (Rosén 2008:17). Larger projects, such as building a new dockyard or keeping a fleet at sea, were a heavy drain on resources. During this difficult period in the state´s economy, maintaining a fleet and building new vessels needed an extremely large amount of funding. In order to cut running costs, Augustin Ehrensvärd insisted on giving up ships that were in poor condition. Due to this situation, at least Göteborg's squadron scuttled some of the old galleons (Nikula 2011:404). It is obvious that critical thought was given to the older vessels also at Suomenlinna.

The galliots were old merchant ships that were modified into warships by the Prussians during the winter of 1758-1759 and used to protect the mouth of the Oder and the strait of Swina. All four ships were armed with 14 guns. Nevertheless they were quickly taken over by Swedes in battle. Among other vessels,

No.	Sample No/wreck	Species	Total	Mean	s.d.	a.c.	m.s.	Years	Pt.	Cut down after year
02	46/unknown	*Quercus robur*	109	184.8	72.1	.727	.211	1540-1648	4	1648
03	61/wreck 1A	*Quercus robur*	107	198.9	67.8	.651	.225	1560-1666	4	1666
04	52/ wreck 2	*Pinus sylvestris*	105	151.8	138.3	.943	.250	1537-1641	¾	1641
05	4/wreck 3	*Quercus robur*	82	134.0	66.7	.648	.272	1539-1674	4	1674
06	16/unknown	*Quercus robur*	86	78.5	44.9	.798	.248	1560-1645	4	1645
07	39/wreck 3	*Quercus robur*	139	148.7	63.8	.791	.209	1588-1726	4	1726
08	21/wreck 1A	*Quercus robur*	143	109.7	48.8	.803	.192	1565-1707	4	1707
09	40/wreck 3	*Quercus robur*	81	179.9	58.8	.815	.168	1615-1695	4	1695
10	44/wreck 2?	*Alnus glutinosa/incana*	126	136.3	101.1	.629	.333	-	-	-
11	50/unknown*	*Quercus robur*	117	84.4	43.8	.737	.264	1592-1708	4	1708
12	38/wreck 1A	*Quercus robur*	79	377.6	108.6	.709	.167	1620-1698	4	1698
13	59/wreck 3	*Quercus robur*	93	200.2	122.7	.942	.160	-	4	-
14	48/wreck 3	*Quercus robur*	142	111.1	32.9	.649	.192	1564-1705	4	1705
15	1/unknown	*Quercus robur*	61	159.5	50.7	.778	.167	1540-1600	4	1600
16	43/unknown**	*Quercus robur*	115	210.3	79.5	.736	.182	1607-1721	4	1721

* matches with other results of Wreck 3

** matches with other results of Wreck 1A

Table 11.2. The Little Wharf, results of the dendrochronological analysis. (Zetterberg, Pentti 2010. Museoviraston meriarkeologian yksikön Helsingin Suomenlinnan Venekerhon aallonmurtajan hylkyjen puunäytteiden iänmääritys, dendrokronologiset ajoitukset F56202-F5U6203, FIU 6204, F5U6205-F5U6209, F5&U6210 ja F5U6211-F5U6216. Joensuun yliopisto, Biotieteiden tiedekunta, Ekologian tutkimusinstituutti Dendrokronologian laboratorion ajoitusseloste 367:1-11)

these four galliots were anchored to protect the Bay of Stettin next to Neuwarp. The famous sea battle of the Bay of Stettin took place on the 10th of September 1759. The Swedish took over the galliot *Prinz Wilhelm* in only twenty minutes. The rest of the Prussian fleet surrendered after the Swedish troops were also able to turn the guns of the *Prinz Wilhelm* on them. (Nikula 2011:273-274). As mentioned earlier, Ehrensvärd was building a new fleet in Stralsund, which also included modifying old vessels. Changes were also made to the galliots in Stralsund under the command of Klundret, the building master. At least one of the galliots was rebuilt into a bomb ketch (Nikula 1933:122).

The Army Fleet, which was created in Stralsund

under the command of Ehrensvärd, sailed into Suomenlinna in 1762. What was the condition of the Little Wharf at that time and did the scuttling of the galliots have a role in the process of building a viable harbour? The development of the Little Wharf can be traced by examining historical maps. The oldest name for the harbour is '*bothamn*' (boat harbour), and it appears on a map apparently dating to 1766 (af Hällström 1959:78), at least two years after the scuttling of the galliots. In other words, the galliots were already scuttled in the area before it appeared on a map for the first time. We can draw the conclusion that the galliots had an important part in the development of the whole area. In this oldest map, the breakwater construction is already in the correct location.

The exact duration of the construction work in this area is unclear. We have clues from historian Oscar Nikula (1933:165), who, in his discussion of building activities after the death of Ehrensvärd in 1772, describes the location of a harbour on the eastern shore of Iso Mustasaari (Stora Öster Svartö), without any further description. In addition, old maps reveal that construction work took place at the latest in the 1790s with a slightly different plan than previously proposed (Petterson 1952:3). From this time onwards the area is marked on maps as 'Lilla Varvet', revealing that the function of the area was "a little wharf". It is also worth noting that in old maps of Suomenlinna, it can sometimes be difficult to distinguish fact from theory. Some of the structures shown in the maps were never actually finished or their construction never begun in the first place.

Now we know that work on the breakwater had already begun before 1764, when the galliots were scuttled in the area. Combining these pieces of information allows us to form a new interpretation: the wooden hulls were recycled as a basement for the breakwater. Recycling indicated economical thinking in a nation facing bankruptcy. In this way, the costs of the fleet could be scaled back. In Karlskrona, old vessels typically had to wait until a decision concerning their future could be made. In Suomenlinna, it seems as though Ehrensvärd made decisions quickly, although it must have been a very hard resolution. In a situation like this, one might think that having a new function for the galliots could have made the decision easier.

An interesting question for future research on this matter is whether the status or the history of the ship affected the way it was recycled. Were 'good' ships, i.e., those that were perceived to have positive associations, afforded a more honourable end than ships that were less successful or humbler in service? What was the common treatment of vessels taken from the enemy? The galliots captured from the Prussians did not last long, being scuttled after serving for only a few years in the Army Fleet. Yet they were identified in their new location by ship type on a map drawn 28 years after they had been submerged. The reason for this may be that the person responsible for the cartographical work, Carl Nathanael Klerck, socialized with Augustin Ehrensvärd as a young officer. Ehrensvärd had probably shared the information about the scuttled Prussian galliots with Klerck. During his cartographic career, Klerck captured this piece of information in a nautical map. We also know from historical sources that after the Pomeranian war, Prince Henry of Prussia visited Suomenlinna in October 1770. Ehrensvärd took him around the islands in a sloop and they most probably passed the site of the Little Wharf. What is left to our imagination is the conversation between these two gentlemen regarding the old galliot ships and their destiny as the recycled basement of a breakwater construction.

It is surprising to find recycling in a historical context. According to historical sources, the landscape of Suomenlinna looked like a disorganized construction site. In some of the old paintings, there were abandoned ships lying on shorelines. All this has not given a positive image of the relationship between man and sea, or the environment on a larger scale. The recycling practices have now been set into a historical context with these galliots. The question remains of how recycling is seen from the maritime archaeological perspective.

Recycling

One way to understand material cultural objects is through their whole existence, the process and cycles of production, exchange, and consumption. This can be called a "cultural biography of objects" in part related to the concept of chaîne opératoire developed by André Leroi-Gourhan. Vessels can also be described this way (Rönnby 2009). The life and death of a ship includes different phases, such as planning, building, equipping, sailing, and an end when the vessel is finally abandoned on the seabed or on the shore (see Rönnby this volume; Adams 2003:30; Flatman 2003:147; Gosden & Marshall 1999; Kopytoff 1986). This "death" of the ship is, however, not always the final end of the story. The biography of the ship can be continued: parts of the hull, equipment and rigging can be reused and even the name of the ship can be perpetuated in other ships. The ship can therefore be "reborn" through recycling.

Recycling means using waste material for a new purpose. Waste is of course a human concept. In nature, everything is part of a continuous cycle and nothing is wasted. Even in death, a creature provides nutrients that can be reincorporated into the chain of life. The idea of waste reflects the belief that some by-products of human activity are useless (cf. Hayes 1978:6-7). A ship is deemed worthless when it has no practical or monetary value at sea any more. Yet even then the ship and hull can still be of practical or symbolic value for contemporary society.

The phenomenon of recycling ships as building material for underwater structures seems to have a long history. Viking Age examples of using old boats as defence blockages are known from Roskilde and Foteviken (Crumlin-Pedersen & Olsen 2002; Ingleman-Sundberg 1983). Old ships have also been utilized in city planning and they were found in the former harbour of Grønnegaard in Copenhagen (Lemée 2006). Marcus Hjulhammar has demonstrated how old ships have played a vital part in the construction of the Stockholm waterfront (Hjulhammar 2010). Other examples include the Norwegian port of Bergen (Christensen 1985) and, beyond Scandinavia: London (Goodburn 1991) and New York (Riess 1991).

However, in maritime archaeological research, the question of recycling has been linked mostly to post-depositional processes. The main interest has focused on the extent of scavenging or recycling of materials that has taken place subsequent to the initial sinking of a ship. Recycling has then been viewed as a way of understanding the processes of site formation. Ships that were intentionally sunk or abandoned after their operational lives were over have not drawn so much attention in maritime archaeological research.

Studies dealing with the recycling of these kinds of post-medieval ships have been rather rare up to now. However, the subject has recently attracted more attention. Significant publications include *Ships' Graveyards,* by Nathan Richards (2008), an in depth study of abandonment which also touches on the subject of recycling. A few case studies have been made in relation to military history, such as Alarik Wachtmeister`s analysis of Karlskrona (1912). Nevertheless, the possibility of gaining new information with archaeological recording is also shown by Richard Gould in his case study of HMS *Vixen* in Bermuda (Gould 1991, 2011:318). A more recent publication, The Archaeology of Watercraft Abandonment, presents several case studies of ship abandonment, exploring the archaeological possibilities (Richards and Seeb 2013).

Discussion

The case study in Suomenlinna has proved that new information can be gained even from abandoned 'skeleton' wrecks, thus allowing these wrecks to be added to a historical context. The wrecks discussed in this article are in their locations for a reason and possess both archaeological and historical information. Combining these sources was a challenging task; new information from written material may still contain surprises.

This case study was based on a small collection of pieces of wood from real ships that were originally interpreted to belong to the time of the Crimean war in the 1850s or earlier. This interpretation was based on a typology of shot fuses. There is no need to overwrite this information, but it should be pointed out that the shot could have ended up in the wood when the ships were already part of the underwater landscape, during the heavy bombing of Suomenlinna in the Crimean war.

Furthermore, pieces of information were gathered

from different sources, such as the hint about the two scuttled galliots in an old map. In addition, a short article written by the historian Petterson already in the 1950s mentions the scuttling of four merchant vessels. This article does not include any references and hence the source of this information remains unclear. The galliot as a ship type is better known as a merchant ship; accordingly, we can assume that Petterson meant galliots when talking about merchant ships. We know from Karlskrona that most of the scuttled vessels had a military origin. By combining this information with the material found in the Helsinki City Auction minutes and Swedish military archives, we can finally draw a conclusion concerning the four scuttled galliots.

These ships were taken from the Prussians in the Pomeranian war. It is possible to find even more information on these ships now that the search is motivated by these real pieces of ships. One problem that naturally has to be taken into account is that ships were often recycled in actively used areas such as harbours and waterways. Consequently, the vessels have often suffered from subsequent dredging and construction activities. For example, the fourth galliot at Suomenlinna was dredged in 1978 and the historical importance of the vessel was not recognized.

In addition to ships, 18th century cannons and chains have been re-employed as fencing at Suomenlinna Church. Cannons and anchors have also been recycled as bollards on the quays. In these cases, recycling was carried out some hundred years after the objects had been in use, proving the potential of recycling to considerably prolong the life of an item. These are not merely cases of a resource recovery system where valuable material is reused because of its physical properties (cf. Hayes 1978: 30). The cannons are not seen merely as recyclable metal, but as historical objects that share the military history of Suomenlinna with its inhabitants and visitors. Constructions such as cannons around a church are embedded with an intuitive symbolism.

Some conclusions

All in all, the re-use and recycling of ships and their equipment have been very innovative at Suomenlinna. This indicates a flexible system in the past, where ships that could not be sold at public auction were harnessed to be of use to contemporary society. This was achieved by using ships as construction material, saving on the building costs of expensive structures such as a breakwater. In the Little Wharf it took thirty years from the 1760s to the 1790s to build a breakwater to shelter the area from north-eastern winds. We can also argue that the construction was not thoroughly finished until

1982, still benefitting from actions taken in the 18th century.

Up until now the harbour at the Little Wharf in Suomenlinna has been considered as an uninteresting area containing a small harbour and 19th century wrecks. Archaeological analysis has led to the identification of some of these wrecks, enabling the public to become familiar with real pieces of galliots and their story in an exhibition at the Suomenlinna Museum. These recent investigations have also shown that the underwater area around the fortress should be treated as a cultural landscape. The wrecks on the seabed form a part of the built environment, containing archaeological meanings that enhance conventional historical interpretations.

Acknowledgements

I wish to thank all my colleagues at the National Board of Antiquities in Finland, students involved with galliots at the University of Helsinki, and the MARIS group around the Baltic Sea, especially Johan Rönnby. I am also grateful to the Governing Body of Suomenlinna for their co-operation over the years. My special gratitude goes to the Kone Foundation, which has made my study possible. I also want to express my gratitude to Anne Ala-Pöllänen and Jon Adams for their editing work and Sarianna Silvonen for revising the language.

References

Adams, J. 2003. *Ships, innovation and social change: Aspects of carvel shipbuilding in Northern Europe 1450-1850.* Stockholm studies in archaeology 24 and Stockholm marine archaeology reports 3. Stockholm: University of Stockholm.

Alopaeus, H. 1984a. Suomenlinnan vedenalaiset esteet. *Narinkka*, Helsinki City Museum 1984: 19-58.

Alopaeus, H. 1984b. Huomioita museoiduista tykistön ampumatarpeista, *Suomen museo* 91:120-123.

Cederlund, C.O. 1983. *The Old Wrecks of the Baltic Sea, Archaeological recording of the wrecks of carvel-built ships.* BAR International Series 186. Oxford: BAR.

Christensen, A.E. 1985. *Boat finds from Bryggen.* Bryggen Papers M.S.1, 47-280. Bergen: Universitetsforlaget.

Crumlin-Pedersen, O. & Olsen, O. (eds) 2002. *The Skuldelev Ships I.* Roskilde: The Viking Ship Museum.

Ekberg, G. 2008. *Djupasund och Stumholmen, Arkeologisk sonarkartering.* Statens Maritima Museer Arkeologisk rapport 2008: 9.

Ericson, L. 1993. Pionjärer och rustningar 1680-1721. In: E. Norberg, *Karlskronavarvets Historia 1: 1680-1866.* Karlskrona: Karlskronavarvet AB.

Flatman, J. 2003. Cultural biographies, Cognitive landscapes and dirty old bits of boat: 'theory' in maritime archaeology. *International Journal of Nautical Archaeology* 32. 2: 143-157.

Gardberg, C.J. & Palsila, K. 1998. *Viapori, Suomenlinna.* Keuruu: Otavan kirjapaino.

Gosden, C. & Marshall, Y. 1999. The Cultural Biography of Objects. *World Archaeology* 31.2: 169-178.

Goodburn, D. 1991. New light on early ship and boatbuilding in the London area. In: Good, et al. (eds) *Waterfront Archaeology:* 105–115. CBA Research report No. 74. York: CBA.

Gould, R.A. 1991. The archaeology of H.M.S Vixen, an early ironclad ram in Bermuda. *International Journal of Nautical Archaeology and Underwater Exploration* 20. 2: 141-153.

Gould, R.A. 2011. *Archaeology and the social history of ships,* second edition. Cambridge: Cambridge University Press.

Hayes, D. 1978. Repairs, Reuse, Recycling – First Steps Toward a Sustainable Society. *Worldwatch Paper* 23: September.

Harju, E-S. & Tiilikainen, H. (eds) 2009. *Kuninkaallinen merikartasto 1791-1796, C.N af Klerckerin johtama kartoitustyö Suomenlahdella.* Jyväskylä: Gummerus Kirjapaino Oy.

Hjulhammar, M. 2010. *Stockholm från sjösidan. Marinarkeologiska fynd och miljöer.* Stockholm: Stockholmia Förlag.

Hornborg, E. 1950. *Helsingin kaupungin historia, toinen osa.* Helsinki: Suomalaisen kirjallisuuden Seuran Kirjapainon Oy.

af Hällström, O. 1959. *Hur Suomenlinna kom till.* Helsinki: Frenckelleska Tryckeri AB.

af Hällström, O. 1986. *Suomenlinna Viapori Suomenlinna, The Island Fortress off Helsinki.* Helsinki: Anders Nyborg A/S.

Ingelman-Sundberg 1983. *Vikingaskepp Foteviken,*

marinarkeologisk undersökning 1982. Malmö, Sjöfartsmuseum.

Kopytoff, I. 1986. The Cultural Biography of Things: Commoditization as Process. In: A. Appadurai (ed.) *The Social Life of Things: Commodities in Cultural Perspective*: 64-91. Cambridge: Cambridge University Press.

Leino, M. 2008. Underwater Cultural Heritage at Suomenlinna: Recent Survey. In: J. Eiring, T. Lind & H. Matikka (eds) *The Future of Historic Dockyards, Round-Table Reports, Suomenlinna 2008*: 96-101, 120. Helsinki.

Lemée, C. 2006. T*he Renaissance shipwrecks from Christianshavn: an archaeological and architectural study of large carvel vessels in Danish waters, 1580-1640.* Ships and boats of the North, 6. Roskilde: The Viking Ship Museum.

Matikka, H. 2008. Shipbuilding at Suomenlinna, In: J. Eiring, T. Lind & H. Matikka (eds) *The Future of Historic Dockyards, Round-Table Reports, Suomenlinna 2008:* 28-38. 120. Helsinki.

Maritime Museum of Finland, 1982. *Short Notes, Annual Report 1982.* Helsinki.

Nikula, O. 1933. *Svenska Skärgårdsflottan 1756-1791.* Doctoral Dissertation. Helsinki.

Nikula O. 2011. *Augustin Ehrensvärd 1710-1772.* Karisto. (reprinted and translated, original publication 1960)

Petterson, L. 1952. *Suomenlinnan telakan vaiheita, Kustavilainen aikakausi.* Valmet 2, perhelehti V vuosikerta. Toim. Yrjö Rantala. (1-3).

Richards, N. 2008. *Ships'graveyards.* Gainesville: University Press of Florida.

Richards, N & Seeb, S.K (eds) 2013. The Archaeology of Watercraft Abandonment. New York: Springer.

Riess, W.C. 1991. Design and Construction of the Ronson Ship. In: R. Reinders & C. Paul (eds) *Carvel Construction Technique: Skeleton-First, Shell-first:* 176-183. International Symposium on Boat and Ship Archaeology 5 Amsterdam, 1988. Oxford: Oxbow Books.

Rosén, H. 2008. The History of the Suomenlinna Dockyard, In: J. Eiring, T. Lind & H. Matikka (eds) *The Future of Historic Dockyards, Round-Table Reports, Suomenlinna 2008*: 16-21, 120. Helsinki.

Wachtmeister, A. 1912. Något om Karlskrona örlogshamn fordom sänkta skepp. *Tidskrift i sjöväsendet* 75: 55-74.

Other Sources

Alopaeus, H. 1982. Original drawings and photographs of fieldworks at the Little Warf site. Archives of the National Board of Antiquities.

Laitinen, M. 1999. Minutes of discoveries from the National War Archives (Krigsarkivet), 2.11.1999. Archives of the National Board of Antiquities, unpublished.

Malinen, I. 1997. *Varakkuus ja valta, varhaiskapitalistinen laivanvarustus Helsingissä 1700-luvun puolessavälissä.* Pro gradu - tutkielma, Helsingin yliopisto, Suomen ja Skandinavian historia. (Master thesis. Dept. of Finnish and Nordic History. Helsinki University). Helsinki.

Matikka, H. 2009. Email correspondence between Matikka and Leino, May 2009.

Rönnby, J. 2009. Unpublished introductory speech "Maritime Archaeology: The investigation, interpretation and historical significance of shipwrecks", 10th Nordic TAG conference at Stiklestad, Norway, 27 May 2009.

Vakkari, E. 2009. Report of recognizing the wreck elements at Hylkysaari, The National Board of Antiquities (in Finnish unpublished).

Zetterberg, P. 2010. Museoviraston meriarkeologian yksikön Helsingin Suomenlinnan Venekerhon aallonmurtajan hylkyjen puunäytteiden iänmääritys, dendrokronologiset ajoitukset F56202-F5U6203, FIU 6204, F5U6205-F5U6209, F5&U6210 ja F5U6211-F5U6216. Joensuun yliopisto, Biotieteiden tiedekunta, Ekologian tutkimusinstituutti Dendrokronologian laboratorion ajoitusseloste 367: 1-11 (Report of dendrochronological datings, in Finnish, unpublished).

Archival material

HKA Ga:7 Huutokauppakamarin pöytäkirja 12.6.1766, verifikaatit 1766, 19.

HKA Ga:8 Huutokauppakamarin pöytäkirja 23.4.1767, verifikaatit 1767, 27.

SKA Serie F. Fartygsinventarier m.m. 1764—1792 Inventarium öfver Krono Orlogs Galliothen Printz Wilhelm upprättat vid General besigtningen och Inventeringen den 21 och 27 Martii 1764. Finska Eskadern: Kammar- tyg och sjömilitiekontoren.

12

From Wreck to Heritage – a Matter of Time?

Mirja Arnshav

In recent years, the cultural heritage sector (national heritage boards, contract archaeologists, county administrative boards and others) has made an effort to extend its sphere of activities and take modern heritage into its care. This is well in line with new research fields, such as heritage studies and the archaeology of the contemporary past, plus a widespread public interest in the recent past (Ferguson et al. 2010:287; Blank 2006:15-23).

This development, however, involves new challenges in regard to selection, assessment and consideration of public interests when it comes to heritage management. The sector has to rethink some of its traditional concepts and guidelines. In the light of this situation, the close connection between great age and high cultural value has become destabilized and requires reconsideration. Attitudes to time have become an issue.

What importance does the age of a find or set of remains hold when it comes to assessment of its status as an item of cultural heritage? This question was recently included in a study that began with a maritime topic – the current movement for protection of a selection of modern (20th century) wrecks and the preferences underpinning the selection (Arnshav 2011a).

This paper is based on some of the results of that study (see also Arnshav 2011b). It is not to be construed as a voice in favour of recent wreck management. It does not set out to interpret the history of recent shipwrecks, or to discuss their potential as archaeological sources. Rather, this paper addresses contemporary issues, dealing with the role of wrecks in present day society. To be specific, the focus on recent wrecks aims at exploring the significance of dating and the attitudes it raises. Whilst drawing on a case study,

it is my belief that the results can provide a general understanding of 'recent heritage' issues (Fig. 12.1).

The arrow of time

A theoretical starting point for this discussion is that the notion of 'modern' is linked to the conception of the western world that the past is something foreign, inconsumable and forever lost. In order to define ourselves as 'modern', we need the past to be alienated and distant. We learn that we are forever separated from earlier epochs, habits and people not only by a certain amount of years, but also by a number of epistemological revolutions. The more distant the past, the more different we imagine it to be (Latour 1993:39, 71-72, 125; Lowenthal 2009; Thomas 2004).

It goes without saying that this notion also involves a linear concept of time – one that for centuries has been the basis of western intellectual and religious thought (Grundberg 2000:13-16), and is apparent in the ideas of human progress, social evolution and the concepts of developed and developing nations. Time is thought to move in a single direction – a phenomenon sometimes described as 'the arrow of time'. Conceived as being one-directional, advancing and non-repetitive, the history of the world is seen as a drama enacted on a single stage, with no repeat performances. In other words, there is no turning back – the past is constantly left behind. A connection is ruptured and the interplay of past and present is merely illusory (Latour 1993:67-72).

True or not, this concept of time and the past is widely adopted in the western world and it seems especially strong among historical scholars and

*Figure 12.1.
A monument of the
Cold War – and
a piece of World
Heritage (©
UNESCO/Eric
Hanauer).*

professionals dealing with the past. It makes the past exotic and fascinating, and underpins the growing interest in history, antiquities and ancient remains (Lowenthal 2009:xvi-xvii, 47, 289-291, 371). However, this view also has a downside. When identifying ourselves as 'modern' (and thereby fundamentally different from the 'unmodern' past), we sacrifice our ties to history. The progress of time causes a feeling of uneasiness, a constant awareness of losing the present to the past. Nietzsche has referred to this condition as modern society suffers from the illness of historicism (Latour 1993:67-72).

At the turn of the new millennium, this feeling definitely intensified. We experience time as rushing faster and faster, until change almost becomes the *status quo* (Benton 2010:1). In the endless creation of the new, even the recent past becomes ancient history. This situation fires us with longing for the past and provokes a desire to slow time down. Nostalgia flourishes as never before and we increase our efforts in studying and reconstructing times past (Edensor 2009:128 [2005]; Lowenthal 2010:4-5 [1996]). Paradoxically, as we observe that we can only grasp the past within present discourse, history becomes artificial to us (Smith 2009:58-59 [2006]). Our understanding of history is reduced to histories about history (Kristiansen 2001:153). The past remains a foreign country.

Heritage assets however, such as ancient remains, offer something as rare and precious as a somewhat intact gateway to the past. Being (potentially) tangible, authentic and spatially fixed over time,

they somewhat bridge the gulf between the past and present. They represent something solid and provide a sense of continuity in a world of chaotic flux. In this respect, the concept of heritage has a healing effect (Edensor 2009:136). As the Stockholm International Antiques Fair alluded to in their latest advertisement 'revitalize your home [with antiques]', there is a special aura associated with heritage assets (Antikmässan 2011). This aura, I believe, has to do with western culture's perception of time.

Time limits

So, what effect does this complex of ideas have when it comes to archaeological and antiquarian praxis? Well, just as archaeology is permeated by the concept of linear time and a belief in the uniqueness of each epoch (hence our inclination to approach the past by means of typologies, chronologies and a focus on change over time), so cultural heritage management is also founded on this way of thinking. One consequence of this mindset is that it allows for the use and justification of fixed time limits as regards our heritage. In practice, such regulations divide up time, distinguishing different epochs from one another.

As already mentioned, this paper is based on a case study of modern wrecks, from here on termed 'recent wrecks'. Needless to say, a regulation like this, separating and classifying a set of remains on the grounds of age, is of great importance for our recognition of heritage status. Hence, ever since it was inaugurated, and even though its relevance has been questioned from time to time, this ruling has certainly influenced the views and affected the practices of the heritage sector. The more recent wrecks have consequently been of little interest to heritage managers and the archaeological community – a fact that makes the 100-year criterion in the Heritage Conservation Act in itself a strong manifestation of how age matters (Arnshav 2011a; Arnshav 2012; Haasum 1998:3). A proposed amendment to this Act will substitute the rolling date of 100 years to a fixed date of 1850, with the provision to protect a selection of very valuable post-1850 wrecks (Kulturmiljöns mångfald Prop. 2012/13:96). To an extent this retains the relationship between date and significance. 1850 represents an assumption that by the time something is that old it will have accumulated cultural significance, while the provision to protect younger sites acknowledges the potential significance of the recent past.

Why then was the line originally drawn at 100 years? Records of the discussions preceding the establishment of the rule indicate a dispute as regards the rights of possession of wrecks (ATA 006074; Prop. 1967/19). Furthermore, at that time 100 years was considered a general boundary between what was considered antique or modern, and it was already used to define antiquities and ancient remains (Janson 1974:22). Furthermore, the time limit may be discussed with reference to numerology, or the symbolism of numbers. When it comes to heritage issues, the phenomenon has been problematized with reference to our inclination to celebrate historical jubilees (Nilsson 1993:44-45). Another example is the compilation of 'the hundred', a list of the 100 'most' valued wrecks in the Baltic (Acta 1267/03-51).

Although the 100-year principle specified for shipwrecks is a clear exception in the Swedish Heritage Conservation Acts, provisions for ancient remains, time limits – either based on age or a fixed year – are in fact rather common within heritage management. In fact, all the Baltic and Scandinavian countries rely on a criterion of age when it comes to classifying shipwrecks as ancient remains (Acta 1267/03-51). In Sweden, there are also fairly formal time limits regulating cultural-historical issues about churches/burial grounds, archaeological finds, ancient settlements, traditional vehicles, memorials, repatriation and exportation of heritage items, etc. (Arnshav 2011a:77-78; Blomqvist 2007:24, 32-33, 37-38). In these cases, the principal purpose of the time limit is to guarantee the historical value of a heritage asset. Apart from this, some time limits primarily serve to control the total number of heritage assets, for the sake of manageability (Holm-Olsen et al. 2010:6, 2011:9). Further, one might also add that in countries where the authorized attitude to heritage is

challenged by alternative beliefs – for instance those of native populations – in a more integrated relationship between the past and the present, time limits are implemented in order to avoid confusing status and to prevent 'incorrect' use of heritage labelling (for examples cf. e.g. Bruning 2010:213 and Smith 2009:54 [2006]).

However, the '100-year criterion' regarding shipwrecks is presently being questioned in Sweden. As the heritage sector strives for more selective and well-founded heritage management (Dir 2011:17), the criterion of time is somewhat troublesome, being too static and categorical. As regards shipwrecks, the main problem under discussion is the lack of power of legislation to protect wrecks younger than 100 years. This focus shows a growing susceptibility to assign even relatively modern remains to the past. In other words – the past is now very close to the present, even if not every single item is deemed worthy of heritage status. Furthermore, criticism of this ruling might be understood as a token of a new order in terms of evaluating 'heritage': great age or a distant past is no longer a predominant criterion. Or is it? (Fig. 12.2).

Figure 12.2. The clock from the wreck of the Hansa which stopped at 05:57 hours, telling the time of the attack. (© SMM/Karolina Kristensson).

Maritime archaeology of the contemporary past

Before we enter more deeply into the particular issue of evaluating age, let us first examine the setting, external conditions and present practice. By way of introduction, it might be worth mentioning that Sweden, and especially the Swedish Baltic coast, offers unique preservation conditions for shipwrecks, due to the absence of shipworms and a propitious environment. There are about 2500 registered and located shipwrecks in Swedish waters. Although a remarkable number of them are of great age, a majority – about 1500 wrecks – date from the last 100 years (FMIS). To complete the picture, one might also mention that Sweden has a long tradition of maritime archaeology. At present, the discipline is well-established in academia as well as in the cultural heritage sector. Despite this, the maritime archaeology of the contemporary past has not yet tried its wings. No archaeological research of 20th century wrecks has been carried out, apart from documentation and studies on site-formation processes (Arnshav 2011a:83-88).

The Freja Project is perhaps the nearest we get to an archaeological survey of a recent wreck in Sweden. The steamship *Freja* tragically foundered in 1896. It was raised (only two years before the wreck passed the 100-year limit), restored and put back in traffic. Before renovation, an archaeologist, Susanne Pettersson, was contracted to excavate the interior for finds which were later put on display at a local museum (SMA). But, as the press reported:

'To tell the truth, the *Freja* is far too modern to interest Susanne Pettersson. Finds that are not even 100 years old hold little attraction for an archaeologist... For even though the *Freja* differs in all essentials from Susanne Pettersson's earlier work and though it may well be of historical interest, one can hardly call it archaeology' (Bäckvall 1994; my translation).

There are, however, foreign examples that illustrate how recent wrecks offer useful contributions to historical knowledge. Submarines, monitors, ironclads and paddle steamers dating from the late 19th and early 20th centuries have been meticulously studied, as well as the famous ship-graveyards of the Great Lakes and the Falkland Islands (Delgado 1997; McCarthy 1998:61-69, 2009; Smith 2000:9-12). The studies of the steamships *Xantho* and *Montana* deserve to be mentioned as examples of ambitious surveys, with results that go far beyond the maritime sphere of interest. The *Xantho*, wrecked in 1872, was investigated by the Western Australian Museum (McCarthy 2009:7-9), while the *Montana*, wrecked in 1884, was investigated by East Carolina University (Corbin & Rodgers 2008:1-2). Another example is the newly investigated *HMQS Mosquito*, a torpedo-boat that was stripped and abandoned on an Australian foreshore in 1913 (Hunter 2011).

Maritime archaeology, in Sweden and abroad, is concerned not just with science and research but also narrative. There is a rich tradition of using modern wrecks to assist historical narratives. The utilization of material culture to enhance histories, known or silent (Burström 2007:15), is one of the main directions in contemporary archaeology. However, when applied to 20th century wrecks, such books and films, etc., seem to be mostly the work of non-archaeologists.

Another closely related enterprise is the management of archaeological remains. As already stated, recent wrecks are not an authorized part of heritage at present, and therefore tend to fall outside the scope of official guardianship. The most apparent cause – lack of formal status as ancient remains – has already been pointed out. But surely there is more to it than that?

As an illustrative example, let us now turn to the Norwegian arctic islands of Svalbard and its proposal for heritage management. Svalbard has a relatively short history. It was first settled in the 17th century, but has only been continuously inhabited during the last century (Dahle et al. 2000:7-8). Thus, the area is comparatively poor in cultural remains, and the majority of these are relatively modern. Furthermore, there is almost no need for development in the area. Due to this situation, it has been decided to protect all physical remains dating from the period before 1945 (Dahle et al. 2000:12). Although the situation at Svalbard is more or less the reverse of the Swedish situation as regards wrecks, it provides several keys to understanding the general prioritizations and principles of heritage management. And it should come as no surprise that the protected modern remains at Svalbard have been the subject of several archaeological research projects (Hultgren 2000; Lejoneke & Rönnby 2005; see also Ruin Memories 2011).

Thus, recent wrecks are at present fairly absent from practical archaeology and heritage care in Sweden. How can this be, when there is so much discussion about modernizing the rules and regulations of heritage management? As already mentioned, heritage management – which is sometimes governed by time limits – has a great impact on our archaeological focus and notions of source material (and vice versa). This might partly explain the archaeological lack of interest in modern wrecks. Another explanation might be that Swedish waters are so amazingly rich in well-preserved wrecks of a great age; young nations or regions that are 'lacking' in ancient remains seem to be more open to studying the contemporary past.

The older the better?

Almost a century ago, Le Corbusier questioned the fact that we dutifully preserve the Colosseum, yet allow locomotives to rust on the refuse dump (Le Corbusier 1925:51, see Lowenthal 2009:143 [1985]). The tendency to overlook the heritage of the recent past has also been pointed out by the heritage sector itself (Janson 1974:50-54, 64). Furthermore, it has been stated that what is presented to the general public as 'authorised heritage' does not include remains from the recent past and yet in a recent poll (Blank 2006:20), when asked to list what they regard as the most important monuments and sites, people mostly listed 20th century buildings. Obviously this reaction will vary across communities but in this case there is obviously a dissonance between the public and the heritage bodies as regards what to assess and protect. People seem to have a greater interest in the history that they can relate to such as things that they or their parents can remember. Such buildings are more meaningful to them, they evoke stories and emotions. Just think of how the 'antiques' market nowadays is flooded with items from the 1950s, '60s and '70s.

What then can recent wrecks tell us about such attitudes? As has already been highlighted, it is customary for recent wrecks to be depreciated by the archaeological community and heritage sector. Now, the sector is beginning to show an interest. Does this mean then that the traditional attitude towards age is becoming outdated? It turns out that even within the limited group of recent wrecks, the heritage sector mainly favours those of greater age; the tendency has merely been transferred to a more compromised time-frame. Of course, until now there has been only a small number of reports on the cultural value of recent wrecks, but a noticeable number deal with those that date to the very first decades of the last century, many of which will turn into ancient remains automatically in only a few years by fulfilling the 100-year criterion (Acta 876/08-95.2; Acta 1267/03-51; Acta 56/2006-51; Ekberg 2004; Statens maritima museer 2011). Also, it would appear that the recent wrecks that are exemplified in these reports are mentioned as a result of an obligatory framework of instruction. When the same curators are asked to make a selection of free choice, recent wrecks clearly fall behind (Acta 876/08-95.2). Once again, the Svalbard proposal for heritage management can serve as a simple comparative example, where great age is considered a prioritized quality, both when it comes to the very oldest remains or the oldest examples of the recent past (Dahle et al. 2000:33).

Why then does the sector favour older remains at the expense of younger? Is it just a matter of oversight, or does it indicate a more deliberate direction? One interpretation, corresponding to the notions of 'bygone days' outlined in the opening of this paper, is that a more distant past is equated with a higher degree of difference and with rarity, which in turn increases our fascination and its sense of importance. This is a perfectly logical, rational way of reasoning, but what happens if we instead try to experience the past?

Pastness

First of all, in Sweden scuba diving to wrecks is a popular hobby –which according to the maritime heritage sector serves as proof of a widespread interest in maritime history (ATA 322-3995-2008; Statens maritima museer *in prep*). However, the attitude that wrecks are cultural heritage is not very common among scuba divers. While the heritage sector tends to refer to age and history (the ship and its context), scuba divers seem more occupied by a wreck's present state (Arnshav 2011a:64-71).

In a way, a ship suffers a sea change by becoming a wreck. It attracts a new audience - people that would probably not have paid any attention to the ship had it still been afloat or simply accessible through archives and photos. Diving around wrecks is to a great extent an experience-based phenomenon. From such a point of view, the wrecks are not just gates to history, but also arenas for aesthetic impressions, fascination with the underwater world, social intercourse, adventure and fun (Arnshav 2011a) (Fig. 12.3).

Having said that, it comes as no surprise that a fixation with age is generally not relevant to scuba divers. Although they mostly dive to 20th century wrecks, this is not because they prefer this historical period, but simply because they see certain qualities in these wreck sites (Acta 1544/05-20). In contrast to old wooden shipwrecks, recent steel wrecks tend to be larger, more intact (three-dimensional) and relatively rich in details and finds – characteristics that make them more intelligible and more of a challenge to diving.

However, this does not mean that the historical dimension is completely absent or unimportant. Knowledge of a wreck's history can add spice to the diving experience or can incite an underwater search for a lost ship. But as a rule, such knowledge is only superficial or limited to the events of the final voyage and the finder. The historical aspect is approached from a slightly different perspective, where importance is instead attached to impressions of 'pastness' (Holtorf 2009:35). In other words, what counts is patina and the ravages of time rather than years, and instead of relating a wreck to a specific life story and historical context, it comes to symbolize

Figure 12.3. The recently raised wreck of the Södra Sverige on display in Stockholm in 1897 (SMM/unknown photographer).

the general passing of time (Arnshav 2011a:92-94). This phenomenon – the allure of the past – has already been noted in several contexts. We are all familiar with the concept of romantic ruins, but this has also been discussed with regard to the streams of tourists visiting scrap-yards for old cars (Burström 2004, 2009). So why not apply it to shipwrecks? Surely they too can possess the aesthetics and existential dimensions associated with the past (cf. Arnshav 2011a:93-96). This finds support in the fact that, before the era of scuba diving, wrecks were occasionally raised and exhibited to the public, their shabbiness and state of ruin being the main attraction (Bergquist 1980:174-177; Wetterholm 1989, 1994:81, 91). The heritage sector, however, has apparent difficulties adapting to such views, as it opposes the traditional tasks of preservation and safeguarding where the aim is to keep the cultural heritage as intact as possible, to prevent it from sinking into decay (Burström 2009:137; Shanks 1992:73-75, 1998:17; Skeates 2000:69-70). Once again, we can trace two perspectives clashing with each other; the wrecks can be considered to represent a closed chapter or an ongoing history, forming part of the present.

Time capsules

Another time-related quality as regards cultural heritage, is the 'time capsule'. These well-preserved sites, where time seems to have stood still, are highly appreciated. Their uniqueness and manifest authenticity appeals to heritage managers, their capacity as closed contexts and peep-holes into history are valued by archaeologists, as much as their intactness and variety of detail make them fascinating to divers. All together, these features lend a special aura, a touch of magic (reflected in names like 'Ghost wreck', 'Ghost town', etc.).

An interesting fact with regard to the significance of time, is that true 'time capsules' tend to be esteemed as such irrespective of their date (compare the widespread fascination with abandoned sites) (Edensor 2009:50-51 [2005]; Jörnmark 2007:5-6, 2010; Rostsverige 2010; Övergivna platser 2010). In other words, importance lies not in age but in a frozen past. Significant events of course hold a prominent position, but, trivial incidents can be just as fascinating on another plane. The briefer the moment and the more frail the traces of action, the more exclusive the physical remains seem – just think of how preserved fingerprints or footprints from past times create chills down the spine. Fragments of lost everyday acts thrill us and enchant into a feeling of presence.

This also applies to shipwrecks. When a ship is suddenly abandoned and sinks into oblivion or inaccessibility as a wreck, it can indeed form a remarkable time capsule – at least if conditions are favourable for preservation. A Pompeii in miniature, full of frozen moments (the moment of impact/fire/explosion, of heaving to, of clearing the pumps, etc.). Recent wrecks are obvious competitors in the category of time capsules, since date and age are somewhat subordinated qualities. The few recent wrecks highlighted by the heritage sector so far, include a number that distinguish themselves by being extremely well-preserved, providing an experience approximating to time travel. One such example is the sunken sailing ship, *Nepolina*, where the wheelbarrow is still stowed away and the spades still stuck into the sand cargo, just as they were left when she set out for Stockholm early in the morning of 8 April 1913 (SMA).

Interesting times

At the Stockholm International Antiques Fair in 2011, some traditional mangle-boards were put up for sale. All equal in size, with carved decorations and dates, yet one was almost twice as expensive as the rest. The reason for this, the antique dealer explained, was not that it was the oldest, the most beautiful nor in the most prime condition; but that it had a particular year, 1632, carved on it. In Sweden this date is commonly associated with one of the most well-known events in Swedish history, namely the battle of Lützen, where the Swedish king Gustav II Adolf – a king with a great posthumous reputation – was shot dead. Scandinavian mangle-boards were not only the standard way of smoothing linen, they were also traditional courtship gifts. Thus, in the year 1632, far away from the battle-lines, somebody was making a mangle-board, hoping to get married. Any historical connection between this incident and Gustav II Adolf's life is of course non-existent. Nevertheless, as far-fetched and anachronistic as it might be, our perspective on history and our cultural concept of heritage make such a connection possible. The mere occurrence of such a legendary date makes all the difference.

This example illustrates two things relevant to our discussion. First, it detects a touch of obsession in our cultural relationship to past times. One can discuss the phenomenon either in terms of religion (history as a religion) or philosophy (the Marxist thesis of reification applied to social relationships). Also, it proves how 'big histories' are important to us, and tend to make themselves heard above the cacophony of 'ordinary histories'.

Returning to the case of recent wrecks, it is clear that there are many 'big histories' accompanying those highlighted as historically interesting. Wrecks relating to the First and Second World Wars clearly excel in attracting archaeologists, heritage managers and tourists, all around the world. The fleets at Scapa Flow, Orkney, in Pearl Harbour and in the 'Iron Bottom Sound' off the Solomon Islands may serve as examples (Delgado 1997:307, 449; Drew 1998; *ScapaMap 1*; *ScapaMap 2*). The 'crossroad' wrecks, that is, battleships of the Second World War wrecked by the nuclear tests at the Bikini atoll during the ensuing Cold War, have also gained a wide reputation, and were recently added to the UNESCO's World Heritage List (Carrell 1991:464-465; Delgado 1997:116-119; UNESCO 2010:206-209) (Fig. 12.4).

The World Wars are prominent also in Sweden. Although Sweden was neutral, the merchant fleet suffered great losses during both wars, as also did foreign ships passing through Swedish waters. Today, the heritage sector as well as the scuba-diving community have a noticeable interest in the World Wars and consider their traces to be of great historical value (Acta 1544/05-20). The torpedoing of the neutral *Hansa* passenger ship, the 'Submarine Massacre' (the sinking of the four German cargo carriers: the *Nicomedia, Gutrune, Walter Leonharth* and *Director Reppenhagen*), and the fatal collision of the German steamship *Ingrid Horn* (due to navigational war adaptations), are all examples of incidents involving recent wrecks, that were put forward by the heritage sector in reference to world history (Acta 876/08-95.2; Acta 1267/03-51; Acta 56/2006-51; Ekberg 2004; Statens maritima museer 2011).

According to this, the possible heritage status of a recent wreck is also due to what we consider to be an important period in the past. In addition, if we can somehow relate it to a significant date, it is very likely it will attract interest and be ranked highly. Who knows, the date '9/11' might very well be such a stimulus for tomorrow's heritage selection.

Final remarks

There are recent wrecks, and there is heritage. In a handful of cases, both positions can apply simultaneously. In this paper I have tried to discuss how perspectives on time come into play when selecting which wrecks should gain heritage status. As stressed in the introduction, cultural concepts of heritage are closely related to cultural concepts of time. Obviously time matters with regard to key episodes in history or necessary time limits. But one can also argue that age does not matter scientifically nor when experiencing heritage. Perhaps the concept of an unbridgeable gulf between modern life and that of the past, together with

Figure 12.4. The wreck of the 'Gutrune 'sunk in 1915 by an English submarine is presently highly valued both by scuba divers and maritime cultural heritage managers (© Ingvar Eliasson).

a fixation on the distant past, is a scholarly perspective rather than a spontaneous one. In any case, date is not considered an important factor governing interest in a wreck among pleasure divers. A survey of scientific studies of 20th century wrecks shows that such studies might very well be of archaeological importance.

Thus, if the heritage sector wishes to approach the public and keep in step with current archaeology of the contemporary past, it has to tone down its insistence on great age, and be prepared to accept other values and views, including different perspectives on time and the significance of age.

Given that an increased number of archaeologists are seeking alternatives to 'the big history' and now embrace 'the material turn' and material culture studies, (thus adopting research not only about what people do with things, but also what things do to us and what alternative stories and perspectives they might bring forth), it is likely that material remains henceforth will have a more prominent position within the study of historical periods and the recent past. In the long run, it is the research focus, rather than the age of remains or finds, that determines the usefulness of a source material. And, to paraphrase a scuba-diving friend of mine: a valuable wreck may simply be the one where you get to see bottles with the kind of tops you remember from your childhood!

References

Antikmässan 2011. Electronic document, http://www. antikmassan.se/, accessed June 04, 2011.

Arnshav, M. 2011a. *"Yngre vrak". Samtidsarkeologiska perspektiv på ett nytt kulturarv.* Huddinge: Södertörns högskola.

Arnshav, M. 2011b. Rost skrot och värdefulla vrak. *Nicolay* 3: 5-10.

Arnshav, M. 2012. Wreck huggers, aqualungs and red tape. A heritage process of the middle ground? In: N. Myrberg, & F. Fahlander, (eds) *Matters of Scale. Processes and courses of events in the past and the present.* Stockholm: Stockholm University.

Benton, T. 2010. Introduction. In: T. Benton (ed.) *Understanding heritage and memory*: 1-5. Manchester: Manchester University Press.

Bergquist, L. 1980. *Per Brahes undergång och bärgning.* Stockholm: P. A. Nordstedt & söners förlag.

Blank, Y. 2006. *Svenska folkets egen K-märkning. En kampanj i tiden?* Electronic document, http://www.lansstyrelsen.se/vastragotaland/Publikationer/Rapporter/2006/2006_19.htm (June 12, 2011).

Blomqvist, M. 2007. *Informationssystemet för fornminnen – lista med lämningstyper och antikvarisk praxis. Version 3.4.* Electronic document, http://www.raa.se/publicerat/varia2007_7.pdf, (November 04, 2011).

Bruning, S.B. 2010. Articulating Culture in the Legal Sphere: Heritage Values, Native Americans, and the Law. pp. 209-224. In: G.S. Smith, P. Mauch Messenger & H.A. Soderland (eds) *Heritage Values in Contemporary Society.* Walnut Creek: California: Left Coast Press.

Burström, M. 2004. Archaeology and Existential Reflection. In: H. Bolin (ed.) *The Interplay of Past and Present*, pp. 21-28. Papers from a session held at the 9th annual AEE meeting in St. Petersburg 2003. Södertörn Archaeological Studies 1. Huddinge: Södertörn University College.

Burström, M. 2007. *Samtidsarkeologi. Introduktion till ett forskningsfält.* Studentlitteratur, Lund.

Burström, M. 2009. Garbage or Heritage: The Existential Dimension of a Car Cemetery. In: C. Holtorf & A. Piccini (eds) *Contemporary Archaeologies. Excavating Now*, pp. 131-143. New York: Peter Lang.

Bäckvall, S. 1994. Första kvinnan ombord på Freja. Fast för arkeologen Susanne är båten väl modern... *Tidningen om Freja,* supplement to *Fryksdals-Bygden,* September 1994.

Carrell, T.L. (ed.) 1991. *Submerged cultural resources assessment of Micronesia.* Southwest Cultural Resources Center Professional Papers No 36. New Mexico: Southwest Cultural Resources Center, Santa Fe.

Corbin, A. & Rodgers, B.A. 2008. *The steamboat Montana and the opening of the west. History, Excavation, and Architecture.* Gainesville: University Press of Florida.

Dahle, K., Bjerck, H.B. & Prestvold, K. 2000. Kulturminneplan for Svalbard 2000-2010. In: K. Dahle (ed.) *Kulturminneplan for Svalbard 2000-2010.* Sysselmannens rapportserie 2000/No 1. Svalbard: Sysselmannen.

Delgado, J.P. (ed.) 1997. *Encyclopedia of Underwater and Maritime Archaeology.* London: British Museum Press.

Drew, T. 1998. Solomon Islands: Guadalcanal shipwrecks revisited. In: J. Green & M. Stanbury (eds), *The AIMA bulletin (The bulletin of the Australian institute for maritime archaeology)*, Vol. 22, pp. 71-74. Papers from the Australian Institute for Maritime Archaeology 17th International Conference The Maritime Archaeology of Long Distance Voyaging; 5-13 September 1997; Fremantle: The Australian Institute for Maritime Archaeology.

Edensor, T. 2009 [2005]. *Industrial Ruins. Space, Aesthetics and Materiality.* Oxford & New York: Berg.

Ekberg, G. 2004. *KMÖ – rapport 2001-2004.* Manuscript on file, Statens maritima museer.

Ferguson, R., Harrison, R., & Rose, D. 2010. Heritage and the recent and contemporary past. In: T. Benton (ed.) *Understanding heritage and memory*, pp. 277-315. Manchester: Manchester University Press.

Grundberg, J. 2000. *Kulturarvsförvaltningens samhällsuppdrag. En introduktion till kulturarvsförvaltningens teori och praktik.* Licentiat thesis. GOTARC, Series C. Arkeologiska skrifter no 33. Göteborg: Göteborgs universitet.

Haasum, S. 1998. Marinarkeologin i kulturmiljövården – ett kronologiskt perspektiv. In: L. Einarsson (ed.), *Marinarkeologi och Kulturmiljövård*, pp. 3-7. Rapport från seminariet i Kalmar 18-19 mars 1998. Kalmar: Kalmar läns museum.

Holm-Olsen, I., Myrvoll, E.R, Myrvoll, M. & Thuestad, A. 2010. *100-årsgrensen for automatisk fredete samiske kulturminner: Status og scenarioer.* NIKU Rapport 40 2010. Electronic document, http://niku.no/archive/niku/publikasjoner/NIKU%20Rapport%20pdf/Rapport_40.pdf (April 25, 2011).

Holm-Olsen, I., Myrvoll, E.R, Myrvoll, M. & Thuestad, A. 2011. *100-årsgrensen for automatisk fredete samiske kulturminner: Casestudier og mulige modeler.* NIKU Rapport 43 2011. Electronic document, http://www.niku.no/archive/niku/publikasjoner/NIKU%20Rapport%20pdf/NIKU%20Rapport_43.pdf (April 25, 2011).

Holtorf, C. 2009. On the Possibility of Time Travel.

Lund Archaeological Review 15: 31-31.

Hultgren, T. 2000. *Den russiske fangsten på Svalbard: en reanalyse av arkeologiske og historiske kilder.* Dissertation. Tromsø University, Tromsø.

Hunter, J.W. 2011. HMQS Mosquito: the rediscovery and identification of Queensland's first warship. *The International Journal of Nautical Archaeology* 40:2: 374–386.

Janson, S. 1974. *Kulturvård och samhällsbildning.* Stockholm: Nordiska museet.

Jörnmark, J. 2007. *Övergivna platser.* Lund: Historiska Media.

Jörnmark, J. 2010. *Creative destruction.* Elektronic document, http://creativedestruction.se/ (November 23, 2010).

Kristiansen, K. 2001. Är kulturarvet en mänsklig rättighet? In: M. Elg (ed.) *På resande fot. 23 forskare skriver om turism och upplevelser*, pp. 144-153. Stockholm: Sellin & partner.

Kulturmiljöns mångfald Prop. 2012/13:96) Kulturmiljöns mångfald. Kulturdepartementet http://www.regeringen.se/sb/d/16860/a/213245

Latour, B. 1993. *We Have Never Been Modern.* Cambridge, Massachusetts: Harvard University Press.

Lejoneke. P. & Rönnby, J. 2005. *Svalbard: marinarkeologisk rekognoscering 1998 och 2000.* Huddinge: Södertörns Högskola.

Lowenthal, D. 2009 [1985]. *The past is a foreign country.* Cambridge: Cambridge University Press.

Lowenthal, D. 2010 [1996]. *The heritage crusade and the spoils of history.* Cambridge: Cambridge University Press.

McCarthy, M. 1998. The submarine as a class of archaeological site. In: J. Green & M. Stanbury (eds) *The AIMA bulletin* (The bulletin of the Australian Institute for Maritime Archaeology), Vol. 22, pp. 61-69. Papers from the Australian Institute for Maritime Archaeology 17th International Conference The Maritime Archaeology of Long Distance Voyaging; 5-13 September 1997. Fremantle: The Australian Institute for Maritime Archaeology.

McCarthy, M. 2009. The Xantho. In: M. McCarthy (ed.) *Iron, Steel & Steamship Archaeology. Proceedings of the 2nd Australian seminar, held in Perth, Melbourne and Sydney, 2006*, pp. 5-11. Fremantle, Western Australia: Australian National Centre of Excellence for Maritime Archaeology and Australasian Institute for Maritime Archaeology. Special publication Australian National Center of Excellence for Maritime Archaeology No. 13; Special publication Australian Institute for Maritime Archaeology

Special Publication No. 15).

Nilsson, G. B. 1992. Fetischism och rationalism i kulturpolitiken. In: *Modernisering och kulturarv*, edited by Jonas Anshelm, pp. 41-57. Stockholm: Östlings bokförlag.

Rostsverige 2010. Electronic document, http://rostsverige.blogs.se/ (September 23, 2011).

Ruin Memories 2011. *Ruin Memories. Materiality, aesthetics and the archaeology of the recent past. Pyramiden Arctic Ruins.* Electronic document, http://ruinmemories.org/pyramiden-arctic-ruins/ (September 23, 2011).

ScapaMap 1. 2000-2002. *Report Compiled for Historic Scotland on the Mapping and Management of the Submerged Archaeological Resource in Scapa Flow, Orkney.* Electronic document, http://www.scapamap. org/docs/ScapaMAP2002.pdf, (September 23, 2011).

ScapaMap 2. *Marine Heritage Monitoring with High-Resolution Survey Tools: Scapa Flow 2001-2006 Final Report.* Electronic document, http://www.scapamap. org/docs/ScapaMAP2006.pdf (September 23, 2011).

Shanks, M. 1992. *Experiencing the past.* London: Routledge.

Skeates, R. 2000. *Debating the archaeological heritage.* London: Duckworth.

Smith, L. 2009 [2006]. *Uses of heritage.* London & New York: Routledge.

Smith, T. 2000. Up periscope: submarine *AE2* makes first contact. In: J. Green & M. Stanbury (eds) *The AIMA bulletin* (The bulletin of the Australian Institute for Maritime Archaeology), Vol. 24, pp. 9-20. Fremantle: The Australian Institute for Maritime Archaeology.

Statens maritima museer 2011. *Yngre fartygslämningar*, manuscript on file, Statens maritima museer.

Thomas, J. 2004. *Archaeology and Modernity.* New York: Routledge.

UNESCO 2010. *Report of the decisions adopted by the world heritage committee at its 34th session.* Electronic document, http://whc.unesco.org/en/decisions/3999/ (February 13, 2011).

Wetterholm, C-G. 1989. *Skrufångaren Per Brahe.* Skärhamn: Båtdokgruppen.

Wetterholm, C-G. 1994. *Vrak i svenska vatten.* Stockholm: Rabén Prisma.

Övergivna *platser 2010.* Electronic document, http://www.facebook.com/home.php?#!/group. php?gid=11027840069&v=info&ref=ts (September 23, 2011).

Archives

Acta 1267/03-51 (Statens maritima museer). Statens maritime museer (2006). *Rutilus. Strategies for a Sustainable Development of the Underwater Cultural Heritage in the Baltic Sea Region;* Bilaga: *Rutilus. Appendix 100.*

Acta 876/08-95.2 (Statens maritima museer). *Fråga ställd till anställda på arkeologienheten. Vilka är de 20 mest intressanta vraken?*

Acta 56/2006-51 (Statens maritima museer). Riksantikvarieämbetet, Naturvårdsverket & Statens maritima museer (2005). *Förstudie inom miljömålsarbetet: Värdefulla undervattensmiljöer i svensk kust och skärgård - samverkanspotential mellan natur- och kulturmiljövård.*

Acta 1544/05-20 (Statens maritima museer). Sportdykarenkät tillhörande projektet Managing Cultural Heritage Under Water (MACHU).

ATA 006074 (Riksantikvarieämbetet). *Motiv till Förslag till lag om skydd för vissa äldre sjöfynd.* Oktober 1965

ATA 322-3995-2008 (Riksantikvarieämbetet). *Skydd av särskilt värdefulla yngre skeppsvrak.*

Dir 2011:17 (Kulturdepartementet). *Översyn av lagstiftning och nationella mål på kulturmiljöområdet.*

FMIS, http://www.fmis.raa.se/cocoon/fornsok/search.html

Prop. 1967/19 (Riksdagen). *Kungl. Maj:ts proposition till riksdagen med förslag till lag angående ändring i lagen den 12 juni 1942 (nr 350) om fornminnen, m.mm; given Stockholms slott den 27 januari 1967.*

SMA Svenskt marinarkeologiskt arkiv (Sjöhistoriska museet). *Freja* (file).

SMA Svenskt marinarkeologiskt arkiv (Sjöhistoriska museet). *Nepolina* (file).